An
Inconvenient
Voice

An
Inconvenient
Voice

One Woman's Fight Against Injustice

A True Story

Ian Thompson

Paperback ISBN: 978-1-7353665-0-0

Printed in the United States of America.

Cover and Interior Design: Creative Publishing Book Design

For Charlie Oliver

Contents

PART 1

Go West, Young Man

CHAPTER 1

Preparing to Launch

Done laid around, done stayed around this old town too long
And it seems like I've got to travel on
Bob Dylan – "Gotta Travel On"

Betty glanced out of the window of her lingerie store at the pedestrians passing on the sidewalk outside. It had been a slow day, and now it was almost closing time. She was looking forward to stopping on the way home to pick up dinner from her favorite Italian deli just down the street. Turning back to the stack of invoices on the counter, she continued to punch numbers into an old calculator that rhythmically kept pace with her keystrokes. It was her last task of the day.

Out of the corner of her eye, she saw two men step through the open doorway. Looking up to greet them, she caught herself in mid-sentence as one of the men reached back and pushed the door shut. Sensing that something was wrong, Betty slowly rose from her seat. The man who had closed the door was tall and unshaven with shoulder-length black hair partially covered by a gray woolen cap pulled low over his forehead. He was also wearing a tan-colored trench coat, which struck Betty as being out of place in the California summer, and most of the people in the store that day had been wearing light clothing. The other man was shorter, much heavier set, wearing an ill-fitting gray suit and dark glasses. Someone who would not have looked out of place providing security at a nightclub.

Any thoughts about who her two visitors might be, however, were cut short when the tall one reached for the "Open" sign in the window and flipped it to "Closed," then set the latch on the door to lock it. Betty's heart started to race, and her hands tightened around the edge of the counter. Sensing trouble, she instinctively scanned the store for a way to escape, at the same time regretting an earlier decision not to keep a loaded weapon at hand, even though the store was in one of the rougher areas of town. "What do you want," she said, trying to stifle the quiver in her voice, but her question went unanswered as the duo began to advance past the racks of undergarments. Betty remembered the fire exit in the storeroom that led to an alley. It was her only way out without going through the two men who were now only seconds away. Turning, she leaped out from behind the counter and ran toward the rear of the store. Three strides into her quest for freedom, she felt a hand grab the back of her hair, and in a flash of pain, her head snapped back, causing her to crash awkwardly to the floor. Struggling to regain her wits, she looked up to see the heavyset man stepping across her as he bent down and grabbed the lapels of her jacket. She could feel his breath on her face and was reminded of the pain in her neck as he hoisted her to her feet as if he was lifting a tray of hors d'oeuvres. Still clutching the front of her jacket, he walked her backward, and, with his partner close behind, used her body to push open the unlocked storeroom door. Soon all three of them were surrounded by the boxes, clothing, and mannequins that provided Betty's livelihood. After a final violent shove, she felt herself lose her footing, and the room swirled before her as she tumbled into the rows of inventory neatly stacked against a wall.

Now defenseless and in a fog of panic, she could only guess at what was to come as the man in the suit stepped back to make way for his partner. The tall one took his position and stood for a second, staring down at her with a mocking grin on his face. Using his left hand to open the front of his trench coat, he reached inside and drew out a matte black shotgun. Supporting the barrel, he cradled the fore end with his left hand, and she heard the double click of the action as a cartridge made its way into the chamber. Betty screamed, but there was no one within earshot. Lifting the gun, he leveled it at point-blank range and spoke the only words the two men had uttered since entering the store: "You can thank your brother." In an instant, the gun was discharged, and her life was over. It was 1983, and I barely knew Betty, having only seen her at a couple of parties where we had exchanged pleasantries. But both of our lives could have been permanently altered had she not been dispatched in such a ruthless fashion. The way we met was triggered by a series of events dating back to 1978, when I was over 5,000 miles away living on a different continent.

I had finished college in 1977, and as a member of the fledgling surfing fraternity in England, I'd left the books behind and taken off for the coast. Spending hours in the ocean in the typically cold and gray English weather spawned a desire to visit exotic lands and warmer waters, images of which filled the pages of *Surfer* magazine, a periodical that made its way across the Atlantic from the U.S. once every two months.

This desire for travel manifested itself in low-budget trips across European borders into France, Spain, and as far as North Africa, where comfortable temperatures, different cultures, and new adventures stoked the appetite of a willing student. Each trip was made possible by earning money doing menial work in summer jobs on the English coast. These included a couple of stints as a pot washer at a hotel called the Water Beach located in the southwestern county of Cornwall. It was there that a high-strung head chef with the nickname "Tweet" created meals for the vacationing guests who were eager to get to the beach, or hungry after a day spent on the sand.

The kitchen typically worked in harmony unless the chef, or a member of his staff, was inconsiderate enough to burn any of that day's offerings. If braising pots or roasting pans became the blackened victims of neglect, or the remnants of scorched boeuf bourguignon clanged its way into my steam-filled purgatory, all hell would break loose. The chef, as captain of the culinary ship, would be the first to suffer the shrieks of outrage from the pot room. "Tweet! What the fuck have you done! You must expect the guests to use carbon dating to figure out what they're eating! This isn't a Cajun restaurant. Heck, you're the only chef I know who can burn a salad."

The waitresses, nonchalantly polishing water glasses on a linen-draped table and dressed in their brown skirts and starched white shirts, would look knowingly at each other as the salvo of expletives streamed from my workspace unabated. Tweet would rush over with a feigned look of disbelief on his face and proceed to inspect the damage with a comprehensive assessment more befitting a seasoned homicide detective than a professional chef. "It's not that bad," he would offer up, hopeful that his confident rationale would defray the verbal assaults that were a hallmark of the interlude after each meal. Scowling, I would counter with a more critical assessment of the foodborne disaster, confident that my description of the difficulty of cleaning up the food, now welded onto the pans, would deter any future instances of such an atrocity. At least until the next mealtime.

Outside the humid environment of dishwashing, breaks in the action were filled with sessions surfing the waves off the local reefs and sandbars, where I would join friends and other members of the staff as we paddled around in the waves until our arms felt like noodles. As the breaktimes neared their end, we would often have to sprint to the confines of the hotel to make it back in time to address the remnants of the most recent sitting.

A couple of miles inland lay an old airfield that had been built before World War I. It had subsequently been commandeered by the Admiralty in the 1930s to become a Fleet Air Arm training facility. In the southwest corner, a complex of buildings had been converted into a wholesale meat-butchering and packing plant. This anomaly, in an otherwise mostly derelict landscape, was owned by an ex–amateur heavyweight boxing champion who had grown up in the gritty East end of London. He'd found his niche in the vast Smithfield meat market in the center of the city before starting his own business. When he wasn't working on building his enterprise, he spent his time boxing his way to prominence amidst the blue-collar environs of London. Some said he could have been a contender for the national, if not world, title. Instead, he chose the business world, establishing his enterprise in the capital before moving it to the airfield 250 miles outside of London.

When the summer ended, and the tourists had all gone home, it was essential to top up the funds needed for the next surf trip. And the meat factory was pretty much the only steady employment in an area where the principal drivers of the economy were agriculture and tourism. A certain amount of folklore had grown up around the factory. Tales of worker beatings and speculation regarding criminal activity titillated the locals, who shared gossip over fish and chips down at the pub. And not all of it was false. These tales, real or manufactured, gave the business, with its remote location amongst forgotten wartime structures, a foreboding mystique.

Getting a start at the meat factory was the easy part. Surviving the first day was a different story, and all the established employees were familiar with the drill. Newbies, arriving in the half-light of early morning, were often greeted by the likes of Black Jimmy, a butcher from Liverpool in the north of England who was usually accompanied by his dog Nelly, an imposing Great Dane who Jimmy referred to as Nelly the Wonder Dog. Alongside Black Jimmy, who coincidentally was neither black nor, likely, named Jimmy, was Black Chris. Strangely enough, Chris was black, and the consensus was that his name was, in fact, Chris. Then there was Terry. Terry was on the run for ducking out of paying child support from more than one marriage. And he was always on the lookout for smartly dressed people in unmarked cars that would ask to speak to the owner of the business. More than once, he was found hunkered down in the chiller behind boxes filled with the results of that day's work, convinced that the local health inspector was either a cop who'd come to arrest him or, worse still, some enforcer hired by an ex-wife to extract payback.

Since technology had yet to introduce its conveyor systems and digital scales to this factory, almost all the work was processed manu-ally. Large eighteen-wheel big rigs would pull up to the loading dock packed front to back with sides of beef. And it would be up to the meat porters to unload the fore and hindquarters from the rig and carry them to a chiller that stood twenty long yards away. As with many tasks that involve lifting heavy objects, technique was everything. At the meat factory, however, there was no training class, no manual, and no encouraging instructor to support each step along the road to competency. Instead, the two to three hundred-pound quarters of beef stood before you like an invading army. Ready to crush any poor soul not capable of embracing, then teasing them off their steel hooks as only an expert could execute without injury or embarrassment.

Adding color to the struggles of a new hire, was a peanut gallery of veterans who had all been through the same first-day initiation. They were fully aware of how to pivot a side of beef until its hook released while gliding under the falling weight to support its center of gravity. They stayed curiously silent, conducting their tasks while keeping a knowing eye on the other fresh meat that had shown up for work that day.

Many a bright-eyed freshman had stood tall on that dock only to have their spirits broken, most admitting defeat by not showing up for work the next day, or by simply walking off the job. If a first-timer came back for a second day, the reason probably fell into one of three main buckets. The first was desperation. There wasn't much alternative work in the area. So, if you could ignore the pain in your shoulders and back, and the bone cuts in your hands that kept you up for the first few nights, you might survive for a second day. Pride and machismo were equally strong motivators for certain novices who endured the first day's misery of struggling with hundreds of pounds of greasy flesh. Better to withstand the pain than have to explain down at the pub why you wouldn't be showing up for work the next day.

History provided the third and, for me, the most compelling leg of the stool. Having had friends who had run this grisly gauntlet and emerged to brag about it had set the benchmark. Defeat was not an option. And it wasn't long before that first day of struggle became a second day of lifting while ignoring the inflamed muscles and bruised shoulders inflicted on day one. Days three, four, and beyond saw improvements in technique. Even the experts on the team, who could recognize when a recruit was going to stay the course, weighed in with a few tips to make the workers' efforts ergonomically effective. This rotation of work, interspersed with winter surf trips across Europe, continued for a couple of years, until the Pacific Ocean beckoned, and I made plans to travel to the surfing meccas of California and Hawaii.

CHAPTER 2

A Question of Credentials

Odd jobs, hard jobs, anything under the sun
Big jobs, small jobs, baby
Bon Jovi – "I Could Make a Livin Out of Loving You."

Flying into Los Angeles at night, my girlfriend and I gazed down at an endless carpet of lights sliced from all directions by the web of freeways that keep California moving. Baseball fields, shopping centers, and the Hollywood Park Racetrack dominated the illuminations, while the traffic created red and white ribbons of color as it moved constantly through the landscape.

After a night in a seedy downtown hotel we caught a Greyhound bus down to San Diego, where I needed to find work so I could stay for the full six-month duration of my visa. After a couple of days spent getting acquainted with the area, I started trolling the beachside restaurants, soliciting managers for work. However, I began to realize that, lacking any evidence that I was legally eligible for employment, I was wasting my time. After a week of denials, and with funds starting to run low, I decided to order a custom surfboard from a local manufacturer called Gordon and Smith. That way, I could at least enjoy the waves before returning to England. Two weeks later, when the board was due to be finished, I showed up at the store to collect it. "Sorry," was the response. "The guy who does the final polish on the boards has a hernia and won't be back for a week, so your board has been delayed." In a flash, I replied, "I can polish boards. Let me fill in for him." At the time, I'd made a couple of boards in my parents' garage. However, my skills were not at the level required by a famous manufacturing company that, as I discovered later, was the largest producer of surfboards in the world. "Nah, the shop manager said. It's dirty work, let me see what else I can do to hurry up your board. Come back on Wednesday."

I returned on Wednesday, and the board still wasn't finished. "I can polish boards. I'll do the work." I repeated my solicitations with the confidence of a seasoned craftsman. And much to my surprise, the manager said, "let's take a drive up there. You can see for yourself what's involved, and we'll have a chat with the boss."

We climbed into his truck and drove about four miles inland, where I walked into a state-of-the-art factory. Rows of craftsmen, shrouded in the whine of power tools, were shaping the foam cores that would become the foundation for the finished product. From other rooms leaked the fumes of polyester resin. Or they were awash in color as artwork was applied to the shaped cores before the laminators sealed them in their fiberglass shells.

The manager of the factory was an Italian called Paul. Paul knew everything about the process of making surfboards. Having worked his way up through the business, he had become an expert in each phase of their construction. After an introduction, we talked for a while, and he showed me the layout of the shop. There were two bays for polishing the boards. One was occupied by a man named P.K. who had driven out to California from New Jersey, eager to test himself against the bigger and more consistent surf that the West Coast offered. I said hi as he peered out from behind safety glasses while brandishing a 5000-rpm grinder, which howled to a standstill as we exchanged pleasantries.

After pitching my expertise at polishing surfboards, Paul offered me a job. But only after explaining that no shop in the world did as many boards as fast and as well as they did and that the work would be hard and exacting. I readily agreed to the terms. "P.K. here will get you up to speed on our tools and our system," he said. P.K. nodded from behind his paper mask as the grinder he was holding stopped spinning for a second time. "Can you start on Monday?" he asked. Yes, I replied, barely able to contain my excitement at having found not only work, but work at a highly respected surfboard manufacturer.

That night, I thought hard about how to handle the job as I had only made a handful of boards in my life. Would I be busted for a lack of technique on my first day and be let go? What if I damaged a board while using one of those powerful hand tools? How long would their patience extend once they found out that I didn't know the correct technique?

I showed up for work, and it turned out that P.K. was a patient mentor, although my apprenticeship came at the expense of a couple of damaged boards that skidded off the racks and onto the concrete floor before I became a competent member of the staff.

The work was dirty and exhausting. Still, I was around the industry and some of its finest craftsmen, and I began to absorb a world-class education on the art and techniques involved in the surfboard building process.

In September 1981, after I'd spent nine months in the U.S, my visa expired, and I returned to England and started my own business making surfboards. But as winter closed in, and the endless days of rain, drizzle, and cold gripped the country, I realized, like legions of others before me, that the weather in California is the real and enduring star of the state. This was before man's disruption of the global climate had incubated the horrifying wildfires and worrisome patterns of drought that now threaten its residents. I'd made my decision: I was going to return, but this time it would be for good.

At the end of that winter, I sold my tools and once again took off for California. During my first trip I had developed a relationship with Mike Eaton, a surfboard shaper at the factory and a world-renowned craftsman who had made boards for some of the world's finest professionals from California to Hawaii and as far away as Australia. He let me stay at his place, and I soon slipped back into my old job polishing boards, along with taking on some additional duties in other areas of the production line. Then, one day, an incident occurred that threatened to derail my plans and promised immediate deportation from the country. It was Friday, and Paul pulled the staff together. He announced that the cash float that he kept in his desk had been tampered with and the money in it was missing. His next words sent a chill down my spine. "The insurance investigators have been called in, and they will be conducting their research starting on Monday to see if they can figure out who took the cash." My heart sank. Of all the things that could go wrong, this was certainly high on the list. If I showed up on Monday, I would be questioned. And since my eligibility for employment was non-existent, I could be exposed on that front.

If I didn't show up, I would become a, if not the, prime suspect in the theft. I tossed and turned for three sleepless nights, consumed with a choice that had little upside.

I awoke on Monday morning, got dressed, and drove off to work, expecting that one way or another, it would be my last day. When I arrived, the other members of the early shift were milling around drinking coffee and organizing their tools. I grabbed some boards and began to work, not looking up from the spinning wool disc before me until break time.

Finally, I put my machine down and wandered over to the office, which doubled as a break room. Two brothers whose job it was to sandpaper the boards to a smooth finish were in the office, along with Robin, the head shaper. They were talking about the insurance company, and it wasn't long before I realized that the perpetrator had been unmasked late on Friday, shortly after the announcement of the theft. No one was saying how. Maybe there had been a confession. Or had there been a mistake, and it wasn't a theft after all? I never found out, and as far as I was concerned, it didn't matter. I just breathed a sigh of relief and walked back out onto the shop floor. I could now get back to planning what my next steps toward immigration were going to be.

Since I was holding down a regular job, I started to develop a strategy and determined that a consultation with a lawyer would be the next step. I collected all the free newspapers that littered the residential area near the beach and poured over the legal ads, finally setting up an appointment with a downtown lawyer to strategize my entry into the new world. In my naivete I chose a firm owned by a single attorney. The justification was that he must be cheaper than the numerous other legal firms in the ads as they sported the names of four or five managing partners, all of whom had to get paid.

On the day of the meeting, I made my way to the address, which turned out to be a house built in the early 1900s that had been converted into four "suites." Professionals, including an accountant, a real estate company, and another law firm, occupied the remaining three offices. I climbed the creaking wooden stairs and, after a brief meeting with the attorney, I was passed along to a paralegal who asked questions about my goals, qualifications, and intentions. "Yes, we can certainly help" was the predictable outcome of the conversation. Even being fresh off the boat, I was suspicious of such a positive response. I wondered if he could seriously help, or if he was merely assessing if I was gullible enough to accept that his law firm could make all my immigration dreams come true, for a price of course.

Probably knowing that the cost of this project could be a deal-breaker, he refrained from mentioning a price as he walked through the steps that would guide me toward my new life. Finally, I confronted him with the question of money, and he talked me through their rates and payment plans. Although the process seemed unfairly tilted toward the law firm receiving full payment without guaranteeing anything in return, I signed up for what I feared could quickly turn into a financial sink hole.

As he wound down his presentation, the paralegal casually tossed out the fact that the process could take some time, and that any delays would most likely be the result of twists and turns perpetrated by the government. I put two and two together and realized that should these twists occur, it could also extend the law firm's grasp on me. "You'll need this surfboard company to sponsor you and they need to fill out these forms," he said, brandishing a set of papers along with a contract that was to cement the relationship between us. With the bundle of forms in hand, I was ushered to the door and told to make an appointment after I had returned the completed paperwork. Encouraged that at least I was making some forward progress, I went home and immediately set up a meeting with the owner of the surfboard business.

The morning of the appointment arrived and I pulled out the smartest attire that I owned: a blue polo shirt, some wrinkled khakis, and a pair of tennis shoes. I'd scrubbed the shoes with a wet rag the night before, which had blended the more prominent stains with the white background—giving an overall appearance of an off-white finish that was at least consistent across both shoes.

Arriving at the corporate office, I was greeted by a receptionist who, after a quick phone call, walked me into the owner's office. The room was surprisingly small and lit by a single fluorescent light that hung from the ceiling. Reprints of ads for the company's surfboards and clothing products lined the walls while at the back of the room stood a desk that displayed a cluster of invoices along with ad copy waiting for approval.

I'd always considered Larry, the owner, to be a somewhat dour figure. On his occasional visits to the surfboard factory, I rarely saw him smile. And as far as I could tell, he didn't often engage in the kind of light banter that typically takes place between people in the workplace. My musings, however, were cut short when he walked into the office and invited me to sit down before asking what this green card situation was all about.

I laid out what I believed to be an irresistible pitch. The proposition was that if he sponsored me for labor certification, his business would secure a loyal and consistent employee in what otherwise tended to be a somewhat flaky labor pool. I explained how the immigration process worked and how minimal his actual involvement would need to be. For his part, all he would need to do was support my application as a European design consultant for his surfboards.

I delivered my proposal in meticulous steps. However, as thorough as my preparation was, I couldn't help but feel that when it was over and silence filled the room, I was dangling at the end of a rope. And as each second ticked by, another strand of the cord was separating, leaving me hanging ever more precariously. Was he about to ask me about my current status since I was already working for him? Would he kick me out without a thought as to my offer on the table?

During the presentation, I had worked my way to the edge of the chair, out of a mixture of excitement, anxiety, and the need to make each point with as much conviction as possible. Now that it was over, I sat back and looked at the CEO, who showed no sign of emotion. He merely looked past me, tapping the end of a pencil slowly on the table. I leaned back and felt the sweat that had accumulated during my speech making its way down between my shoulder blades.

He pushed his chair back from behind the desk, alternating his gaze between me and the framed ads on the wall. "Will it cost me any money?" he asked.

"Not a dime, I replied. I cover all the expenses. You'll probably need to go downtown for an interview, but that'll be it."

Eager to downplay any burdensome activities that might derail a positive outcome, I painted a picture of a smooth ride through the bureaucracy chaperoned by accommodating Immigration and Naturalization Service agents, all the while disguising the fact that I didn't have a clue about what the process involved. I waited to see if he would bring up my current status in his workforce.

"What're the next steps?" he asked, bending forward as if he was looking for that one flaw in my arguments that would cause the whole proposition to collapse like a house of cards in the hands of a two-year-old.

"Just sign the forms as a sponsor, that's it."

He sat back again and held me in a cold stare that read, *do I trust this foreigner, where's the downside and who is this dude anyway?*

I could feel the last strands of the rope giving up the fight and was sure that the sweat that was now wicking through my polo shirt would signal that I was a serial liar who had no idea what I might be getting both of us into. I began to analyze what I could have done differently and what kind of a Hail Mary I could throw since, at this point, it felt as if my future was slipping through my cold, sweaty hands.

"Alright," he said. "Where're the forms?" His body language up to that point had suggested no deal, and I was taken aback by this sudden turnaround. Collecting my thoughts, I reached for the crisp manila folder that I'd purchased from the office supply store the previous day. Shuffling through the set of papers that lay inside and pushing past the old magazine ads for my surfboards, I pulled out the forms he needed to sign. Assembling them neatly on the desk in front of him, I said, "I've marked where you need to sign." In my naiveté, I expected him to fire off his John Hancock right there and then, so I hovered awkwardly over the table, fidgeting like an accused offender waiting for the jury's verdict. "Let me have my legal guy look at these. I'll get back to you."

Not yet experienced in the ways of business, this was not a step that I'd anticipated. Still, quickly realizing that it was pro forma, I thanked him for his time, shook his hand, and left the office, hoping that the sweat on the back of my shirt was not yet visible. I thanked the receptionist on the way out to the parking lot and received a practiced smile in return.

A week later, a number of us were convened in the surfboard factory's office. The manager, between sips of coffee, turned to me as if he was surprised that he'd remembered and said, "Oh yeah, this came for you from the corporate office." He grabbed a large brown envelope and tossed it across the room. I opened it and slid the top paper out only to the point where I recognized the contents as the immigration forms I'd left with the owner. Not wishing to explain what was in the package, I slid the paper casually back into the envelope and placed it on the seat next to me. No one questioned why I'd received something from corporate, and before the break was over, I slipped out to my car, tucking the papers under the front seat until I could examine them in greater detail at home. That evening I reviewed the forms, and sure enough, the owner had signed them. The following morning, they were dispatched to my attorney for review before being forwarded to the INS.

Time passed, and days turned into weeks, weeks into months. Finally, it became evident that my visa was going to expire and that I would have to leave the country. I checked in with the attorney and set everything up for my absence. I then spent the next couple of weeks putting together a plan to fly to Australia while my paperwork weaved its tenuous way through the first stage of the immigration process.

It wasn't long before I was on a flight to Sydney, where, after almost a year in the land down under, I received an urgent request from my attorney to return to the States. He'd received notification from the INS about a date for an interview where both the owner of the business and I needed to appear in person.

I hastily applied for a new visa at the U.S. Embassy and, within days, was boarding a plane bound for Los Angeles. As promised, an interview ensued and Larry accompanied me to the federal building downtown to answer questions as to the validity of my application. We left the interview with no indication as to whether it had achieved the desired result or if we'd missed the mark. The INS instructed me to standby, saying that they would contact my attorney, who was acting as my agent.

I returned to work in the factory and again began a wait that turned from days to weeks and finally months with no updates coming from any source. I badgered the attorney who, condescendingly, seemed only mildly interested in where my petition was heading. This lack of progress was a growing concern as I was still making regular payments to the law firm while earning a modest hourly wage.

There was nothing I could do to speed up the process, and so the weeks dragged on. Then one day, while reading the local newspaper, I learned that my attorney had driven the wrong way down an off-ramp and onto the freeway, where he had been struck in a head-on collision and killed. Tests on the body had revealed alcohol intoxication. I had only met him occasionally, since the day-to-day processing of my petition was handled by his paralegal—a contact who, despite repeated phone calls, went silent after the death of his boss.

It had now been over a year and a half since I'd applied for labor certification and, as the time ticked by, I realized that my latest visa would only last for a few more months. I needed to decide to move on to a new plan or return to the colder confines of England. I wrestled with the options and evaluated other countries in which I might build a future, an exercise I'd been through many times before. And I grappled with the realization that I was in the right place, but was this the right time.

CHAPTER 3

Society's Dark Underbelly

Homicide, drugs, money, sex, what you 'bout?
Cousin Stizz - "What You Bout"

Due to the friendships I had made on my first visit, along with an expanding number of acquaintances, I became more exposed to San Diego's social life. Mike's house was a hub for impromptu gatherings that would draw in neighbors, surf industry workers, and friends from the multiple interests he pursued. Mike lived in one of the more affluent areas of San Diego. One Friday night, he decided to invite a few friends around to his house overlooking the ocean, which stretched out beyond the cliffs at the bottom of the street. During a conversation about the party, Mike, speaking from underneath a long gray mustache that gave him the aura of a latter-day gunslinger, mentioned, "You'll get to meet Maggie. She's someone where, if you're ever feeling down, she'll pick you up by the bootstraps and give you a good shakin'. You'll get a kick out of her." Then he smiled, with a twinkle in his eye.

That evening the guests started to arrive and, as with most parties, a crowd assembled in the kitchen. Some gathered around the butcher-block island in the center of the room, while others, in smaller groups, were scattered around the house locked in conversation, clutching glasses of wine and picking at the snacks laid out before them. A trio stood in the front room admiring the sunset, a view made possible by a panoramic west-facing window that provided a 180-degree view of the ocean. Captured in this view was a sliver of the city where homes blanketed the hillside, only stopping at the land's margin with the sea.

Smooth jazz played in the background as the last guests merged into the festivities. One of the late arrivals was a tall woman with a broad smile accented with bright-red lipstick and wearing a dress by Norma Kamali, a hip designer of the day. The dress featured substantial shoulder padding, which gave the wearer a look reminiscent of a National Football League player who'd forgotten to remove their pads after a game. It was a silhouette that I later discovered was a must-have amongst the avant-garde of the time. The dress, a vibrant teal color, was offset by a shock of curly red hair coiffed slightly above the shoulder. Wearing a pair of flaming red heels, she clacked across the wooden floor, working the crowd and greeting old friends, often with shrieks and hugs, before moving on to more unfamiliar faces. Standing by a window, chatting with a local photographer, I missed the introductory tour and remained ignorant as to who she was, outside of recognizing that here was someone who certainly knew how to make an entrance.

As the guests settled into their conversations, the sun slowly sank behind the horizon in a blaze of orange and we migrated to a cozy living room at the back of the house, where sliding glass doors led to a deck equipped with a Jacuzzi shaded by trees that protruded over the fence from the neighbor's yard.

I slumped into a comfy armchair and struck up a conversation with a shapely yoga teacher who had just scored a swimwear modeling assignment. As we talked, I briefly contemplated taking up yoga, but my thoughts were interrupted when her photographer husband showed up. As she pirouetted and glided away, I glanced around the room and spotted a group huddled around the coffee table where a mound of cocaine, the size of half a ping-pong ball, had been deposited. This was the early eighties, and as I spent more time in Southern California, I realized that many a party was energized by this magic powder.

I took a slug from my bottle of imported Danish lager and, out of the corner of my eye, saw the teal dress heading my way. The wearer swooped in and knelt on the carpet in front of me. Sporting her bright red smile, she said, "Hi, Ian, I'm Maggie. Mike tells me you're from England. How's your trip going so far?" I responded with some generic response about how great the weather was and how much I enjoyed the outdoor lifestyle. Undaunted by an answer that seemed plucked from a tourist brochure, she continued to pepper me with questions. "How long are you staying, have you been to Mexico yet, what's happening in the music scene in England, we're always so far behind England when it comes to music and fashion, do you work with Mike, how long have you been in town, what have you seen since you've been here?"

It wasn't long before I started to understand what my roommate had meant. This was a high energy, intelligent, and curious woman, and I was beginning to get the impression that she just might be an extrovert. We chatted, or more accurately I was chatted to, for about ten minutes until the dynamics of the party changed and we found ourselves mingling with other guests. I didn't think much about the exchange until a few weeks later.

The following week I was sitting in the kitchen, enjoying a beer with Mike, and started ruminating about my stalled immigration plans. I joked that at this rate, I would need to find someone to marry me to avoid having to leave again. A flippant remark delivered in jest slowly led to a serious conversation, and we began to discuss the possibilities of such a wild notion. That debate then morphed into a game plan, where the idea of an arranged marriage would be floated amongst carefully selected members of our social circle to see if it would generate any interest. The goal, of course, was to see if there might be a single female interested in a brief marriage that had a financial upside but no long-term strings attached. I'd no idea what something like this might cost, and neither did Mike. It wasn't as if either of us had traveled this road before. But, without any further delay, the message was crafted and carefully relayed to selected targets.

As our circle of confidants shared the information with their networks, the first feedback came in the form of estimates as to what it might cost to create this kind of arrangement. Prices started at a few thousand dollars and escalated to hundreds of thousands. I thought to myself that at multiple thousands of dollars, the candidate would have to be a Hollywood A-lister. All the numbers seemed very speculative, and I realized that in this murky arena, there were no rules and certainly no price sheets. I sat back and let the jungle telegraph continue to do its work, waiting to see what would come of this curious twist in my affairs.

In about a week word arrived that Betty, the lingerie store owner was interested in talking about a possible arrangement. Betty didn't disappoint when it came to feminine allure. Full figured and with flowing dark hair, she would show up to social events always impeccably dressed. I remember witnessing her arrival at a party some months earlier when she'd swooshed up to the curb in her classic 1960s Cadillac convertible, brilliant white and long enough to consume two parking spots. Betty had exited the car to shrieks of delight from her appreciative female friends who were amongst the crowd gathered on the front yard.

The intermediary for our communications was Debbie, the yoga teacher I'd met at Mike's party a few weeks earlier. She'd known Betty for some years and had met her through her patronage of the lingerie store Betty owned on the outskirts of downtown San Diego. Debbie would pass messages on to Betty and bring back her responses. Through this process, we started a dialogue. Encouraged by the early progress and eager to dive into the unknown territory of negotiating a marriage, I gave some dates and times when I could meet and eagerly awaited her response.

News arrived a week later, a much darker report than I'd been expecting. It turned out that Betty's brother was a somewhat shadowy character with links to the underworld. Over time, he'd become involved in the drug trade, and his business had escalated to the point that he was now a significant player. Something had gone awry with one of his recent transactions, leaving an aggrieved party who had not taken kindly to being wronged. One afternoon, two guys had walked into her store and shot her.

This callous act was a signature of the drug trade. Operating under its own rules, and governed by brutal and often instant justice, its violent structure was propped up by fear and intimidation. If you were in the business and strayed beyond the fluid confines of its practices, the penalties were typically swift and often deadly. Betty was innocent of any wrongdoing. However, due to her relationship, she became the collateral, selected as compensation for the misdeeds her brother had visited upon some unknown who, in turn, felt compelled to set the record straight using the one tool that got everyone's attention.

Appalled at the proximity of this act of retribution, it took a while to refocus on my mission. Still, the plan was in motion, and it was only a few days later that I returned from work to find Mike sitting at the kitchen table. "Hi," I said, greeting him as usual, even though I could detect from the broad smile that creased his face below the overhang of his mustache that he had something to share.

"Guess what?" he said.

I played along nonchalantly, not wanting to appear eager to hear what he had to say. Mike was a notorious jokester, so this was most likely some new gag he'd just gleaned from the postman, a visitor who always seemed to have a bottomless cache of new material. At least Mike's smile indicated that it wasn't bad news. So I pulled up a chair on the opposite side of the kitchen island and politely waited for his next move, half expecting to have to roll my eyes at yet another painful one-liner.

"Guess who I spoke to today?" he said with a glint in his eye.

"Dunno," I replied, still puzzled at where this was leading.

"Maggie."

"Oh yeah, the redhead who wears the designer dresses."

"Yeah, that Maggie. Well, it looks like she's struggling with some bills right now, and with a young kid, she could use some extra income, so she's interested in this whole marriage thing. She wants to meet you and find out what your game is. It looks like you might have a hot one." He passed me a used envelope with a telephone number scribbled on the back of it. "Now it's up to you," he said with a grin.

PART 2

Escape to the Beach

CHAPTER 4

The Odd One Out

Well, I know what's right
I got just one life
In a world that keeps on pushin' me around
But I'll stand my ground
"Won't Back Down." – Tom Petty

Maggie had grown up with an older brother and a younger sister in a meat-and-potatoes suburb, just east of downtown Long Beach. The regimented clusters of houses were situated within walking distance of transportation networks and cookie-cutter retail outlets, along with the schools and parks that had been added to support the growing population. Mid-tier hotels and motels, a recent addition, mainly punctuated the neighborhoods closest to the beach. Here, they announced their presence with colorful flags that flapped nonchalantly above awning-shaded entryways, each banner bearing the name of a hospitality chain, all eager to entice members of a new era of post-war traveler who arrived in their late-model automobiles carrying discretionary income.

Many of these tourists had traveled from points inland eager to take advantage of their two weeks of annual vacation. They were quick to spread their towels on the warm sands of the local beaches, where they were joined by the city's youth, equally as bent on enjoying the freedom that the sandy retreats offered. These young folk were part of a demographic that had grown up listening to their parents talk about the struggles they endured during the war years. No matter where time would ultimately lead them, these members of the next generation were going to live in the moment. It was a generation establishing itself not as a body of obedient offspring, but as a movement of non-conformists underpinned by a desire that their goals, aspirations, and vices be of their own making. They were wary of the regimented lives they witnessed their parents leading and yearned to carve out their own futures. Futures that would be built on their decisions rather than on the dogma of the establishment's expectations.

Reinforcing this newly assumed right to self-determination was the ominous presence of the ongoing and politically suspect Vietnam War. The violence and carnage precipitated by the conflict were delivered nightly to their black-and-white TV sets, where the likes of journalist Walter Cronkite would peer amiably from the screen while informing the viewers of "Today's Vietnam story in a moment." The camera would then cut to film of Marines scouting out North Vietnamese encampments or to more graphic scenes of body bags and injured soldiers.

Both saddened and increasingly outraged to see so many of their peers being sent into harm's way, these young people had become keenly aware of the value of life. In so doing, they had decided not to live by the societal mores of the day, much less blindly adhere to the rules of bureaucrats and the ever-present corporate machine with its dress codes, timecards, and exploitive hierarchies.

Maggie was born in June of 1948 in Hollywood, California, making her a part of the Vietnam generation. Her father was a retired naval petty officer who later settled into a job repairing business machines, and her mother was a nurse. They had met during the Second World War and had married shortly after it ended. Larry, her father, was of Irish descent and one of five children. Growing up in Omaha, Nebraska, he was the son of an alcoholic father who spent more time riding the rails and drinking than he did tending to family. This lack of parenting, combined with only intermittent detours into the world of work, left his wife and children with a small and irregular income. On more than one occasion, Larry was admitted to the Omaha Boys Home for Orphans, an institution that included many children of the destitute. He once recalled that "In those days we were so poor that a nice black family on our street used to give us bread crusts because there were times my mother couldn't get enough cereal from the factory to feed us." Childhood experiences like these had molded a resilient but insular patriarch for the family.

Marguerite, her mother, was raised on a farm in Nebraska, distant from any centers of population and in an environment where children, and most certainly girls, were meant to be seen and not heard. It was the time of the horse-drawn plow, long before agribusiness moguls had acquired most of the expansive farmland in the Midwest to grow soybeans for the Chinese market. The motto on the farm was "spare the rod spoil the child." This practice had left visible effects on the young girl by suffocating any emotional development that may have been hiding beneath the surface. The austerity of her upbringing had produced a hardened and stoic personality.

These backgrounds could have combined to create a grim childhood for Larry and Marguerite's three offspring, but that wasn't entirely the case. Larry showed great interest in his son John's development, fully embracing a child who, like his father, possessed an interest in all things mechanical. Michelle, the youngest daughter, had emerged as the parental favorite and enjoyed the kind of support and encouragement that would bypass her older sister.

When it came to Maggie, the well of understanding had run dry. Her mother seized on every opportunity to criticize the most willful of her offspring and attempted to keep her in check by assigning a daily list of chores that would occupy the child and keep her confined to the house for hours. She seemed fearful that Maggie might enjoy the kind of freedoms that she had been denied. Freedoms that through determination and guile, the child would still manage to taste. But they came at a price. Only by devising a rigorous schedule of waking early in the morning, while the rest of the household slept, and striking off her list of chores one by one before the sun came up could she escape. And at the close of the day, she would work into the night to complete her school homework. This system paved the way to that sweet payoff when she could quietly close the kitchen door behind her, rush out into the street, and make her way to the corner, where she and her friends would gather before heading off in pursuit of that day's adventure.

Growing up in Long Beach, California in the fifties had its perks. Sparse development, ample open space, and light traffic allowed kids, with the tacit approval of their parents, to not think twice about riding miles on their bicycles or walking long distances to meet friends, often at one of the beaches that lay south of the busy harbor. And it was before America's children were burdened by the need to continually grasp a smart phone as a conduit to paranoid parents.

These instances of escape, though hard-earned, were the panacea to a restrictive home life that was almost devoid of unconditional affection. Instead, it remained dominated by a father determined to raise his children in a manner that he saw fit and a mother who acquiesced to the control of her spouse.

By the time she was four years old, Maggie's curiosity about the world had begun to develop. But it was her brother, John, a full year older than she was, who would be the first to attend school. Watching him leave to spend all day surrounded by teachers and other students was almost more than she could bear. On that first day, John broke into tears. He didn't want to leave home, and he certainly didn't want to go to school. Maggie, in contrast, sat in her bedroom sulking because it would be an entire year before she would embrace this rite of passage. For her, school would provide another form of liberation from the rigors of her home life. The year would eventually pass, however, and what had seemed like an eternity finally came to an end as she stepped across the threshold of Charles A. Buffum Elementary.

As the early years of school slipped by, Maggie began to exercise her passion for learning by poring over magazines and quietly flipping through the meager library of children's books that lay around the family home. When she had exhausted these resources, she took to badgering friends and relatives, in the hope that they might part with some of their old or unwanted publications. It was during one of these solicitations that she hit the mother lode. One of her friends had an older sister who had in her possession several completed textbooks that she would happily pass along. Maggie dropped by her house that evening and left with armfuls of history, math, and English coursework.

This newfound trove of knowledge was manna to a young and eager mind. And within a day, she had erased all of the answers, notes, and doodles penciled in by the previous owner. She paid for the pristine pages with one large and painful callous. Despite this momentary discomfort, work began in earnest to sift through the puzzles, problems, calculations, and essays contained in the books. And it was only a few weeks until the material was absorbed and the publications stacked neatly in the corner of her bedroom as she embarked on the hunt for more.

During breaks in the school's academic calendar, one of the tools the district used to bring education into its pupils' homes was a bookmobile that toured the surrounding neighborhoods. A perceptive librarian, Ms. Peterson, drove the bus that traveled to Maggie's. Ms. Peterson was quick to notice the extraordinary appetite for books that the energetic kid on Pepperwood Avenue displayed, and she watched as the child would leap onboard the bus and move systematically from the shelves at the front slowly toward those at the back, pulling specific titles out and returning the ones that didn't fit that day's agenda. It was like a candy store for her. And she would pepper Ms. Peterson with questions about that day's inventory, specific topics, and when a book she had heard about might become available.

Realizing that this was a child with a curious mind and the drive to satisfy it, Ms. Peterson soon became familiar with the subjects that interested the girl. She would arrive on the street and greet her student with a cry of, "Margret, I think you're going to love what I've found!" She would then hand over selected publications featuring animals, American Indians, and specific periods in history. Maggie would pick out which ones she wanted and carry the books into the house, where their contents were eagerly absorbed. At the next visit, she would return the journals and pick up a new set. The work of this savvy librarian would help cast the young girl's future interests by introducing her to the mysteries of the world from the printed page.

When Maggie was seven, a job opportunity presented itself. Eager to earn her own money and in the process gain a sliver of independence, she jumped at the chance. Any allowance emerging from the parental porthole at the time was scant and typically came with strings attached. The job was ironing clothes for a neighbor, and the money earned was immediately spent with the Government Printing Office, where it was possible to order a book for a quarter. It wasn't long before a cluster of paperbacks and magazines formed a mini library in the corner of her small bedroom, with an entire section dedicated to astronomy. The ability to read the night sky by reading a book reinforced her thirst for enlightenment and betrayed an inner wish for escape. She craved the time when she could shed the suffocating list of chores, arbitrary restrictions, and criticism, and experience the sensations conjured up by an active imagination. It was a longing fed by the promise of the real-life adventures that beckoned from the words and pictures in her books. When asked by an instructor what her favorite subject was, the quick reply was, "Everything!" And it was no surprise when Margret would ask a teacher for next year's coursebook so she could study it before the semester commenced.

The staff at school fostered this curiosity and fed her thirst for knowledge not only by teaching the disciplines of math and science but also by attending to the creative side of the brain, exposing their students to unusual artistic pursuits such as gourd-painting. It was not just splashing on watercolors so the expression of a child's inner Van Gogh could feature on the family mantel. Rather, they had the children paint the gourds with symbols from different languages and then explain what the symbols meant.

Social studies class was another creative favorite. Here, the teacher would take the brightest students from the class and have them write to their favorite author. In Maggie's case, she chose Marguerite Henry, the author of fifty-nine books based on true stories of horses and animals. Much to her surprise, Ms. Henry took the time to reply, and her first letter became the catalyst for an ongoing correspondence that lasted over a year. Ms. Henry's letters received a reverence usually reserved for a scholarly archive, with each note carefully folded and kept within a binder tied up with a strip of cloth tape that was placed in a prime position on Maggie's bedside table.

This consumption of knowledge and a keen fascination with the world beyond her neighborhood continued through elementary and middle school until high school beckoned. And it was here that a new set of interests would consume her attention.

As a teenager, the various experiences of high school started to mold her outlook while the beach began to dominate her free time. In the hot summers, she would hang out on the sand on the weekend and show up to school on Monday morning to share tales of her adventures, and of the dangers that she and her friends had survived in the pounding surf.

Maggie's parents were never the kind to pack up the car with swimsuits, towels, and a packed lunch and haul the family down to the sand for the day. They were more likely to be found cussing over a stuck piston in the cluttered garage or chuckling over a game of cribbage with a friend than getting covered in sand and sunburnt. If Maggie wanted to get to the seaside, she had to use public transportation or walk.

Her attraction to the beach occurred at the same time that the sport of surfing was starting to creep into Southern California's coastal life. Surfboards had evolved from heavy redwood hulls, which would often take two people to haul them to the waterline, to sleek new lightweight foam and fiberglass models that were showing up at surfing spots along the coast. Featured on the hugely popular *Ed Sullivan Show* and added as a novelty filler to sports channels and print media, surfing was taking its first steps to becoming the defining element of California's beach culture.

The rebel spirit created by the freedom-loving lifestyle of the surfing community was intoxicating to California's youth. Society considered riding waves, basking in the warm sun, and lazing away the summer on the sand a waste of time. Nevertheless, it delighted the early adopters of this new pastime.

Many surfers of the day were returning Vietnam vets. And they were intent on living in a manner that was a polar opposite to the stark and bitter existence they had experienced on tours in the jungles of Southeast Asia. No rules, no uniforms, no overseers, and any danger was of their own making, typically defined by the size of the day's surf. Over time, the waves, parties, and camaraderie spawned a strange new surfer dialect with names for specific maneuvers performed on the waves and for the various elements of their surfboards. This linguistic evolution, in turn, created a tribal feel to what was an emerging youth-driven subculture.

Now in high school, Maggie was a part of the surfer crowd. But not to the point where she would miss cheering on the jocks during the school's football games or fail to show up at the Friday night dances, where live bands played for the energetic students all eager to perfect the latest dance steps.

When the weekend arrived, she would get up before dawn and take care of her chores. After packing away cleaning supplies and dust rags, it was a short bus ride to the beach to catch up with the gang.

And it wasn't long before Maggie's friends began passing their driving tests, which, for any teen, pried open the envelope of discovery. Car ownership provided quick transportation, not only to the nearby ocean but also to undiscovered territory up and down the coast.

Maggie took to the water with the same passion she directed toward her schoolwork. First, it was bodysurfing at the rock groin in Seal Beach, a twenty-minute drive down the coast, where some local experts took Maggie and a couple of her friends under their wing. They showed them how to survive the bigger and more powerful surf by swimming to the sandy bottom to avoid the impact of a breaking wave, and how to pick just the right shaped peak before turning for shore and kicking off with their swim fins to match the speed of the swell. They would bob around in the surf for hours, launching into waves up to ten feet high before they crashed into the shore in an explosion of water and foam, accompanied by the excited shrieks of the girls.

The calories burned by their exertions were enough to light a small house and resulted in the trio emerging from the water with gnawing appetites that could only be satisfied by one reliable source. After a quick towel-off, they would head to the French bakery on Main Street, where the smell of freshly baked goods perfumed the air.

Bloodshot eyes would eagerly watch the hot crusty loaves as they were picked from the racks by gloved hands and packaged up in brown paper bags. The next stop was the convenience store across the street to grab a quarter pound of butter to complete the buffet. After a short walk back to the beach, the warm, soft dough drenched with ample helpings of melting butter soon vanished beneath colorful tales from that morning's session.

While body-surfing provided a gateway into the surfing community, it was the stand-up crowd that ruled the waves. These riders were the athletes of the beach. Carving their ten-foot platforms deftly around the whitewater and out onto the unbroken green faces of the swell, they would stroll to the very front of their boards and pose as if defying the rules of physics. And just as the energy center of the wave changed, they would rapidly back-pedal to keep their boards from digging into the water and launching them from their perches. The surfers would continuously adjust to the playing field that moved beneath them—twisting, crouching, and using their center of balance to gain maximum speed and maneuverability until it was time to flip the board over the back of the wave and paddle out for the next one.

Physically fit and comfortable in the ocean, Maggie was not oblivious to the fact that at that time it was unusual to see a woman in the waves. Despite the lack of a peer group, she decided to buck the status quo and learn how to surf standing up. Local board riders had yet to adopt the territorial mentality that would creep into the sport as crowds increased along with the competition for waves. And as a result, the boys looked with curiosity at a girl who wanted to learn to surf. A couple of them spent time loaning her their boards and giving advice until she could scramble to her feet and stand up for a precious few seconds. Her muscle memory, not yet attuned to the split-second balance needed to be competent, meant she paid her dues, often steering the board into irrecoverable positions from which she would be pitched awkwardly into the water.

By the age of sixteen, she had managed to save up enough money to afford a second-hand board. With the surfboard industry in its infancy, there were only a few manufacturers up and down the coast, with each business typically bearing the owner's name, such as Velzy, Bing, Gordon and Smith, and Hobie. Maggie picked out a model called the Soul Invention from the racks of the Jacob's surfboards factory, which proudly bore the manufacturer's logo and sported orange panels on either side of a wooden strip down the center. Now equipped with her board, the young surfer's technique quickly improved as she spent many long summer days surfing the local breaks.

Contrary to the nature of her upbringing, Maggie had turned out to be an extrovert and was never shy to engage a stranger in conversation. And it was during one of these chance encounters that she met a resident, much older than she was, who lived near the beach. His curiosity at seeing this young girl tackling what he viewed as a very manly sport led to a conversation between the two. He ended up offering to let her leave her board at his rental cottage, not far from the sand. This act of kindness meant she would no longer have the hassle of relying on a friend with a car to haul it to and from her house. She jumped at the chance.

Turning sixteen also meant going to nightclubs, where security guards would check each person's age at the door before allowing them to enter. Those old enough to purchase alcohol had their hands stamped. Without a stamp you couldn't purchase alcohol, but you were still on the hook to buy a quota of one soft drink every hour.

In nearby Seal Beach, a converted Quonset hut had become a music venue that housed the vibrant Airport Club. A litany of emerging acts included the club in their touring itinerary as they worked to realize their dreams of getting that elusive big break. It was here that Maggie first saw artists such as the Rivingtons, Jimmy Reed, Ike and Tina Turner, the Four Tops, and Little Richard. Some of the musicians did emerge from these humble beginnings to become icons in the world of music. However, on the nights they headlined at the Airport Club, they were typically newcomers not yet famous enough for the bigger auditoriums.

At another venue called the Lighthouse Club, near the pier in Hermosa Beach, jazz acts such as Art Blakey and Mongo Santamaria played to packed crowds. One evening the featured artist was Les McCann. Backing Les on drums was Bill Cosby, the comedian, quietly playing in the background. Later that evening, Les sought out Maggie in the crowd and ended up asking her for a date, which she managed to evade. She decided that going out with someone who was more than ten years her senior likely wasn't going to end up being in her best interest. Nevertheless, seeing McCann and Leroy Vinnegar up close in a dimly lit club, alive with dancing and music, was a treat not to be missed.

A few years later, there were trips farther afield to the Shrine Auditorium in Los Angeles where, under its massive chandeliers, Maggie would see both emerging and established rock artists like Electric Flag, Blue Cheer, the original Cream, Janis Joplin, and Jimi Hendrix. Another favorite haunt was the open-air Greek Theatre, which hosted the likes of Crosby Stills Nash and Young. With exposure to these artists, the world of music soon joined her other passions and it would spark a vinyl record collection that would grow into the hundreds.

It was at one of these early shows at the Airport Club that Maggie and some friends got tickets to see Ike and Tina Turner. On stage, Tina Turner roared out some of their early numbers, including River Deep Mountain High and It's Gonna Work Out Fine. Behind her, the Ikettes sashayed through their synchronized dance moves, the gold fringes of their dresses swishing from side to side in unison. Meanwhile, out front, the five-feet-four-inch fireball was busy stomping, sneering, and kicking up her heels—much to the delight of a crowd squeezed together in front of the stage in a bond of sweaty admiration.

Also at the show that night was a group of Cholos, Hispanic toughs who wore a uniform of khaki shorts and long socks, usually accompanied by flannel shirts fastened only by the top button. This particular group came from the north side of the Seal Beach pier, an area they had staked out as their territory. There was tribal friction between the surfers and the Cholos, but it had never manifested itself in any substantial violence outside of a few choice words and the odd shoving match.

Amongst the females was an overweight woman who went by the nickname Big Mama. Big Mama had a ritual of arriving at the beach in the morning, where she would have a fellow gang member apply zinc sunscreen in the shape of the number 69 on her back. She would then lie out and bake in the hot summer sun as the number, isolated by the sunscreen, became temporarily tattooed onto her skin.

On this particular evening, Big Mama had arrived at the club with ill intentions and as the night wore on, she became uncomfortably interested in the exuberant redhead who was typically out on the dance floor. Big Mama fixed her threatening stare on Maggie and made a point of bumping into her during frequent visits to the bar. Finally, after a particularly violent jostling that almost knocked Maggie from her feet, Big Mama decided it was time to "choose her out," street vernacular for selecting an opponent for a fight. In a flash, it was on. Tables crashed to the floor, drinks spilled, and patrons leaped out of the way as the duo struggled with handfuls of hair and nails clawed at exposed flesh. A childhood spent fighting with an older and stronger brother had provided enough smarts in the art of brawling for Maggie to stay on her feet. And, after she'd withstood the initial rush from the zinc-embossed tsunami, it was only a matter of seconds before two burly security guards approached. Maggie's friends jumped in, grabbed a limb each, and hauled her off to the bathroom. Just in time for her to avoid the ignominy of being tossed out onto the sidewalk in the middle of the night.

As her hair was adjusted and her makeup repaired, a smartly dressed attendant entered the bathroom. Spying Maggie at a wash-basin, she crisply announced, "Ms. Turner would like to see you in her dressing room. Come this way, please." Assuming that she was about to get reprimanded for disrupting the show, Maggie dutifully followed the attendant out of the bathroom, down a dimly lit corridor behind the stage, and waited as she knocked on a door beside which hung a paper sign marked "Ike and Tina Turner." The door swung open, and as her eyes adjusted to the bright light inside, she could see Tina sitting in front of a makeup mirror, dabbing cotton wool on each eye. Ike was in the corner with what looked like a business type signing some papers, and the Ikettes were milling around a stand-up table enjoying a post-concert drink. At the back of the room, Maggie spotted Willie, a singer from one of the local bands, talking to Ike's bass player, and she nervously waved hello.

Tina looked up and said hi as the attendant left the room, pulling the door closed. After getting her name, Tina yelled out an introduction to everyone in the room, then pointed to a chair beside her and gestured to Maggie to sit down. "Honey, you're a good fighter, but you're too clean. Girl, if she got you down, you were in trouble." Tina then went on to share stories of her earlier days as a bartender and how she'd learned to defend herself against drunks and unfavorable advances. "If anyone plays with you, you dip your finger in their eye. Somebody's comin' after you, you gotta hurt 'em. You can't play. That out there wasn't playing, that was serious, but I like your style." Maggie couldn't believe it. Here she was getting the lowdown on how to inflict some serious bodily harm from a woman who only minutes earlier had been revving up the crowd with her signature high-octane performance.

They continued to chat until the same attendant came to escort Maggie out into the ballroom, where cleanup for the following night's performance had already begun. After that meeting, it became a ritual for Maggie to attend Ike and Tina Turner concerts whenever they came to town. And she would always get as close to the stage as possible and wave hi. Tina would respond with, "Waddya wanna hear tonight?" That was before the days of superstardom—before crowds in the thousands, high prices for front row tickets, and security personnel put an end to that kind of intimacy.

CHAPTER 5

Far Too Soon

Heavy metal thunder
Racin' with the wind
And the feelin' that I'm under
Steppenwolf – "Born to be Wild"

It was only a matter of time before a handsome fellow student began to attract Maggie's attention. Bill Johnson, clad in a leather jacket and jeans, could often be found roaring around town on his motorcycle. And it was this rebel persona that proved irresistible to a girl who had grown up within the boundaries of a conservative household.

The two were often seen together at school dances or at one of the fast-food joints around town, and Bill soon became Maggie's first deep relationship. With success in school, her love of the beach, and now a handsome partner, she felt her life was heading in the right direction.

On the evening of October 3, 1964, after the two had been dating for a few months, Maggie was invited to hang out with some girl-friends on a Saturday evening, and she told Bill about the invitation. Bill hadn't seen his friend Eddy in some time. And he'd just purchased a new lightweight motorcycle that he wanted to show him, so he agreed that they should go their separate ways that night.

Maggie got dressed up and stepped out with the girls, listening to music and then seeking out one of the local restaurants for a late-night snack. It was shortly before midnight.

At the same time, Bill, now seventeen years of age, was riding around town with his friend Eddy Hoffman, one year his senior, on the pillion seat. They'd called on a couple of friends, but as it was getting late, they decided to climb aboard the bike and head for home. As they drove down empty streets bathed in orange light from the streetlamps, Bill became aware of the lack of traffic and turned up the throttle. The freedom of the speeding bike, the wind in their faces, and the absence of other vehicles made it feel as if they were the only people in the world. They turned a corner and began to approach the intersection of Willow Avenue and Lakewood Boulevard. Bill could see that the traffic light ahead was green, so, without hesitation, he continued to speed down the road.

Waiting to enter the intersection, and stuck at a red light, was twenty-seven-year-old Toussant Parker of Los Angeles. Parker had been waiting at the junction for what seemed like an eternity. And as the seconds ticked by, it dawned on him that the light must have malfunctioned. The typical time at a stoplight is around two minutes, but by now, Toussant had been waiting for over four with no indica-tion that anything was about to change. He scanned the streets around the intersection to see if there were any cops in the area. Slumping back in his seat, he continued to wait, eyes fixed on the static red light ahead of him. It was a big intersection, and he began to weigh his chances of crossing it on the red without encountering another vehicle. The neon-lit gas station on the other side of the road was empty, except for an attendant emptying some trashcans. The restaurant on his left had its interior lights turned down and appeared to be closed. As it was almost midnight, no other cars were waiting and there were no pedestrians in sight. With his patience now exhausted, Toussant glanced around the intersection one last time. Deciding the odds were in his favor, he stepped on the accelerator, and the car leaped forward just as Bill and Eddy roared through their green light. Bill was killed instantly.

Maggie didn't know about the collision until the following afternoon when Maritza, one of her closest friends, came by the house. When Maggie answered the door she could see from the tearful look in her friend's eyes that something was wrong. She stepped outside, closing the door quietly behind her.

"What is it?" she asked. Maritza gave her the news between sobs.

"I don't know how to tell you this." She paused, fighting to maintain what little composure she could muster. "Bill was in an accident last night on his motorcycle. I'm so sorry…but…but he didn't make it. He passed away."

Maggie stood on the porch, looking at her friend in disbelief. Her knees felt weak, and all the strength in her body evaporated. In a shallow voice, she started to ask half questions, "Where did…who… when…" and finally the tears came as she lowered herself onto the top step of the porch, laying her head in her hands as her body shook with grief. Maritza stayed on the patio for over an hour sharing what few details she had in between bouts of sobbing. When she finally left, Maggie pulled herself to her feet using the railing next to the stairs and went into the house. Walking silently past her parents, who were watching television, she entered her bedroom, closing the door behind her. It would be weeks before she could reconcile herself with the loss.

The next day the newspaper headlines read "Youth in Fatal Cycle Crash. One Dead as Cycle Hits Car." Eddy had survived the accident, missing any contact with the car, but he had finished up pinned in the wreckage of the bike. The following morning, he awoke in the hospital with skull and leg fractures. The police later confirmed that the stoplight had malfunctioned, and their report stated that when they arrived, all lights were stuck on green or red. Both sets of parents sued the city for the malfunctioning lights, but no lawsuit could ever return a deceased child.

Shaken by the loss, Maggie found solace at the beach, where the surfing culture was continuing to increase in popularity. Along with it, a related phenomenon began to emerge, not by any grand design but as part of the natural evolution of its youthful participants and their willingness to try new things. Individual clubs and party venues in the area started to feature rock bands with a particular style of reverb-drenched guitar playing, enhanced with fast picking, which emulated the sound of breaking waves. It was the incubation of a music genre called the surf guitar, where the focus was on the instruments, with most tracks typically omitting any lyrics. Places like Harmony Park in Anaheim and the Rendezvous on Balboa Island in Newport Beach put on shows by Dick Dale, the Ventures, the Chanteys, and the Challengers, and crowds packed the halls.

At the same time, a separate and competing form of surf music emerged in which harmonies were added to the original guitar sound. Bands such as the Beach Boys and Jan and Dean brought this vocal variety into the mainstream, much to the disdain of many in the hard-core surfer crowd who considered this music to be a sellout of the surfing underground.

With their unique style of music established, the surf crew took another step forward and came up with a new and spirited form of dancing. And it wasn't long before bleached-blond participants were rocking local dance halls, moving to the high-octane beat of the surf guitar while dancing the Surfer Stomp, the Frug, and the Watusi. The Surfer Stomp went on to become a coast-to-coast phenomenon in the early sixties with "Surf Stomp" events a staple in many beach and even urban venues, often accompanied by the leader of the surf guitar movement, Dick Dale, and his band the Del-Tones.

The evolution of surf culture had reached a peak with a unique language, specialized music, dance steps, and its own casual fashion. The word was getting around that surfing was cool and with this new popularity, the surfboard-manufacturing industry was quick to respond. Many businesses left their garages and backstreet workshops and expanded into stylish main street storefronts. Innovative T-shirts bearing the logos of board builders flew off the shelves. And it seemed like everybody from the kid next door to a favorite uncle living inland wanted to own a board, whether they could surf or not. Surfers had even gravitated to a functional form of transportation, the "Woody Wagon." These spacious wooden-sided vehicles, made by the likes of Pontiac, Plymouth, and Buick, were big enough to sleep the driver and often a handful of friends during surf trips up and down the coast. Upon arriving at a remote beach, the occupants would spill out of the wagon and into the water, often doubling the size of the crowd already riding the waves. This was still a time of innocence, where surfers would welcome visitors to their local break so they could share waves in the Hawaiian spirit of Aloha. And it was a time to be cherished, as it wouldn't be long before the popularity of the sport would see crowds of fifty or more competing for the waves at any given spot.

For Maggie, high school, the time to push through the perils of puberty with all of its social and emotional changes, was drawing to an inevitable close. It was time to consider higher education. Her grades had always been exemplary, despite an almost complete lack of support from her parents. They had come to view her scholastic achievements with a wary eye. Neither of them had pursued higher education. And now, faced with a daughter who was on track to become their intellectual superior, they were not about to encourage this well of knowledge. Instead, they chose to marginalize it, sometimes in a heartless way.

With the stellar scores she had achieved throughout high school, an Ivy League education was the logical next step. Glowing recommendations from the school and select members of the community would provide validation to an admissions committee that here was not only an exceptional student, but also a stand-up citizen. But even with a full scholarship, there would still be expenses. And in an attempt to defray some of these costs, she had worked all summer and saved $700. Her aspirations were high, but not unreasonable considering her grades. And she had chosen the study of medicine as her objective.

To apply for scholarships, Maggie needed her father's signature on the financial disclosure papers. "I'm not giving the government information about how much money I make," was his terse response when she proudly slid the forms in front of him at dinner that night. Maggie was shocked by her father's words, even though she had long realized that he had little interest in her academic development. His concept of the world was one where a woman's place was in the home, standing obediently behind a pile of dishes or a basket of laundry. This degree of intransigence, however, still came as a complete surprise and It dawned on her that he alone could destroy her aspirations, all for the sake of a signature. It wasn't as if she was asking him for money. She was only asking him to prove to the necessary admissions authority that, due to her family's economic situation, she was eligible for financial support. All it would take was a moment to sign the form. She pleaded, negotiated, argued, burst into tears, and asked again, but it was all to no avail. Sitting across the table unshaven and wearing an undershirt, her father remained adamant. The pleading and the tears only caused him to dig in his heels. In that single moment of denial, her aspirations evaporated, and excitement turned to disbelief, dismay, and then abject disappointment. The tears continued to flow. However, her father remained unmoved, becoming yet more strident in his arguments against divulging personal information to what he considered to be the deep state. Or was there another reason for his refusal? Maggie suspected his real motivation was resentment that a daughter of his could rise to the upper echelons of academia and then on to a prestigious career as a doctor. Or perhaps a concern that she would step out from behind the shadows of her brother and sister. Whatever his logic, he refused to sign, and Maggie withdrew to her room so she could work through this latest setback.

In the days it took to come to terms with her father's decision, her therapy, as it had always been, was the beach. Slowly she started to put the disappointment behind her. And it wasn't long before she became curious about the surf trips, known as Surfaris, that members of her ever-growing circle of acquaintances were taking. On these trips up and down the coast, the explorers would search out new beaches with different surf breaks and coastal attractions.

Now seventeen and eager to explore new turf, Maggie and some friends travelled south on a surfari to a small beachside community at the north end of San Diego County called Leucadia. Nestled beside the Pacific, Leucadia got its name during a period of Greek revival in America. The community was named after an island in the Ionian Sea, and many of the street names came from Greek mythology. It was in Leucadia that Maggie was introduced to a group of people who lived by the beach on an acre of land that they had turned into a mini farm, enabling the tenants to be almost self-sufficient. The operations of the farm fascinated Maggie, so she decided to stay on for a few days.

Leucadia, at the time, was part of a division of the coast bordered by Cardiff to the far south, Encinitas immediately adjacent, and Olivenhain to the east. The entire town was primarily split between farms and modest coastal dwellings. During the spring and summer months, the hillsides behind the beaches were vivid with color as local growers would shepherd crops through their final phase, ultimately cutting and shipping the vibrant begonias, birds of paradise, ranunculus, and roses across the country.

Interspersed with the flower fields were orchards of avocados and other fruits, while meadows, populated with cattle rhythmically grazing their way through the lazy summer days, completed the tapestry. With its Mediterranean climate perfectly suited for agriculture, Encinitas had adopted the moniker of "Flower Capital of the World."

Since the town was still a relatively undiscovered haven, the traffic was sparse enough that kids could play baseball right out on Highway 101, a road that ran through these coastal communities. Or they would swim in the lake at the top of Woodley Road, now called Leucadia Boulevard, just before the grade plunged eastwards toward the village of Olivenhain, a community originally settled by German pioneers. All of this existed before the interstate freeway system carved the city in two with the different halves of the town linked by underpasses and bridges.

A short walk from her new friends' farm were sandstone bluffs beneath which lay Beacons Beach. Standing on top of the bluffs, she could see the endless swath of the Pacific Ocean as it reached into the distance, and the sound of waves, crashing on the empty sand, made its way up the cliff and into receptive ears. This place seemed like a slice of paradise to the young surfer, and it wasn't long before she was grabbing her board and picking her way down the winding dirt path to the sand and into the sparkling waves. But the thoughts of her lost education, and now the lack of a plan for the future, were never far away.

When the visit finally came to an end, Maggie returned home and decided to collect catalogs from local schools where it would be possible to study and work while still living with her parents. In this way, she could cover the costs of higher learning while sidestepping the need for a signature from her father. Somewhat begrudgingly, she chose Long Beach State University. It was close, she felt she could handle the cost, and it wasn't a bad school by any measure. But the visions of Harvard or Yale were still tough to shake off.

Without the need for her father's cooperation, the application process was a breeze. She would start in the fall, studying psychology and later anthropology. These courses of study weren't the noble path to becoming a doctor that she'd envisioned. Still, it would set her on a path to a qualification that would serve her well later in life.

After Maggie's acceptance to Long Beach State, her mother stepped forward with a gesture that left Maggie confused as to their relationship. Unbeknownst to her husband, she had cashed out a savings plan that had been opened when Maggie was born. And she called Maggie into the house and handed her a sum of money to help pay some of her college bills. This act of kindness, when there was seldom any praise or support for her efforts, put Maggie psychologically on her heels, but not to the point where she refused the gift. The money would come in handy, and she was thankful for anything she could get, particularly considering this unlikely source.

Soon after commencing her studies, the world of student politics beckoned. And there was no shortage of initiatives, gripes, and causes that needed championing. The first step toward a political position, however, meant applying to become a member of a sorority. Maggie shunned the necessary kowtowing to be accepted, however, and remained an independent student throughout her tenure at the school. "You're never going to be elected to any student body office if you're not in a sorority," she was told. Her response was, "I'm not the sorority type, I don't fit in with sororities."

Nevertheless, in her first year, Maggie was elected to be a senator, and in her second year, was given the honor of being the Associated Women's Most Valuable Woman for her contributions to the student body. The excitement of representing others and fighting for just and equitable causes such as free speech helped to mold her worldview. And this commitment to justice would reappear in a different manifestation as her life progressed. "Never overlook the power of getting to know the voters" was her mantra.

PART 3

The Road South

CHAPTER 6

When Poverty Comes Knocking

Like a fish on a hook,
Like a bug on a dirty windshield, it's ok
It's time to take your chips and cash them all in
'Cause it matters where you're going
Not where you been"
Carrie Underwood – "One Way Ticket"

Maggie's social life continued to revolve around the beach. Here, the collection of characters ranged from surfers and tourists to businesspeople escaping the rigors of their jobs, if only momentarily. Rounding out this eclectic mix were the hippies and the homeless, who saw the beach more as a sanctuary than as a venue for recreation and socializing.

It was amongst this diverse network that a charming and popular surfer began to take an interest in the one-time redhead now turned blonde. He'd spotted her on the beach and made a point of introducing himself when he bumped into her a few days later at a party at a mutual friend's house. Maggie was bowled over by his charisma, and it wasn't long before the pair started dating.

Harry Theobald was a successful salesman for a local coffee business, and the company had him fast-tracked for greater responsibility. Sociable, and well known to many of the party people in the South Bay of Los Angeles, he captured Maggie's heart. And after a brief courtship, they decided to get married. The ceremony, quite a grand affair, took place in the Crystal Church on the Palos Verdes Peninsula, not far from where Harry's parents owned a spacious home close to the ocean. On the day of the wedding, the church was filled with friends from the beach and Harry's business associates, along with both sets of relatives. The bride was resplendent in a full-length white gown and veil, accompanied by the groom, who cut a dashing figure in a charcoal suit with tails.

Maggie quit school, and after almost a year of marriage, the couple bore a child named Chris. The newborn brought joy to the family, but cracks had started to appear in the relationship. As early as their honeymoon in Mexico, Harry had begun to reveal a brooding temperament that Maggie had not seen before, but she was quick to brush it off as a symptom of his adjusting to married life. She had moved on, determined to make the best home she could for the family.

Her husband's dark side continued to raise its ugly head, however, and only increased in intensity. The emotional abuse was bad enough, but then Harry started going out and not returning for days on end, leaving Maggie with a young child and the maintenance of the household. On one occasion, he took her beloved car—a rare Citroen 2CV, one of the only ones in the LA area—parked it at a party, and never brought it home. The city promptly towed the vehicle. With Harry being the sole breadwinner in the family, no one else could liberate it from the tow yard, and Maggie was left without transportation. It was as though Harry resented being tied down to family life and was pushing back in the only way he knew how. His party lifestyle continued and he became a fixture at events where drugs were an integral part of the scene. And it wasn't long before his ability to stay up late, while consuming large quantities of intoxicants, prompted his inner circle to bestow on him the nickname of "No brakes." Maggie turned to her parents for help and confided in them that she was thinking of leaving Harry. They'd been married for less than two years.

Her parents, hearing of her plans to separate, were appalled. They had been raised with the expectation that a woman must stand by her man through thick and thin. And they were not about to offer any support to a disrespectful wife who saw separation as the only way out of an abusive relationship. A relationship that had not yet devolved into physical harm, but that had the potential to put the couple's infant into threatening situations—a scenario that Maggie was going to avoid at all costs.

In a last desperate effort to find some financial help so she could secure her independence, and to facilitate her exit from the marriage, she turned to Harry's parents. However, she soon learned that he could do no wrong in their eyes. They had created an entitlement mentality in their son, which had led him to believe he could have a wife and family, and still party as he pleased, without restraint. All of his extracurricular behaviors were evidence that he'd been a privileged child raised in a financially comfortable setting where he wanted for nothing and was denied very little.

Thwarted by entrenched thinking and the loyalties of enabling parents, Maggie had limited options: stay and face a life where the safety of her child could be threatened, or head out and find a place where she could create a new future for her family.

Fear of the challenges that a fresh start would present to a single mother, and a poor one at that, triggered second thoughts. But, after assessing the pros and cons of her situation, Maggie made her decision. It would alter the course of her life and set her on a path that would test both her instincts and her resilience.

With her mind made up, she climbed into the aging red and white Chevy station wagon that a friend had sold her and made a final visit to her childhood home. The wagon had seen better days. Rust was starting to seep through the rear fenders, a caustic reminder of the car's advancing years and lack of maintenance. A section of the headliner hung down, having long ago surrendered its attachment to the roof, and in a final act of defiance, it partially obstructed the rearview mirror. But the price had been right, and Maggie needed a car so she could execute her plan.

After enduring the disapproval of her parents, it was soon time to leave. Jumping behind the wheel, she reversed down the shared driveway, past a front yard yellowed by the heat of the summer sun, and felt the car lurch awkwardly over a drainage culvert as it came to rest in the street. Two rows of identical houses built shortly before the end of the Second World War greeted her, each home displaying the same beige walls topped with brown shingled roofs that looked down upon modest lawns. They were homes initially occupied by the blue-collar workers who had toiled in the nearby Douglas factory churning out aircraft before the post-war peace slowed demand, triggering a series of downsizings that would continue until the plant was finally shuttered in 2015.

Alongside Maggie, wrapped in a blanket and strapped into a gray plastic child seat, was her eighteen-month-old son Chris. Two cats, incarcerated in cardboard carriers and meowing indignantly, were parked on the back seat and beside them, panting in anticipation, sat Buddy the dog. Buddy was a mongrel whose mix of breeds, remained a topic of some speculation, although he seemed to be mostly terrier. Buddy had been rescued from a neighbor who, having tired of the novelty of owning a pet, was about to turn him over to the local animal shelter.

Maggie had refused to hand off her small menagerie of animals to sympathetic friends, despite facing a perilous financial situation and an uncertain future. On the floor beside her lay a well-worn suitcase that was stuffed with all the clothes she owned. A couple of black garbage bags, tossed behind the back seat, held all the supplies needed for the immediate care and feeding of her charges. In her pocket, she carried just short of $400. All the money she had in the world.

Glancing briefly at her childhood home, she could see the rusty black railings that led to the front door, supports that had doubled as climbing bars when she was a child. A wooden gate divided the oil-stained driveway, where an always-open padlock hung awkwardly on the latch. Nearby, the limbs of a mature plumeria tree, a sentinel that had stood guard outside the kitchen for as long as she could remember, cast its spindly shadow across the concrete below.

She turned her attention to the cats, and after making the last of a series of futile attempts to calm the furry duo, she gunned the car and headed north toward the city of Long Beach before looping around the housing development and picking up the ribbon of asphalt that was Highway 1 South toward San Diego.

A friend's house in Oceanside would be the first stop. A way station before making her final push to Leucadia, where she would begin work on establishing a new life. She knew that there would be no turning back, and since she would carry the stigma of the one who walked out on the marriage, there would be no help or support from either set of parents. Maggie would, in effect, become a pariah in their eyes.

Highway 101 (certain segments of which are called highway 1), in its heyday, had been the primary connector between San Diego, Los Angeles, and the rest of California. From the Mexican border, it ran the length of the state, taking in mile after mile of ocean views on its way to Canada. Similar in historic value to the old Route 66 from Chicago to Santa Monica, it was once part of the backbone of the interstate road system. Now, parts of it had been turned into housing and other developments. And the new Interstate 5 had made portions of its original path obsolete while forcing drivers onto the new multi-lane highways.

On the trip down from Long Beach, Maggie could have driven the freeway to Oceanside, where its final section linked the north county towns of Oceanside and Carlsbad to San Diego. Instead, with a heavy heart and a feeling of trepidation, she decided to take Highway 1 to remember the old surfari days. A slower cruise down the coast would also give her time to think about how she was going to get by when she arrived at her final destination.

The drive took her through the towns of Huntington Beach, Newport, and San Clemente. The further south she went, the more open space and greenery met her eyes, while to the west, the Pacific beckoned. Occasional stops at beachside parking lots to change the baby and let the dog out provided moments of contemplation. Times when she would sit quietly beside the vastness of the ocean, piecing together ideas for finding a job and accommodations for her family when she arrived in her new hometown.

Later that afternoon, the station wagon pulled into her friend's driveway in Oceanside, where she would stay for a week. Enough time to collect her thoughts and figure out how she was going to make what little money she had last. The generosity of her friends was a big help, but it was soon time to move on, and the day for farewells arrived. The baby was loaded, along with the dog and the fretful cats, and the family continued their journey south. It was November, but the winter chill had yet to fill the air and the sun pierced the windows of the car, bathing the skin of exposed arms in reassuring warmth as the town of Carlsbad slipped by and Leucadia came into view.

Accelerating past the empty sands of the nearby beaches, Maggie harbored a growing sense of anticipation, along with some concern as she prepared to search for a place for the family to spend the night. By now, against the backdrop of the quickly disappearing sun, the car slipped beneath the vast canopy of eucalyptus trees that covered the northern stretch of Highway 101 leading into the village. Over the years these trees had acted as a welcoming committee for thousands of visitors, helping them transition to the rural vistas that awaited them just up the road.

With a population of retirees, students, flower growers, artists, and farmers, the place had a laid-back feeling reinforced by its history as a center for the healing arts. In 1936 the Swami, Paramahansa Yogananda, had moved into his Self-Realization Fellowship on the bluffs above one of the local beaches. And he had often walked the neighborhoods blessing the streets. Even to this day, some say you can still feel his aura in the atmosphere of the town.

After searching the streets closest to the coast, Maggie picked out the Travelair Motel for a roof over their heads. The weekly rate was as cheap as she could find, and, despite the sign that said no pets, she would smuggle the animals into her room under cover of darkness. After a few days at the motel, she realized that the manager knew she had the troika of a dog and two cats. But having understood her desperate situation, he had decided to turn a blind eye. The animals stayed in the motel while Maggie, with Chris along for the ride, searched the farms and small businesses for employment. After hitting dead ends for a week, she finally scored a position at the Compass West Print Shop, helped by her friends from Oceanside, who vouched for her lightning-fast typing skills. She had placed fifth in an all-city typing contest when she was in high school and had included the award on her sparse resume.

Working at the printing business was monotonous, but there was an upside. Maggie was allowed to bring her baby to work as long as he didn't disrupt business operations. Cloistered in the back room of the shop and standing for most of the day, she folded and collated trifold brochures, catching those whose print work was defective. Or she would be assigned typing projects creating content for the marketing pieces and other publications that the shop produced. As she became familiar with the work, Maggie started learning about the local flower-growing industry since most of the work she checked came from the farming community. In the material, she read information on such pursuits as growing epitheliums or grafting poinsettias.

Her boss at the print shop was a moody individual, perhaps with good reason. His life had been changed by the death of his daughter in a car accident in Europe, and it was an event from which he'd never recovered. The tragedy had left him harboring a bitterness that came out in his relationships with others. Maggie would make sure to arrive at work on time to avoid any confrontations, despite the early-morning struggles to get the baby dressed and the animals fed and watered.

Work would end at 5:30, and there was a thirty-minute lunch break when she would speed back to the motel to let the dog out. Despite the mundane working conditions, she was happy to have the security that the steady, if small, income provided, as it took some of the pressure off her new living conditions.

After a few weeks of work, she spotted an ad in one of the free local newspapers. It was for a teller position at a Bank of America branch, just around the corner from the shop, and the pay was a step up from what she was presently earning. She applied and was scheduled for an interview a couple of days later.

On the day of the appointment, she arranged for an extended lunch and took off for the bank, where she was to meet with the assistant manager in charge of the tellers. A smartly dressed receptionist helped her sign in and then escorted her across a spacious lobby to an office where a sallow looking man, despite the sunny conditions outside sat behind a large wooden desk. Pushing some papers to one side, he rose from his chair, revealing an ill-fitting gray suit accented with a red paisley tie. He greeted her and pointed toward a chair on Maggie's side of the desk. She sat down as he proceeded to inquire after her education, achievements, and pastimes. All the while comparing her qualifications to the needs of the bank and the risk to his career if he was to make a bad hire. After the interview, she rushed back to the print shop to await the bank's decision. A couple of days later, a staff member called with the news that she was hired, and she gave Compass West her two weeks' notice.

Away from the dim and dingy isolation of the print shop, Maggie socialized with the bank's employees. She soon made friends with a girl almost six feet in height who went by the name of Tall Sharon. Sharon knew a lot of the younger people in town and was soon introducing

Maggie to the beach crowd, many of whom were also new to the area, and had also been attracted by its laid-back feel, great surfing, and growing cadre of artists and musicians.

One of the people Sharon introduced Maggie to was Lynda, the wife of a fisherman and carpenter. They had spent time on their boat plying the waters off Alaska and Washington State before deciding to make a life in Encinitas. Lynda worked the tables at a local café called Alfredo's, where many of the surfers and employees of the town's surfboard-manufacturing industry would regularly gather for breakfast. Since it was the seventies, and this was Southern California, drugs were present. And many amongst the younger crew knew who the importers, distributors, and dealers were. Lynda would often wait tables for a group associated not only with the surf industry but also with some of the most significant movement of drugs in town. They had been christened "the coke for lunch bunch." Not that they were ever aware of this distinguished handle, or the other names the staff bestowed on them as a result of their sparse tipping habits. Maggie soon became firm friends with Lynda and her partner Jimmy, who would often babysit Chris.

With her new job, and after spending almost three months in the motel, it was time to find different accommodations. Maggie began combing the ads in the newspapers and on the bulletin boards at the laundromat and grocery store. One sure way to get a leg up on anyone else looking for a rental was to head down to the offices of the local newspaper, the *Coast Dispatch*. If you arrived at their building shortly after 3 a.m., you could get first dibs on any new postings that were due to appear in the paper that day.

It was on one of these early-morning forays that Maggie came across an ad for two rooms and a bathroom on Cornish Drive, a location that overlooked the town's main street. A couple was renting the rooms for $80 a month. Maggie quickly jotted down the contact information, and that morning she drove over to the property to submit her request to rent the accommodations. After a quick once-over by the owners, she was accepted. It was only after moving in that she confessed to having a dog and two cats, fearful that the landlords would have turned her down if they had known of her entourage in advance. The couple hemmed and hawed for a while but finally acquiesced and allowed the furry trio to be an unsigned part of the deal.

On their first night, after they had finished moving their limited belongings into the rooms, it started to rain. "Let's go outside and get wet," Maggie said to Chris, and so they sloshed off into the backyard, jumping and dancing until they were thoroughly soaked. It felt good to let loose and celebrate the momentary cloak of security that surrounded them.

The new accommodations were sparse and lacked a kitchen, so a second-hand hotplate, borrowed from a friend, became their only mechanism for heating food. Chris would later dub their home as "The house without a kitchen."

Their new landlady also had a young child, and since the bank wouldn't allow children in the workplace, Maggie started to look for an additional job so she could pay the landlady to babysit Chris. A friend passed along a tip about a jobs program up in Oceanside, where she might get a lead on something she could do part-time. So, on her next day off, she drove up to the Employment Center and registered at the front desk. After a short wait, an employee ushered her to a cubicle and started asking questions about her skills and her current financial situation. As she was answering one of the questions, the interviewer interrupted and cut the conversation short, saying, "I have someone here I think you ought to talk to." Maggie got up and was ushered to another cubicle, where a middle-aged woman in a flowered dress sat typing. She stopped and turned to greet the couple as the original interviewer handed her the partially completed paperwork. After looking at the forms, she asked Maggie if her husband paid her any child support or provided any financial assistance.

"No," Maggie replied. "He works, and he could pay, but he doesn't, so I only have my clerical job at the bank."

"Did you know we have a program for women in your situation?" said the woman.

Maggie gave her a blank stare and said no, curious as to what she meant by "program."

"Yes," said the woman in the flowered dress. "We can help you find part-time work. And we can also provide you with some financial assistance to help you get through this transition period." Maggie's jaw dropped. She couldn't believe what she was hearing as the woman described the details and restrictions of the program. "You qualify for the transition plan. Your financial and family situation makes you eligible, and you can expect your first check in about six days."

Maggie had found this place through a friend and had arrived in search of a part-time job, unaware of any social programs that might help a single mother. Now the state had assessed that she didn't take home sufficient income from the bank to feed, clothe, and put a roof over her small family, which, as it turned out, was good news. And she wasn't about to turn her nose up at this unexpected lifeline.

Two weeks later, the agency followed up. "We've found you a part-time job working for a gentleman close to where you live. He would like you to iron his clothes one night a week. The pay will be $5." Without hesitation, Maggie took the work. In the meantime, she had also found a job stuffing and addressing envelopes. A third opportunity opened up when some locals discovered that their bank teller was a very effective seamstress who specialized in making garments to order. It was a skill Maggie had perfected years earlier when she lacked the funds to spend on new clothes.

She had learned how to sew using the old Vogue paper patterns of the day, and many of her outfits were so good they had become the envy of her college friends when they saw her arrive in a fashionably pleated blouse or ankle-length skirt. This skill now turned into an essential source of support as she struggled to stay afloat in her adopted town.

In Cardiff, one of the communities south of Leucadia, Maggie approached the manager of Swami's Beach Bag, a store that made products for beachgoers. A number of local businesses used the name "Swamis" in their titles. It was a name derived from the Self Realization Fellowship, whose religious courses and prominent buildings on the nearby bluffs had grown to become a major regional attraction. Maggie knew that with the bags and bikinis they made, they had to have scrap material. And if they were willing to give it to her and her friends, they could come up with their own garments. Luckily, the business was happy to get rid of their offcuts. With this new supply, the diligent recipients quickly went to work, turning the materials into quilts while using the larger pieces to create dresses and other articles of clothing. One day, a woman who was going to an event called the Witches Ball saw one of Maggie's creations and immediately purchased it for $30—a windfall in those days, with the funds providing Maggie's family with groceries for an entire week.

Thanks to these various jobs and the bonus of a welfare check, Maggie could pay her bills while community clinics provided her family with healthcare. But unexpected expenses like a punctured tire or car repairs still presented a challenge, and her struggle to maintain a decent existence for herself and her family continued.

CHAPTER 7

Return to the Books

Barely gettin' by, it's all takin' and no givin'
They just use your mind and they never give you credit
It's enough to drive you crazy if you let it
Dolly Parton – "9 to 5"

It was 1971, and a new cadre of acquaintances started to emerge from Maggie's time at the bank where, during her assignments on the drive-up window, she met many of the local merchants and flower growers. One customer who regularly visited the bank was a man called Art Glover. Art was a long-time farmer who knew how to grow everything from cacti to peanuts. And whenever he visited the bank, he would insist on leaving Maggie a two-dollar tip with strict instructions to "Go buy yourself a soda now." Maggie would quote the bank's policy against accepting tips, but Art would stand firm. "If I need to, I'll come in and make you take it." Given a choice between accepting the tip and enduring a scene with the bank's management, she would acquiesce and quickly plunge the $2 into her pocket while glancing around the main office to see if anyone was watching.

One day as she reached for the document container that traveled by vacuum between patron and teller, a precursor to today's ATM, she realized that she'd become the unsuspecting recipient of a marijuana joint. Not sure what to do, she made a split-second decision and the contraband was hastily shot back down the tube. Over the intercom, she informed the customer, "There's an error in your deposit. Can you check your math, please?" If the bank's management had found out there were drugs near the business, the authorities would have been summoned and heads would have rolled, not only her own but maybe some of her friends' as well.

The management at the bank was always conservative in its policies. However, on one notable occasion, it showed a remarkable lack of sensitivity, and by today's standards probably violated state labor laws. While working at the drive-through, Maggie detected an anomaly with a one-hundred-dollar banknote. The smooth texture of the paper didn't feel right, and she picked up the phone to call the bank's assistant manager. As she lifted the receiver, she heard the squeal of tires. Realizing that his plan to pass off a counterfeit note was unraveling, the customer had hit the gas and was fleeing the scene.

The following day a couple of suits from the U.S. Treasury came to the bank and, after some testing, confirmed that the note was a fake—part of a pattern of activity that was showing up in the local area. However, after a few days of nosing around, they failed to identify any leads, and the incident was forgotten. About a month later, the same customer showed up, and Maggie, quickly recognizing the car, decided to take matters into her own hands. As an extracurricular part of the transaction, she asked the client for his ID, which, to her surprise, he naively handed over. As she reached for the phone, the same scenario from his original visit played out. The driver, realizing what was happening, took off to a chorus of shrieking rubber, heading south toward San Diego. This time, however, the bank had his ID, and later that day he was apprehended.

Having been at the center of the event, Maggie was asked to testify at the perpetrator's trial and went down to the San Diego courthouse to present her recollections of both incidents. After the court completed its business, she returned to the bank and worked for the rest of her shift. When it came time to leave, she started to wrap up her final transactions. In the process of collecting her belongings, the operations manager appeared in front of her desk.

"Where are you going?" he asked.

"To pick up my son," she replied."

"Well, you can't leave now. We had to bring in two people to cover your shift while you were downtown, and now you need to make up the time."

This show of inequity came as a shock. Here she was having provided enough hard evidence to enable the authorities to apprehend a forger, and yet she was being punished for taking time off to testify on behalf of the bank. After overcoming her surprise, she proceeded to plead her case, explaining that she couldn't possibly afford the additional time that the babysitter would charge. Eventually, there was a begrudging acquiescence by the manager and she was allowed to leave. But the saga left her with a distrust of the organization's treatment of its employees.

This incident, coupled with other arbitrary behavior she'd experienced, confirmed Maggie's growing suspicion that this conduct was a symptom of the male domination of the bank's management. It was also somewhat of a reflection of society and how it viewed women in the workforce as second-class citizens. The misogynistic behavior of the bank's management, however, didn't stop at a zealous application of the rules. That winter, at the bank's end-of-the-year holiday party, the assistant branch manager, presumably having consumed his fair share of alcohol, followed Maggie into the bathroom and attempted to grope her. It took a well-timed slap, followed by a forceful shove, to send the startled official staggering into the washbasins, which quickly cooled his ardor. He stumbled out of the bathroom, but not before shooting a menacing glance in the direction of his victim turned assailant.

The other women in the bathroom stood slack-jawed at what they had just witnessed. "You should never have hit him," one overweight teller with a beehive hairdo exclaimed as she paused in her application of bright-pink lipstick. "You're in for it now," said another as she turned toward the mirror to add the final touches to her makeup. This reaction startled Maggie as she had assumed that her co-workers would support her stand for female dignity. She was sorely disappointed.

That following Monday, the bathroom incident dominated gossip around the water cooler as the staff waited to find out what the consequences of such an outrageous act from a subordinate would be. Maggie arrived and began processing checks while quietly awaiting the condemnation that was sure to come from a self-righteous bureaucrat who would surely accompany his dressing down of the upstart teller with a swing of the termination ax. The day went by, and nothing. The next day was quiet, and the next. It became apparent that the erstwhile groper must have thought better of his actions, deciding that taking the issue further would probably reflect poorly on him. And so the whole incident was conveniently brushed under the table.

During her time outside of the bank, Maggie met many of the artists in the area, including Rick Griffin. Rick had risen to fame, creating posters for musical artists such as the Doors, the Grateful Dead, Frank Zappa, and other popular bands from the Haight-Ashbury era in 1960s San Francisco. Rick was also the first cartoonist to feature regularly in a new magazine called *The Surfer* that was gaining in popularity with the beach crowd. Jim and Lana Evans were also friends with Jim carving out his own niche doing rock era and surf-themed poster work. Since few amongst the beach crowd had much money at the time, the young families shared babysitting responsibilities and social events, which typically involved a potluck, a fire pit, and, if they were fortunate, a guitar or two.

As life settled into a comfortable routine, Maggie attended many of the local gatherings and impromptu parties that were a hallmark of the town's younger set. Chris was always brought along, and, as it was a more innocent time, he would sleep in the car parked outside the house, the girls at the event taking turns to check on him throughout the night. It was at one of these shindigs that a local dentist took an interest in the animated newcomer, sliding into a seat beside her at the fire and striking up a conversation. That encounter sparked an invitation for a date. And it wasn't long before the two were attending parties or hanging out at the beach together. One morning, after learning of her past life and of the academic aspirations that she once harbored, the dentist said, "There's no excuse for you. You need to go back to school. Your life will only get better. You've got the brains and the aptitude, and you love learning. You gotta stop this. Just go down to UCSD (University of California San Diego) and check it out, see what they have to say, you've got nothing to lose."

The idea struck a nerve. Maggie had given up on school after getting married and had never seriously thought about it again. And now it had taken someone else to paint a picture of a future that in her struggles to get by she had dismissed. Agonizing over the idea, she realized that going back would be tough. It would mean borrowing money to pay for what would be a new chapter in her education and giving up her full-time job at the bank. More part-time work would take its place in her schedule. And there was Chris. She certainly wouldn't be able to afford childcare. Would the professors allow an infant to accompany her to lectures?

Having worked at the bank for almost a year, Maggie concluded that she would need a higher qualification to get her out from behind a teller's desk. So, she decided to go down and talk to an admissions counselor at the new university.

The verbal interview went well, and she sat and completed the essay part of her evaluation. With two years of college already finished, excellent grades, and the Scholastic Aptitude Test passed years ago, she was feeling good about her chances. A few days later a counselor called to tell her that she had been accepted.

She greeted the news with both delight and concern. Here was a shot at a new life, but the sacrifices needed to get there threatened to plunge her back into the same struggle that she'd spent the last year trying to escape. She wrestled for days with the decision, trying to find ways to overcome the obstacles that would appear along the way. She finally decided that this was probably her last chance to carve out a decent future. But it was with some misgiving that she accepted the university's invitation to join the student body.

After applying for grants, loans, and scholarships, Maggie managed to cobble together a subsistence revenue stream. These resources, along with part-time jobs cleaning houses, ironing clothes, making garments, and babysitting, gave her the backing necessary to move forward with her decision. The path to a degree would mean long hours and a sparse social life, but the sacrifice would be worth it, and she prepared for her first semester.

During all this planning, what she hadn't taken into account was the length of time she had been outside the educational system. Two years older than the other students, she struggled with the prep courses that provided the foundation for her chosen study of anthropology. These were hardcore upper-division classes, which meant she spent the first few months of university life buried in books playing catch up to other undergrads. She had chosen anthropology partly because of her fascination with the American Indian culture, an interest that had developed during her early years in school and one that would continue throughout the rest of her life.

Childcare turned out not to be the challenge she expected. Most of her professors, on hearing of her situation, allowed Chris to come to class, as long as he wasn't disruptive. Luckily Chris was, for the most part, well behaved. He would spend the lectures counting the gobs of gum stuck under the study tables or playing with the hand-me-down toys that Maggie had scrounged from friends.

With this new combination of multiple jobs, a small social security payment, and a full course load at the university, Maggie's somewhat fragile existence continued as she executed her plan of short-term sacrifice for a better life down the road.

CHAPTER 8

Boot Scootin' Boogie

I take her out dancing in my pickup truck
We rub them belt buckles till they shine like chrome
Doing it to country songs
Blake Shelton – "Doing it to Country Songs"

At the end of her final semester, Maggie learned that she would graduate with highest honors and a place on the Dean's list. The question now was as hard as any she had answered during her time at university: what to do next. UCSD offered her a position in their graduate anthropology program. But with a young child, no family support, and the knowledge that such a program would require long stints abroad, it was with regret that she turned it down. Another alternative was to stay on and study for a master's degree. This wasn't attractive either as it would mean a further dose of the hardscrabble life that, by now, she was eager to leave behind. The question that remained was what to do with her newly acquired qualification? She couldn't afford more time in school. And the prospect of relocating for an entry-level position didn't appeal, so she set out to find a full-time job that would provide for her immediate needs.

One afternoon, while deep into her search, the phone rang. It was Maggie's contact from the employment center in Oceanside. Unbeknownst to her, they had continued to track her progress and now had news about a work incentive program, a program that was in place in the very university library where she'd spent time studying for her degree. It was a job that promised a regular paycheck, a position right on campus, and a reasonable commute.

"Sure," she replied without bothering to find out all the details. "I'll take it!"

"Not so fast," came the response. "It's not a done deal. You have to interview first."

The job involved typing up cataloging cards for books in the central library. By no means a taxing role, but it offered a level of financial security that had so far been fleeting, and it came with the benefit of health insurance. Maggie wrangled some letters of recommendation from her professors, and the following week showed up for the interview. The woman conducting the meeting couldn't understand how someone with such impressive qualifications would need to apply for such a low-level job until she became familiar with Maggie's economic situation. "How about this," she said. "We have another position in the library where you would analyze and catalog the books instead of just working on the cards. I think that would be more suitable for you." Maggie agreed, and with the employment center paying the first six months of her salary, her new career as a catalog librarian was about to begin.

With this newfound income and the promise of a more stable future, it became feasible to find better accommodations. And after a brief search, the family moved into a small cottage on La Veta Avenue, two blocks from the beach. The two-bedroom cottage cost $140 a month, including utilities, which would eat up a chunk of the money she earned. However, she was determined that the family's standard of living should improve, and she moved ahead.

From the house, they could hear the ocean, and on moonlit nights the two of them would walk out to the front yard and watch the bats who lived in the cliffs above the beach come out for their evening hunt. Often the shadowy creatures would swoop down close enough that Maggie and Chris could hear the sound of wings slapping against the cool night air. On rare occasions, they would treat themselves by strolling into town, where they would grab a soda from the fountain in Dietrich's drugstore. Or they would drive over the hill to the happy hour special at Borelli's Italian restaurant where, once seated in one of the red upholstered booths, a customer could eat all they wanted for $1.75. Chris, who by now was undergoing the first of a number of growth spurts, would spend these outings eagerly consuming enough pasta and salad to satisfy a small rhino. And after extinguishing his appetite, he would disappear under the table to indulge his favorite passion of counting the wads of gum squashed under its rim. During these searches, he would frequently check with his mom to see if any recent records were in jeopardy. These outings were a relished treat, but on bad weeks, when unforeseen expenses depleted the weekly budget, Maggie would visit the local bakery, where the owners knew of her situation and would give her leftovers and damaged goods from that day's business.

Another uncommon but much-anticipated luxury was a visit to the La Paloma movie theater in downtown Encinitas. The building, constructed in 1928 in Spanish colonial revival style, was touted to be the first rural theater to install sound equipment. Maggie would rustle up Chris, pick up a couple of his friends, and they would drive over with their beach chairs and blankets. Upon arrival, they would walk past the mish mash of seating, which ranged from old church pews to makeshift benches, and set up camp on the floor in the open space at the side of the theater. Comfortably situated, they would munch on the snacks they had brought while watching the movie until one or more of the children fell asleep, only to be awakened when the show came to an end. The kids would then be bundled, bleary-eyed, into the back of the car and dropped off at their respective homes. Or they would be brought back to the La Veta house to continue their adventure by way of a sleepover. This lifestyle of making the most of sparse resources was typical of the way the community worked. Married or unmarried, surfer, businessperson, or struggling artist, everyone seemed to share the mantra of live and let live, whether it was potlucks or big dinners at each other's houses, bicycling, or visits to the beach while taking care of each other's kids. People made do with what they had and didn't obsess over what they lacked. It was a time rich in friendships and camaraderie, all the while surrounded by the natural beauty that the small coastal town provided.

While studying anthropology at UCSD, Maggie's affinity for the culture and plight of the American Indian had only grown stronger. These were the pioneering days when the indigenous people barely survived the influx of European settlers that began with Columbus in 1492. During her studies, she realized that the popular portrayal of the Indian as a horse-rustling, murderous savage was not entirely accurate. It had been the white Europeans with their culture of individuality and acquisition that had collided with the sharing and group focus followed by most of the Native tribes. And the persecution and deliberate spreading of disease that followed resulted in a genocide that accounted for more deaths than the Holocaust, although the size of the American Indian population during this period has been the subject of much scholarly debate.[1] If an old Western show appeared on TV, she would rail against the early pioneers who would shoot Indians as if they were vermin. The reality of that period in history was equally as disturbing. Often the pioneers would destroy whole villages along with their winter stores simply because they were a threat to the settlers' accumulation of farmland. Survivors would flee into the surrounding area with many perishing without a food source to sustain them over the cold winter months that lay ahead.

If an American Indian stole a horse because they were starving, their entire village would be torched, and its inhabitants, including women and children, gunned down. American Indians were pushed off their gold claims during the California gold rush of the 1800s. And war was waged against the tribes, first by vigilantes and militias sponsored by the state, and later by federal troops.[2] Such was the desire of the new settlers to claim the West and its riches for themselves.

Maggie's research led her to appreciate the many contributions that these indigenous people had made to civilization, including the world's food source. Around 60 percent of all foods consumed on the planet today are a result of the discovery and use of plants by the American Indians.[3] Things like potatoes, tomatoes, and corn were all discovered and developed by the original occupants of the Americas. Who could imagine Ireland without potatoes, Italy without tomatoes, or the African continent without corn? As the years went by, her respect for American Indians manifested itself in the type of jewelry she wore and the art she used to decorate her living spaces.

This knowledge of how early Western culture had evolved resurfaced when she met a girl from Tucson, Arizona, who had a love of country and western music. And one night, they decided to go to the Stingaree, a local club that hosted country music events. That night, the headliner was Clay Baker and his Texas Honky Tonk band. Maggie was fascinated by the cowboy dress code of Wrangler jeans, western shirts, and boots, with long skirts providing an alternative to jeans for the women.

She sat on the side of the dance floor, keenly observing the flair and precision the dancers displayed with their gliding steps, synchronized turns, and behind the back rotations. It wasn't long before she and her friend were bribing one of the club's leading male dancers with offers of food and wine. If outside of the club, he would teach them how to conquer the choreographed steps that the experts performed with such ease.

After many weeks of eating, drinking, and dancing, Maggie had mastered many of the more popular steps. And after honing her skills at the club, she began to stand out, even when dancing side by side with the best. It wasn't long before her expertise prompted bystanders to ask if she could teach them a step or two. Taking individuals and couples aside, she would spend a few minutes showing them the basics of a step and then mentor them from the sidelines before cutting them loose to mingle with the other dancers in the confines of the crowded dance floor.

Through a contact at UCSD, Maggie was introduced to Jeff Howard, a landscape architect and, more importantly, an expert at country and western dance. Realizing a common interest, the two concluded that they should start teaching dance. So they offered six weeks of tuition at the Stingaree for $12, with classes held during the intermission, just before the main band took to the stage.

Word spread, and the classes quickly filled up. It wasn't long before they had outgrown the space that the club offered. So the duo embarked on a search for a bar with a larger dance floor that could accommodate the growing demand for their services. Just south of Encinitas, in the neighboring city of Solana Beach, there was a club housed in an old Quonset hut called the Belly-Up Tavern, affectionately referred to by the locals as the BUT. They approached the owner, and he agreed to their request, realizing that their dance sessions would bring in additional business. The price for a twelve-week course on Tuesdays and Thursdays increased to $18 for a party of six. Once you had completed one course, you could take as many as you wished, free of charge. And it wasn't long before class sizes ballooned to fifty, sixty, sometimes seventy participants. All this was happening before the cult movie *Urban Cowboy*, starring John Travolta and referred to as country music's version of *Saturday Night Fever*, catapulted the dance style into the popular consciousness. After the movie was released, dance clubs and schools specializing in teaching the Texas two-step, country polka, and the cotton eyed Joe sprang up across the country. And they were soon packed with boot–wearing urbanites eager to connect with their cowboy alter egos.

It was 1979, and Maggie was making more income through part-time dance instruction than she was pulling down at her day job. When the *Coast Dispatch*, the local newspaper, got wind of the new dance phenomenon happening in their backyard, they ran an article on the front page. In it, they touted the demise of the foxtrot, cha-cha, and watusi while heralding the new country and western trend. They quoted Maggie as saying, "It used to be that everything 'country' was considered as hick or backwoods, but now that's no longer the case. In fact, they tell me that the cowboy look is back in the fashion industry. We get everybody [at our classes], doctors, attorneys, construction workers, artists, professors of history."

When time permitted, Maggie and Chris would take trips out to the desert or the mountains, where they could explore the region's many natural attractions. On winter days, when the rain turned the neighborhood gullies and streambeds into rivers of muddy runoff, the duo would head for the top of a nearby hill where one of the ditches was adjacent to a well-traveled road. Almost as soon as the rain would start to fall, a procession of frogs, unaware of the dangers that modern transportation presented, would hop clumsily out of their hideaways, clamber onto the road, and head for new territory. When these migrations occurred, many a frog would become an unwitting victim of the traffic, fortunate enough not to recognize the dangers that lurked on the blacktop until a passing vehicle was already upon them.

Maggie and Chris would spend hours hunched over the fringes of the road, corralling frogs that were in peril and transporting them to safer ground. Soaked to the skin but encouraged by their efforts, they would finally leave the hill with the young boy having experienced an essential lesson regarding the value of life in all of its forms, no matter how big or small. He would never have to wonder how his mother would answer the question, "Can we keep it?" when he returned home with an injured animal. And when these requests occurred, shoeboxes and tissue paper were quickly assembled, along with a call to a local wildlife rescue group for advice on medical care.

As time passed, the many forays to help injured or distressed animals set Maggie apart. One camp of friends saw her as an inspiration and felt their conscience pricked by her example. Others regarded her as an eccentric who would stop at nothing to rescue animals or to fight for their welfare. No one, however, could dismiss her innate conviction for helping all beings that were vulnerable or in peril.

PART 4
A Strange Union

CHAPTER 9

There's No Playbook

I'm going to take my money, play it all on red
I'm just getting started
Queensryche – Get Started

After Mike had given me the piece of paper with Maggie's phone number, I had put it in a drawer. Arranging a relationship, however artificial, with this high-voltage woman was going to involve some thought. She wasn't someone I found immediately attractive. I imagined her to be opinionated and overbearing, a woman who would probably drive me nuts with all that energy. And she had a kid to boot. What did I know about children? However, I wasn't in a position to be choosy, and we weren't marrying for real, so one evening, I dug out the paper with her phone number and called her.

"Hi, Maggie, this is Ian, Mike's friend."

"Oh, yes. Hi, Ian, how's it going?"

The conversation meandered around with the typical small talk as we both skirted the real purpose of the call. As the exchange started to become labored, I jumped in and brought up the subject of a possible arrangement, asking if I could take her to dinner sometime where we could chat face to face? She agreed, and we arranged to meet later that week at a cozy Mexican restaurant in the La Jolla district of San Diego called Su Casa.

The following evening, I picked her up from the parking lot of the University of California San Diego, where she worked in the central library. UCSD is an institution of considerable size with multiple libraries, so you had to know which one to ask for. Otherwise, you might end up on the wrong side of its sprawling campus.

She emerged from the library in more subdued attire than when we'd first met. This time it was conservative and business-focused— blouse and slacks with a colorful scarf around her neck. For my part, I'd laundered the same shirt and khakis I'd used for my business negotiations with the owner of the surfboard factory.

I greeted her and asked superficial questions about the unique architecture of the library as we walked across the parking lot to my car. I secretly hoped she wasn't disappointed with our transportation for the evening, as she sunk into the faded brown upholstery of my aging 1960s American Motors station wagon.

On the way to the restaurant, I experienced a strange mix of emotions. Here I was, intending to close a deal with my dinner guest. On the other hand, here I was, taking an attractive and intelligent woman out on a date. She was certainly not the stereotype I had in mind when the bizarre idea of this arrangement first surfaced. I had visions of an unemployed single mother or a down on their luck blue-collar worker. I shook off the conflict, however, as I deftly steered the car into a parking spot below the restaurant, coming to rest flanked by a black BMW on one side and a silver Mercedes on the other. As I got out, I wished I'd invested in some of that white stuff that you squeeze onto tennis shoes to cover up the stains. Still, it was too late. We were on our way into the restaurant, where a cheerful receptionist greeted us.

At my request, we were led to a booth at the far end of the restaurant, next to a large fish tank where we could expect some privacy for our negotiations. The waiter arrived and asked what we would like to drink. "What would you like?" I asked Maggie. "A kalua and coffee." I went for a house draft, and it wasn't long after the drinks arrived that we slipped into an easy conversation and started discussing the marriage. It suddenly seemed tawdry, amongst the elegant setting of the restaurant, surrounded by what could only be BMW-driving champions of industry and other lofty professions. But my date took it all in stride as we dug deeper into the details of an arrangement with which neither of us had any prior experience.

The waiter returned and asked if we would like to order. Maggie went for bean tacos, and I put in a request for a seafood burrito. It turned out that bean tacos weren't on the menu. Her explanation to the waiter was that she was a vegetarian, with the inference that she wasn't about to embrace any of the meat choices that made up the bulk of the restaurant's offerings. I immediately questioned not only my choice of location but also my selected dish. Heck, I'd never been here before. I couldn't afford it. But it seemed like the kind of swanky place that might make a good impression. And here we were, nothing on the menu for a vegetarian and with my date's request for bean tacos hanging in the balance. "No problem," said the waiter as he turned and walked toward the kitchen.

It was not the start I had planned for. I apologized for not knowing her dietary choices, and she graciously told me not to worry about it. "Most places can make something for vegetarians," she said as we once again slipped into conversation as the fish in the nearby aquarium glided by.

As we discussed the details of our possible partnership, we covered topics that included her son Chris and how this might impact him, where she lived, and what the immigration process was, or as much as I knew about it. It turned out that Maggie had done some research, and she pointed out several downsides, ways in which the whole arrangement could fall apart unless it was carefully managed throughout the statutory two years before the INS would consider it legitimate. Horror stories abounded of disgruntled hosts who had turned in their co-conspirators after the reality of being together tore apart any notion that they might actually get along during the time needed to seal the deal.

Trying to avoid this outcome, I said that I wouldn't be living with her, but that I would need to know her habits and those of her son. At some point, the INS would put us in different rooms and ask each of us the same questions regarding mundane things like a brand of toothpaste, color of underwear, and what a typical breakfast looked like. Any variation in our answers could lead to disqualification and my ejection from the country, never to be allowed back in—not to mention the ramifications for her. What we were cooking up was a violation of federal immigration law, and that went both ways.

"Don't worry about me," she said. "If it comes to that, I'll just tell them you lied and duped me into marriage." Calculating, but fair enough, I thought. She's smart to have designed an escape route if this whole thing flames out. For a moment I pictured the authorities battering down the door where I lived, intent on shackling me into the back of an agency cruiser for a trip downtown and a speedy hearing in front of a judge, from whence it would be off to the airport and back to the mother country.

The conversation finally turned to the subject of the payoff. "I don't have much of an idea about what this kind of thing goes for," she said, much to my relief. "I've heard numbers from a $1,000 to $15,000." The momentary relief I'd just enjoyed evaporated, and I swallowed hard. If this thing went over a few grand, coupled with a generous payment plan, I'd be sidelined.

"Yes," I replied without missing a beat. "That's kinda the range that I'd heard." Yeah, I'd heard that, but the high end of that range meant I'd have to rob a bank to come up with that kind of cash. And since I was already dipping a toe into something illegitimate, a leap to a full-on bank heist was an aspiration I had yet to explore.

The conversation stalled, and I was saved by the waiter, who stopped by to ask if we would like more drinks. "Sure," I replied and looked at Maggie, who had already consumed two kalua and coffees and was in the process of declining a third. "This is on me," I interjected, in the hope that more alcohol might bring about a decline in the ask price for my venture.

"Umm. OK," she said, obviously unsure about what effects a third glass of the creamy liquid might have on her ability to stand up to my negotiations. "Look," she said. "I'm not just doing this for the money. I've met you, and I know Mike and the folks you're with in San Diego. It would be neat if you could stay, but I've got some bills that I could use some help with, including some major car repairs that I need to take care of, and I still need to talk to some friends before I commit to anything or come up with a price."

I unwound this last entry from the conversation and found both good and bad buried within her statement. She wasn't in it for the money. That was encouraging. She empathized with my situation, which was also good, two strikes in my favor. The whole part about bills and checking with others on a price was a shift that made me uneasy. Were they major car repairs like an engine rebuild or body damage? Who were these friends she spoke of? By association, they would be inclined to look after Maggie's best interests. That may be a bad thing. They might talk her out of it, or into charging such a high price that she would at least be left with a generous war chest if the arrangement went off the marital rails. There was nothing I could do, however, and trying to talk her into a quick decision would only make me appear to be an opportunist. So I agreed with her measured approach, and we moved on to dessert and back into the kind of small talk that people indulge in when they're getting to know each other.

When the evening was drawing to a close, the waiter nonchalantly slipped the bill onto my side of the linen tablecloth. As he walked away, I glanced at it in disbelief. How the heck? Then I remembered how many drinks we had quaffed. And put two and two together to come up with the three-digit answer that stared back at me from the innocent-looking slip of white paper. Not to worry, I knew that one downside to the evening might be a hefty bill, so I was carrying enough cash to cover it. However, there would be no luxuries on my calendar until the next payday.

We made our way out into what had become a cool moonlit night and wobbled toward my car, the BMW and Mercedes having long since departed.

"I've had too much to drink," Maggie confessed.

Since I was also having trouble holding up, we both slumped into the front seats, giving ourselves a moment to collect ourselves before we set off for the UCSD parking lot. The fresh air took a toll on both of us, and it was only after we had sat in the parking lot for a while that I summoned up the nerve to start the car.

As we arrived back at the library, there were only a couple of vehicles illuminated beneath the harsh sodium lighting.

"Which is your car?" I asked.

"It's the silver Ford over in the corner."

We pulled up beside a full-size pickup truck, and I became aware of another dimension of my date's character. She didn't seem to fit any mold I'd imagined. Not an academic, not a party girl, certainly not a socialite. All that was left was a vegetarian fashionista librarian who drove a full-size pickup truck. This one was a puzzle.

I made my uncertain way around the car, occasionally leaning on its cold steel for support until I was positioned next to the passenger side door, which I opened as much for my support as to provide an exit for my companion. "I don't think I'm fit to drive," she said. I looked at her. Even in my compromised state, I could see that she was right and that she would be more of a danger to others if she drove than I would, although I was only a couple of degrees better off. So I climbed back in, and we set out for Encinitas in the trusty wagon.

Twenty minutes later, we made our way off the freeway and onto the unlit rural lane where she lived. Feeling responsible for her condition, I wondered if the next day, when all of this came flooding back, she would view my overtures as being clumsy and overzealous since our negotiations had been lubricated with enough alcohol to tranquilize a water buffalo.

I escorted her to the door of a modest ranch-style house that was fronted by a grassy yard dominated by a large pepper tree. She fumbled for her key under the dim porch light and eventually opened the door. Two medium-size dogs came bounding out and after welcoming their mistress with jumps, licks, and wagging tails, they turned their attention to the stranger. Having grown up with many a canine, I could tell they weren't about to bite me, and we quickly made friends. After walking inside the house, Maggie promptly collapsed onto the couch and slipped into the kind of sleep that only an excess of alcohol can induce.

Since I was still wide awake from the drive, I spotted a couple of dog leads and decided to take my furry new friends on a stroll. They couldn't believe their luck. A walk, this late at night! I held on as they towed me up the street, patiently waiting as they stopped to examine every tree, post, or stone that made up the margins of the road. Arriving back at the house, I entered as quietly as possible with two excited dogs on hand. Fortunately, Maggie was still comatose, so I lay on the floor with the dogs, only separated from the concrete slab by a well-worn carpet. Despite the cold making its way through the floor covering, it was only a few minutes before I too drifted off to sleep.

After a fitful night's rest, I was awakened by the sounds of someone trying to step quietly around the house. I shifted my position on the floor and realized that one shoulder, along with the corresponding side of my neck, had become partially paralyzed by the austere sleeping conditions. As I lifted my upper body off the floor and onto one elbow, I winced at the increasing pain. It felt as if a stiletto was being inserted into my neck just above the shoulder.

The unknown figure turned out to be Maggie's thirteen-year-old son Chris. I whispered good morning, which was a mistake. The dogs leaped up and greeted Chris then, directing their attention to the stranger on the floor, started a rain of keenly directed tongues onto my exposed face. Maggie was next, and within seconds, we were all wide awake fending off further tongue-lashings from the saliva-toting duo.

Chris seemed to take what must have been an odd scenario in his stride. Apparently, for him, waking up to find a strange man sleeping on the floor while his mom slept on the couch was nothing unusual.

After we were formally introduced, he changed gears and disappeared into the kitchen, where he started sifting through cupboards in search of cereal while asking his mom if she'd been to the store the day before. She hadn't and suggested that he make toast for his breakfast. In that short interaction, I could tell that this was an active single mother who was often absent from some of the day-to-day parenting duties. And that it wasn't out of the ordinary for Chris to have to fend for himself, which he appeared to be more than capable of doing.

Over time I would discover the love, enhanced by the utility of their lifestyle, that existed between them. Maggie was a devoted mother who was busy not only providing for her son, but who also had a full calendar of activities outside the home. This absence of a full-time parent gave Chris freedom, but also meant he would often have to take care of himself when it came to meals. Maggie apparently provided a loving home, but out of necessity fostered in Chris an independent spirit that was required to cover the times when Mom wasn't around. Her need to earn an income as a single mother determined how much they would be together. When Maggie offered me toast that morning, I declined, cautious about depleting what might have been scarce supplies.

After a quick shower and a change of clothes, Maggie was ready for the trip down to UCSD to pick up her truck. We climbed into the car, pulled out of the short gravel driveway, and joined the road that led out of town. On the drive, we chatted about Chris, animals, and the town in which she lived. And it wasn't long before we were pulling into the parking lot, which looked a lot bigger now that it was illuminated by bright sunlight. I stopped at her truck, and when we said goodbye I arranged to call her sometime during the week.

CHAPTER 10

Meeting of the Minds

There's always just a mystery that locks you in a trance
No matter what the future brings you're booked, and lawd you're bound
Be steppin' softly when you know the deal is goin' down
ZZ Top – "Deal Goin' Down"

By now, Mike was in a serious relationship with a new girlfriend. I could see that it was time to move out. PK, who I'd met at the surfboard factory, was living in Ocean Beach, and his roommate had left to go back east. The timing couldn't have been better. It wasn't long before I'd shifted my few belongings into his apartment about a mile away. At night, the occasional biker from one of the local gangs would roar up the alley beside the apartment block, making enough noise to wake the dead. This new neighborhood was not like the quiet residential area I'd just left, but its occupants were a lot more colorful. It turned out that our neighbor was an exotic dancer from a local club called Pacers. Her story was that she was a professional dancer and was only stripping to make extra cash. Looking at her figure and the way she sashayed around the building, I would have believed anything she said. The location of the apartment was only a few meters from the beach and a short walk to the eclectic main street, where surf shops, restaurants, and retail stores flanked a dusty thoroughfare.

Bordered by the San Diego River to the north, the Pacific Ocean to the west, and the stylish residential area of Sunset Cliffs to the south, Ocean Beach, or OB as it is nicknamed, is a convenient drop-off point for visitors from the east eager to embrace the beach lifestyle. Freeway 8 terminates in OB, and it is where many migrants initially find their feet in San Diego. Some of these visitors then move on to other parts of the county after being initiated into the diverse beach population where attorneys and doctors rub shoulders with surfers, students, and personnel from the numerous military installations around town. Some of these transplants, however, never transcend their initial introduction to beach living. The lure of drugs and the relaxed vibe make for a seduction that has driven many a youthful dream into ruins—prompting a return to family and their cities of origin, or to points outside the Southern California beach scene. San Diego is a place where you can have it all. It's a buffet of opportunity, enlightenment, and sensation. However, like many large and vibrant cities, it's also a source of many distractions that can lead impressionable young minds down some treacherous slopes.

I called Maggie the next week, cautious not to apply pressure but nevertheless eager to find out what she'd discovered and if she'd decided on her next move. We chatted about events that had transpired since we'd last met and finally got down to business. She said, "I've spoken to some folks, and I'll do it for fifteen hundred bucks." I couldn't believe my ears but quickly agreed, doing my best to appear unfazed by what seemed to be a bargain-basement price. This was something I could actually afford without having to sell the car. After hanging up the phone and skipping through a lap of the apartment, I sat in one of the two threadbare chairs in the front room and wondered, not for the first time, why this woman would put herself at risk. And now, as it turned out, for such little compensation. I racked my brains to come up with the answer but could find nothing that would rationalize her decision.

Over the next few weeks, we discussed the faux wedding, agreeing that it would need to look real. And that we would have to rustle up a sizeable contingent of guests along with a legitimate preacher and take lots of photos. The photos would form part of the evidence that we would show to any skeptical immigration agent who might doubt the sincerity of our union.

Word of the marriage soon spread, and a couple that we knew offered up their cliff-top house overlooking the ocean as a location for the event. Others signed up to provide a cake, food items, and decorations. I was to provide the remainder of the food and the booze while Maggie decided on the color scheme, which she decided would be red and black. A member of the surfboard-building community had a mother who was a preacher at one of the new-age churches in town, and she agreed to conduct the ceremony. With all the arrangements now in motion, we set a date for October. The challenge that still lay ahead, however, was how do you break this kind of news to your family? You're about to be married . . . sort of.

Maggie's family was as predictable as the sunrise. They didn't want to know, end of story. No tears were shed over their decision. Serendipity, however, played a part with my parents. During my time away from England, they had frequently followed me around the globe, taking a few weeks of vacation here and there to enjoy the sun and see the foreign lands where their son was holed up. This time they were planning to visit San Diego after the English summer. They had picked October and would be arriving shortly before the ceremony.

By the time they were due to arrive, I'd rehearsed the delivery of my news a thousand times and was still finalizing the presentation as I drove up to the Los Angeles International Airport to pick them up from their flight from London.

I met them as they emerged from the international arrivals hall and helped carry their bags to the curbside, then went to get the car from the parking structure. Dodging the buses, vans, and other vehicles that packed the airport oval, I returned to the curb and loaded the bags, then we made our way out of the complex and onto the Southbound 405 freeway.

Lots of talk ensued about family and friends in England, how the summer had been, and what the neighbors were up to. Finally, it was my mother who hit the hot button. "How's it going with your attorney and getting your paperwork?" she asked, secretly hoping to hear that it was failing and that I would soon be returning to England.

"Not well, I replied. I think the process is going to take forever, and there's no guarantee of approval even then. I think the only way to make this work is to marry someone."

That statement ushered in a silence that descended over the car. I imagined that in their minds, such a wild notion would have been briefly evaluated and then quickly dismissed; however, the doorway to full disclosure had opened, and I stepped through it. "You're invited to the wedding next weekend." Not the delivery that I'd carefully rehearsed, but it was done. Now I could only sit back and see how they were going to react. The silence continued unbroken, but this time for a whole different set of reasons.

Finally, my mother spoke. "Oh really," she said, her voice wavering, hoping that I would come out with a punch line and that this moment of horror would pass. Father sat in the front passenger seat, staring stoically ahead, not saying a word. I could only assume that he saw this as another unfathomable decision that his wayward son had made, this one so outrageous it was bound to end in disaster.

The dynamic between my two passengers was diametrically opposed. A supportive and somewhat progressive mother, who had been denied the opportunity for adventure in her youth due to loving, but overly protective parents, juxtaposed with an old-school father, rarely seen without a collar and tie, who typically acceded to the wishes of my mother. Much to the benefit of family serenity.

"Yes. We're getting married in a place that overlooks the ocean. Should be fun," I said, trying to make light of the emotional grenade I'd just tossed into their lives.

"Oh," replied my mother.

I glanced at the rearview mirror but was spared what I could only imagine was an expression of horror as the reality of her son falling into a tawdry arrangement with some unknown floozy began to sink in.

The grimy neighborhoods around the airport slipped by as we navigated the suffocating traffic heading toward San Diego. "Who is she?" my mother eventually asked.

"She's a librarian in the UCSD central library," I replied. "Very smart. Teaches country and western dancing and loves animals." I tried to paint a picture of a wholesome and hardworking pillar of society to defuse any idea that this was just another down-on-her-luck opportunist, eager to take advantage of a naïve foreigner. "I think you'll like her," I offered up weakly, still trying to break through the sense of impending doom that hung over the car. Finally, I dropped the second grenade and said, "I've arranged for us to have dinner this week so you can meet her."

After another awkward silence, the conversation finally picked up, meandering amongst talk of wedding arrangements, the fact that Maggie was divorced with a child, and what her parents thought about the whole thing, before easing into questions about friends, work, and life in California. But it felt like we had picked up an unwanted hitchhiker who was now present in every conversation.

We pulled into a motel in Ocean Beach where I'd booked a room for them. After helping with their bags and checking in with the manager, I left, planning to return later that evening so we could go to dinner. I imagined the conversation in that small motel room after I left, my parents on the bed, surrounded by partially unpacked suitcases. "Why, how could he? Should we be doing anything to prevent this? Should we let him get on with it? He's an adult; is there anything we can do anyway? You know how strong-willed he can be." The family drama was undoubtedly playing out in the absence of its principal actor.

Later that week, the dinner took place at the Cotton Patch, a budget restaurant just North of downtown. It was a Southern-themed eatery complete with red-and-white-checkered tablecloths and wait-resses wearing frilly skirts. Under awkward circumstances, Maggie behaved with surprising familiarity. I was amazed at her composure, animation, and ability to converse on topics ranging from politics and Europe to family and childhood. She embraced every subject and didn't shy from any sensitive question or from revealing who she was with complete transparency. If first impressions are tough to change, my business partner was off to a great start. I felt that some of the outer layers of uncertainty about this unusual arrangement were peeling away. I was finding that what lay underneath wasn't the tawdry desecration of the sanctity of marriage, just the reckless actions of two people too young to understand what they were cooking up. It was a giant step forward.

CHAPTER 11

The Hotel Incident

Turned away on your side
Is my timing that flawed?
Joy Division - "Love Will Tear Us Apart"

October 8, 1983 arrived. It was a classic fall morning, and a clear blue sky greeted us along with a light breeze blowing in from the Pacific. PK had traveled back to New Jersey to visit family, so my folks had moved into the apartment. They were getting settled in, having just exchanged pleasantries with the nice young woman who lived in the unit next door. I took off for a run along the coast road to burn off some of the energy that was building for the big ceremony. This marriage was the grandest event I'd ever concocted. Come to think of it, it was the only event I'd ever concocted, and I was aided and abetted by a cadre of willing and generous helpers. Why, I'm not sure. Could it have been the thrill of being part of something clandestine?

Was it the novelty of witnessing an arranged marriage? Or was it just the desire to be part of a great party?

After a couple of miles, I turned a corner, ran up the hill a short distance, and turned into the entrance to the wedding site. A long gravel driveway crunched beneath my running shoes as I walked the last few steps toward the rear of a quaint bungalow. At the front of the property was a sweeping view of sandstone bluffs that transitioned into the broad sweep of the Pacific sparkling under a warm sun. In the distance, a handful of surfers rode a small but well-formed wave that unwound as it crashed onto a reef just below the surface.

As I walked through the open door, I could hear laughter ringing out above the clinking of glasses and the sound of water running in the kitchen sink. Tables partially obscured by paper plates, cutlery, and an array of condiments sat alongside the wall in the main room. The sliding doors to the front of the house were wide open, giving a seamless feel to the outdoors. And the homeowners, helpers, and delivery people milled around adding the final touches to the event. Suddenly a loud voice yelled, "Whadda you doin' here!" It was Tom, the host. "Where's the food?" he barked good-naturedly.

I was bringing some special tortillas that would be the foundation for tacos that his partner Jenny was preparing for the Mexican feast. "Just stopping for a peek," I replied, sliding out past a keg of beer that was being carefully squeezed through the back door.

Returning to the apartment I took a quick shower and jumped into the car. Realizing that time was getting short, I was soon speeding toward San Diego to pick up the tortillas from a restaurant five miles away, just off the freeway. There was a line at the door as I arrived, not what I'd expected. The restaurant was renowned for its food, and this was early lunchtime. I hadn't allowed for the crowd. I slipped into line behind a large man wearing a San Diego Padres baseball cap and reading a newspaper who seemed oblivious to two scruffy kids peppering him with questions as they hopped around playing dodge, using his substantial girth as cover.

I fidgeted nervously and glanced at my watch. Two o'clock and the event starts at three. I peered inside the restaurant. There were two staff members in white bakers' outfits sliding stacks of warm tortillas into brown paper bags. Others passed bundles of take-out meals to the hungry customers already intoxicated by the mixed aromas emanating from behind the counter.

Let's see. I have to get the food, get it to the party so they can set up, zip home and change, bundle the folks into the car, and get back to the party. I wished I hadn't gone on that morning run, but it was too late to change things now. I figured that if I could secure unfettered access to the apartment bathroom for ten minutes, I could change and be ready. And if there was a parking spot near the event, we should make it just in time. The line continued to crawl along until finally money was exchanged, and I was cradling the warm, fragrant package as I made my way to the car.

Placing the food on the passenger seat, I slipped one of the tortillas out from the stack and rested it carefully on top of the bag so I could enjoy it during the trip back to the venue. After a quick U-turn, I was speeding home while keeping an eye on my valuable cargo, making sure it didn't end up arrayed across the floor if I had to brake suddenly for some errant driver. Pulling up to the clifftop house, and careful not to tear up the gravel in my haste, I dropped off the goods and took off for the apartment.

The party was only a couple of miles away, and after picking up the folks, we drove along the cliffs beside the ocean. As we drew near, I pulled up to the curb, parking just a few spaces from the entrance to the driveway. The street was filling up with cars, and I could see the gravel area leading to the house filled with an array of vehicles. I paused for a second. *Am I having second thoughts? Is this the right thing to do? What must be going through the minds of all of these people?* Then I suddenly thought about Maggie. *What if she's had second thoughts?* I crunched down the driveway for the third time that day, giving a guided tour of the area to the folks as we passed the cars parked by the bushes until one of them caught my eye. It was a classic bright red Dino Ferrari. *Who the heck is that?* Knowing that it probably didn't belong to any of the crew from the surfboard industry, I surmised that it must be someone from the considerable circle of friends Maggie had attracted through her activities inside and outside of work, including country and western dancing and her involvement in a multitude of animal initiatives. Anyway, there was no time to find out as I could see people lined up at the front door, slowly filing past a trio that was acting as the welcoming committee, busy hugging, kissing, and shaking hands with the latest arrivals.

Walking through the entryway, I looked over the crush of the immediate group and into the main living area, where a sea of people was standing shoulder to shoulder—most of them wearing colorful summer attire with a variety of aloha shirts and flowered outfits on display. Interspersed in the throng, I could pick out the bridesmaids, distinct with their bright red dresses and black scarves in keeping with the color scheme of the event.

The huddle closest to the door had spotted the freshly scrubbed groom, and a cheer went up that caught the attention of those standing in the center of the room. I waved above the heads of the welcoming committee and shuffled forward into the crowd. On the way, I introduced my parents to everyone I knew and introduced all three of us to some unfamiliar faces that had shown up, curious to see how this unique scenario was going to play out.

As I reached the middle of the room, I turned and realized I'd lost my parents to a conversation with someone they had met on a previous visit. I moved on, navigating my way through the well-wishers, shaking hands along the way with the crowd that thinned the further I got from the kitchen. The surf contingent was immediately recognizable as most of them were wearing Hawaiian shirts and shorts while clutching cans of beer. They contrasted with the other guests who wore more formal attire and stood cradling wine glasses in well-manicured hands. Many of the women dressed as if this was a real wedding. I wondered for a second if everyone was up to speed on what was about to go down, but it didn't seem to matter as the guests, huddled in their animated groups enjoyed the party.

I felt a tug on the sleeve of the cheap polyester suit I'd picked up earlier in the week at one of those overstock stores. It was Tall Sharon, one of Maggie's long-time friends from her days at the Bank of America. "Your brides arrived," she winked knowingly.

I looked toward the door where a group of women was bustling around the star of the show. Finally, she broke through the crowd, and someone pointed to where I was standing out on the deck. I waved and smiled, curious as to what I would pick up from her expression. Was she nervous, having second thoughts? She had her trademark shock of red hair pulled back from her face revealing black lightning bolt earrings that flashed every time they caught the sun. Below her signature slash of red lipstick and gleaming smile, a bright red Anne Klein dress with black buttons covered her slender figure. Black high heels completed the ensemble. *Geez,* I thought, *she's looking hot. The photos are going to be perfect.*

We hugged, as our familiarity had not reached the point where either of us was comfortable kissing. We had been on a few "business" dates and had met at an occasional party. Still, we were no more than friends and co-conspirators, hence demonstrations of affection were awkward at best and I was always respectful of our roles. We took a moment to check in with each other as to our comfort level with the plan before peeling away to schmooze with the crowd.

I made my way to the back patio in search of a drink and found Chris, at thirteen years of age, serving behind the bar. "How's it going?" I said as I fished for a beer in an ice-filled cooler sitting on the floor.

He didn't have a chance to answer before one of the local surfers turned away from a group that was leaning against a nearby wall and piped in. "He's a pro! He knows all the drinks and he's fast. I want him at my next do."

I winked at Chris, who was sporting an "I could have told you that" look. Making my way back into the house, I wondered for a second what kind of a long-term effect this whole bizarre episode would have on his development. But the thought quickly faded as I was swallowed up by a crowd that was getting bigger by the minute.

It was soon time for the ceremony, and the guests migrated to a grassy area at the front of the house, just feet from a public pathway that meandered along the edge of the cliffs. Stragglers were ushered from the bar, and slowly, everyone settled into their chosen positions as Maggie and I assembled in front of the pastor, who I believed was the only person at the event who didn't know the whole thing was a setup. She opened with some general remarks to the crowd and then launched into the ceremony.

At this point, I felt strangely guilty as I witnessed phase one of the plan coming to fruition. The talk of two people joining together, the many people who had turned out to support us. And my folks standing off to one side, who knows what going through their minds.

It was soon time to say our vows. Of course, this presented a problem. Although I'd joked with Maggie that she would have to say she was going to honor and obey me until the day she died, that idea had been greeted with a disparaging smile. There wasn't about to be any of that honoring and obeying nonsense and certainly no "till death us do part" stuff. Instead, we'd both constructed some contrived verbiage about partnerships and friendships, which we quickly dispensed as we hurried through that part of the ritual. Now it was time for the ring.

In all the rush and excitement of planning the event, I hadn't given the ring a second thought until my mother mentioned it on the morning of the wedding. *Oh crap!* The prominent symbol of commitment, and a central part of the ceremony, and I didn't have one. I didn't even know the size of her ring finger. What was I going to do? In the midst of the panic, my father said, "I've got an idea. Is there any spare electrical wire around?" I went into the kitchen and fished around in the junk drawer, coming up with a length of red plastic-clad wire that looked like it might have been the power conduit for some long-gone appliance. He pulled a folding knife out of his back pocket and deftly stripped the plastic from the core, revealing its inner bundle of bright copper threads. I could see where this was heading. Skillfully he wrapped the wire around my mother's ring finger, calculating that this circumference would approximate that of my fiancé's corresponding digit. Within a couple of minutes, we had averted disaster. Although a clumsy facsimile of the real thing, this new piece of folk art, gleaming in the light, was destined to save the day.

The four-year-old son of one of Maggie's friends from Long Beach was the official ring bearer. He'd become bored during the early part of the proceedings and had wandered off. As the ring ceremony neared, a ripple went through the crowd. And after a brief search, he was frog-marched up to the front of the wedding party, ring in hand, while sporting a large smudge of dark chocolate across most of the lower half of his face. He gleefully reached up and handed me the loop of coiled wire, which I quickly covered with my fingers, fearing that the pastor might catch a glance. An up-close examination of this symbol of our union would only raise unnecessary suspicions.

I turned to Maggie with a smug smile on my face, and as I raised the ring to place it on her outstretched hand, a rogue thread from the wire caught in her dress and snagged. Panicked, I dropped my hand. Through some divine intervention, although we certainly didn't deserve any, the thread released. Phew. I stole a glance at the pastor—no visible reaction. I pulled Maggie's hand toward me in an awkward effort to conceal the ring from the light, and from what I perceived to be the increasingly curious gaze of the minister. I moved the ring onto her finger as the light flashed off the tightly wound threads of copper, boldly advertising that this was an artifact better suited to gripping the positive terminal of a bedside coffee maker than symbolizing the union of two young lovers.

The ring slipped smoothly over the first knuckle of her finger and quickly ground to a halt. The next small knob of bone and cartilage that bears the medical name of the proximal interphalangeal joint was now threatening the entire ceremony. Maggie's digit was more substantial than my mother's. I pushed, and Maggie winced. I couldn't tell if the wire was biting into her flesh or if she was just embarrassed at my fumblings. I pushed again, and she laughed while reaching down to assist with my desperate attempt to shove the darn thing onto her hand.

By now, the pastor was taking a serious interest in what was going on. But with a final emphatic shove and another wince from the bride, the wire slipped over the bump of flesh and onto her finger. Maggie held it up to take a look, not at the ring, I found out later, but to see if her hand was bleeding. *Nooo,* I thought as the pastor slowly evaluated the folk art for signs of legitimacy, of which, of course, there were none. But hey, this was California. Anything goes, right? Off to one side stood my best man and former roommate Mike, tickled pink at the struggle unfolding before him as he gleefully observed the theater of which he was the original architect.

"You may kiss the bride," came the closing statement from the pastor. I pulled Maggie toward me and was about to plant the customary smooch on her lips when I realized that she was genuinely uncomfortable with that kind of intimacy from me. Especially in front of a collection of her friends and co-workers. However, we struggled through a kiss worthy of a couple of fifteen-year-olds on a first date. And with that symbolism dispatched, the deal was struck. Some papers were signed, and the party, now approaching its crescendo, swallowed us up one more time as the sun sank toward the horizon.

Later that afternoon, after a brief cake-cutting ceremony, I made my way out to the bar in the hunt for another beverage. I arrived to find my father on the receiving end of an explanation of the workings of energy on the human body from an animated guest practiced in the art of Chinese medicine. "Hold out your hand," he said. My father dutifully complied, eager not to offend but with a skeptical look in his eye. The practitioner then passed his hands over my father's outstretched limb, one above, one below. "Feel that," he said, looking confidently into my father's eyes, expecting a positive affirmation of his powers. "No," replied my father in a measured fashion so as not to offend. I could tell that the doctor didn't recognize the conservative nature of his patient. My father was as old school as the day is long, and human-generated healing fields were sure to be anathema to him. After another couple of failed attempts, the practitioner tried it on the photographer I'd met earlier in my stay, who had just strolled over to join us. His jovial, but demeaning response caused the conversation to devolve into a friendly wrestling match that progressed to the point where both participants ended up grappling on the floor of the patio.

My father, seeing his chance, stepped over the writhing bodies and slipped into the central part of the house. Meanwhile, I skirted the struggle going on below and headed for the cooler in the corner.

"Hey, Chris, still going, OK?" I asked.

"Yup," Chris said as he poured a margarita from a pitcher, all the while looking uncomfortably like Tom Cruise in the movie *Cocktail,* rather than a thirteen-year-old boy who was rapidly approaching his bedtime.

As the night wore on, the party started to draw to a close. The last of the guests were lounging on couches finishing up their observations on the day or making plans to meet again in the future. Some had found their way to the kitchen, where they leaned on countertops draining a final cocktail before meandering out of the house. Maggie and I decided it was time to go, but we faced one last problem. In all the excitement, neither of us had paid much thought to where we would spend the night. We couldn't go back to my place as my folks, who had left earlier, were there. And driving to Maggie's house at the north end of the county would have been foolish with all the drinking we'd been doing.

"What the hell are we going to do?" said Maggie. "Tom and Jenny would probably let us stay here, but I don't think that would be fair, and I'm in no state to drive."

I nodded in agreement as by now, I was feeling the fog of having had too many drinks. "Don't worry, I've got some blankets in the back of the wagon. We can crash there and leave early in the morning."

She took a moment to assess the pros and cons of this suggestion, but based upon a lack of any other options, she agreed. So, after thanking our hosts and acknowledging the last of the bleary-eyed participants, we staggered out into the moonlight and weaved our way up to the car, being careful not to end up in the bushes.

The road outside Tom and Jenny's was quiet. Most of the vehicles that had parked there for the wedding had long since departed, and the wagon stood alone, bathed in silvery light from a full moon. A car made the turn at the bottom of the hill, accelerated, and rumbled past where we stood. As it approached, I could make out two figures in the front seats staring straight ahead. I could also see how the car's headlights streamed into the interior of the wagon, illuminating every smudge on the windows and outlining every curve of the cracked upholstery. I said, "We'll have to keep our heads down if this is going to work. You're not allowed to sleep in vehicles along here." I opened the tailgate, and we kicked off our shoes and clambered in, tossing the blankets over ourselves while at the same time pulling the door shut as quietly as we could, fearing that a nearby resident, out in their kitchen for a late-night snack, might find it curious if they glanced out of the window to see two people climbing into the back of a nearby parked car. A call to the police would inevitably result in a black-and-white cruiser paying us a visit.

No sooner had we lay down than another car came speeding up the hill, bathing us in the glare of headlights set at full beam. Fortunately, the sides of the wagon, beneath the glass of the windows, were high enough that if we stayed in the prone position, they blocked the light from hitting us directly. "Welcome to the Hotel American Motors," I joked, leaning over to give my bride a peck on the cheek. At that point, Maggie's face had turned toward mine. Sensing an opportunity, I went in for a full-on kiss. I was surprised to receive a warm and unexpectedly long reception. Encouraged, I maneuvered closer and attempted a repeat performance. "What the hell are you doing!"? Came the sharp response. Recognizing the signal and chastened by the ringing denial of my advances, I could only mumble something about this being our wedding night as I retreated to my side of the hotel, dragging my makeshift pillow back to its rightful position. It wasn't much later that even the passing of an occasional vehicle ceased, and all fell still as we drifted off to sleep.

The next morning, we awoke to the bright light of the early-morning sun. Clambering out of the back of the car, we took in the same magnificent view we had enjoyed the day before—a crystal-clear sky reflecting a deep-blue ocean. The air was crisp, and the only other people around were a couple of surfers at the bottom of the hill checking out the breaks before deciding where to paddle out.

We stood on the sidewalk for a moment, reminiscing about the incidents, conversations, and people that made up the storyline of the party. Then, after walking Maggie to her truck and applying a conservative hug, followed by an even more conservative peck on the cheek, we both went back to our separate lives. We promised to meet the next week to talk about how things were going to work now that we had made our contrived partnership official.

CHAPTER 12

Is There More to This?

Do a little dance, make a little love,
get down tonight, get down tonight
KC and the Sunshine Band - "Get Down Tonight"

It was October 8, 1983 and I'd woken up that morning as a freshly minted married man, complete with plans for the future, just like any new spouse. Only in my case, it wasn't children, a house, soccer Saturdays, and an annual vacation. It was the start of getting to know my wife and stepson's daily habits down to their favorite TV shows, most enjoyable meal, the name of the irritating supervisor at work, and the best and worst teachers at school. Familiarizing myself with the subtleties and nuances of their behavior, along with their likes and dislikes, would be my project for the next few months. I would need to get close to both of them if my plan was going to work. A thorough knowledge of their lives was a necessity in case the INS decided to question us about the validity of our relationship. I intended to be ready for them. But how? It was already a problem that we lived apart from each other. And it would be a challenge to fully understand the depths of their psyches over a cup of coffee and dinner once a week. After mulling over this wrinkle, one idea stood out as holding the most promise, and I decided to propose it to Maggie the next time we met.

The opportunity came when I was invited to dinner at the Houlihan residence later that week. Chris was excited about the visit. Not because I was coming to dinner, but because unbeknown to me, his mom, a strict vegetarian, was going to compromise her beliefs and make chicken tacos for her carnivorous guest, even though I would have willingly eaten something that accommodated her ethics. Chris would have to prepare the meat—Maggie wasn't willing to go so far as cook meat herself. I was aware that the consumption of animal flesh was usually taboo in their house. And it left me with a feeling of guilt since I was going to disrupt that long-held commitment, even if it was only for one sitting.

During the dinner, Chris performed his usual feat of woofing down enough food to feed a platoon of soldiers. After talking nonstop between bites, he finally finished eating and asked permission to step out into the yard, where he set off to practice his fly-fishing technique. Minutes later, I could hear the swish and snap of eighty feet of double-taper fly line whipping back and forth across the front lawn.

Maggie and I chatted about everyday events until I spotted an opportunity and jumped in with my proposal. "You know that the INS will probably interview us in different rooms to find out if we really know each other?"

"Yes," she nodded, fully aware of what pitfalls our plan had lying in wait.

"How would you feel if I was your roommate for a couple of nights a week so I could understand more about your lifestyle? I would pay rent, which would help you out, and I could fix a few things around the house." I threw this last carrot into the mix as she'd told me that the landlady had an implied clause in her lease which meant that if Maggie took care of anything that broke on the property, the landlady wouldn't raise the rent. This agreement had worked to their mutual satisfaction for the last three years, resulting in dripping faucets, broken tiles, and a twisted screen door that had collided with one of the dogs as it rushed out to greet some unsuspecting wildlife in the backyard.

At one of our earlier meetings, she'd shared with me that her roommate Bob had only recently moved out. This situation suggested that she might be open to having a stranger in the house, and that my proposal wouldn't be as poorly timed as my attempts to consummate our marriage had been a few weeks earlier. After a couple of questions, she agreed to the arrangement, which included a monthly sum for rent, and I suggested that I would stay with her on Tuesdays and Wednesdays. She agreed. The following week, I appeared on her doorstep with little more than a toothbrush and a change of clothes.

We quickly slipped into this new routine, and I managed to get a job working in a surfboard factory only a few miles away from her house. But it wasn't long before a financial problem arose, only this time it was mine. After a couple of months of this new arrangement, I realized that paying the full monthly rent on my principal residence, and partial rent on my second home, was draining my sparse funds. So I came up with a solution that I felt would be a win-win for both of us. "I'm having a struggle making both of these payments," I told Maggie. "What do you think about me moving in here full time?" I secretly knew that the extra money would help the financial struggle that she was having. And so far, I'd made sure that I was a model roommate, washing dishes, listening attentively to Chris's tales of school, and taking the dogs on occasional walks. She agreed, and I broke the news to PK down in OB. After PK found a replacement, I shifted my few belongings into my new home, where I quickly fell into step with the routines and lifestyles of my new partners.

It wasn't many weeks after this change in living situation that our relationship took another twist. Chris was out for the night, attending a sleepover at a friend's house, and Maggie and I were enjoying the last of a bottle of cheap wine, having just finished a dinner of pasta followed by a huge bowl of homemade custard. The dogs lay resting on the carpet, twitching to their dreams, while the pet bird provided theme music from its cage in the corner of the room, occasionally peering through the bars, annoyed at the lack of engagement from the beings below.

The conversation had been rich. And with a belly full of wine, I looked at Maggie next to me on the couch and thought I detected a new look in her eye. She was an attractive woman who, as I got to know more about her struggles and achievements, I respected on many different levels. And with the alcohol working its magic on my libido, I decided to see what would happen if I moved closer. She toyed with the spoon resting in her dessert bowl and, not missing a beat, continued the conversation. But she had to be aware of my encroachment into her personal space. I turned toward her, looking for a sign that this time, my advances would not meet the same surgical rebuff I'd suffered on our wedding night. Her brown eyes looked into mine and we kissed, but this time, it wasn't for the cameras.

Within minutes we were shooing a large grey tomcat off her bed as it meowed in protest, utterly unaware of the obstacle he was presenting to our amorous intentions. By the following morning, we had consummated the marriage. Years later, Chris told me that after getting up to pee one night, he could tell something was up, having spotted my well-worn flip-flops outside his mom's bedroom. It was an event that, much to my relief, he'd been quite happy to see.

That night proved to be a turning point in our relationship. The dynamic between us was about to flip. For my part, I was okay with cruising along the way we were, each of us focused on work and our extracurricular activities while we explored our newfound relationship. Maggie, on the other hand, was less committed to its casual nature, and the state of our relationship seemed to make her uneasy. We had something going on, but what? No longer was this the business arrangement we had agreed to some months earlier. However, it wasn't the typical boy meets girl romance either. One evening after dinner, the issue finally elbowed its way to the forefront in decisive fashion.

Chris was in the kitchen, and it was evident that Maggie wanted to talk, so we decided to drive down to the beach. It was late when we arrived at the parking lot, which was dimly lit by a nearby streetlight. One other car stood at the far end of the asphalt with what looked like a couple of teenage lovers inside. The faint light from the streetlamp outlined their murky silhouettes, which were partially obscured by the condensation on the car's windows.

I shut off the engine, and Maggie turned to me. "I don't know where I stand with this relationship. I need to know if we're a couple, or if we should agree that this is still just a business arrangement and that you'll be my roommate until you move on. I have to think about Chris. And I need to know where this is heading, for both of our sakes."

And there I sat, having thought that we had all adjusted to our new familial status. That was not the case, however, with Maggie, who, I learned, had come to harbor a gnawing concern regarding this new phase of our relationship. I was now under pressure to make a decision, right here, in this dimly lit, mist-shrouded parking lot. The decision was not insignificant—a lifetime commitment to someone who had started out as a business partner, or an awkward future that could be short-circuited by either of us at any moment. What if I chose a business relationship? By now things had changed between us. A mutual bond of affection and respect had developed. To try and return to the old way would be awkward and would certainly fracture our newfound kinship. I paused as visions of possible outcomes flooded my brain, but I couldn't sit here all night weighing the odds. I only had a few seconds to think while preparing to appear supremely confident in my decision, whatever that was going to be. "I think what we have is pretty good," I replied honestly. "Let's make it for real." And with those five words, our futures became intertwined.

"OK," was the response, delivered in an almost offhand fashion. It struck me that up to that point, I'd only speculated that Maggie might want a serious relationship. I had avoided asking her any questions about her feelings or concerns regarding our partnership for fear of pushing us into this very situation. And here we were—no clasping each other in a physical act of agreement. No lingering kiss to confirm the maturation of our relationship into something real. We just sat in silence until I started the car and drove out of the parking lot. On the way home, we talked about everything but what had just happened. We'd struck a new deal, this one with no strings attached or financial advantages to one over the other—an agreement not based on a single goal, but centered on a relationship between two former strangers with no emotional ties who had become partners, then lovers, and now a married couple committed to sharing their lives for better or for worse. Maybe even till death do us part.

CHAPTER 13

Paperwork

Welcome to the Hotel California
Such a lovely place
Such a lovely face.
Plenty of room at the Hotel California
Any time of year you can find it here
The Eagles - "Hotel California"

About a month into our new relationship, we believed we had a solid knowledge of each other's lifestyles, and we got ready to fill out the immigration forms for my green card.

"We need to find a decent attorney," I said one evening over some excellent Mexican food, vegetarian, of course.

"No, you don't," said Maggie. "Look, when I split from Harry, I couldn't afford a fancy divorce attorney. I handled the whole thing by getting self-help law books, and I figured it out myself. I couldn't afford an attorney then, and we can't now. You get the forms, and we'll go over them together. We can work this out ourselves."

I rounded up INS form I-485. And we spent a few nights entering passport details, immigration and employment history, who my parents were, my marital background, and other biographic information. As we became familiar with the paperwork, the intimidation factor dissipated. On the fourth day of research, after digging through personal papers to finalize all the necessary information, the form was completed, neatly folded, and slipped into an envelope with its supporting documentation. The next day the package was sent via certified mail, and once again, my future rested in the hands of the federal government.

Outside of her university work, Maggie had not been idle. She had recently become aware that local animal shelters were selling relinquished family pets to medical research laboratories. The prospect of a person's onetime companion animal being turned over to a lab to be burned by chemicals, or to have its limbs broken so that a new drug or surgical procedure could be tested, horrified and incensed her. She could not view with detachment the pictures that she would find in the library of monkeys with electronic data probes inserted into their brains as they endured isolation, drugs, or pain.

Finally, after talking to animal shelter employees and other knowledgeable sources, she approached a local civic leader on the town council to see if she could muster support for stopping the practice. With a well-researched and somewhat graphic description of the perils faced by pets in the local shelters, she found a willing advocate to fight the injustice in councilor Pam Slater.

Encouraged by finding a like-minded person in a position of influence, Maggie was ready to move on to the next step: organizing.

She joined forces with a couple of residents who she had met during her research, and the group cobbled together a grassroots organization called Stop Taking Our Pets or STOP. The new organization then launched its first foray into activism and political involvement by working toward legislation that would halt the selling of shelter animals for commercial or medical research.

Empowered by the structure of their new organization and bolstered by community support, the group ventured out and began lobbying shelter executives, the Director of Animal Control, and politicians in the hope of passing a new law that would halt the sales. Early success came in the form of hearings in front of the county board of supervisors. At these meetings, STOP educated the lawmakers not only on the practice of selling shelter animals, but also on the lack of public education. Families relinquished their pets with the false expectation that another loving family would adopt them.

It wasn't long before the board saw that a vote against legislation banning the sale of pets would condemn them in the eyes of their animal-loving constituents. So, with little downside to imposing new restrictions, the board voted to create a shelter system that was prohibited from selling its animal occupants to medical and pharmaceutical companies.

As this crusade was taking place, the group also turned its focus to creating a more humane environment for the animals. They encouraged the directors of each shelter to work more closely with the animal rescue groups that existed in San Diego and to increase the range of services each shelter offered to the public. Today, the San Diego Humane Society is one of the leading animal support organizations in the country, and it is often held up as the benchmark of excellence for others to emulate.

These successes, made possible by the group's grassroots mobilization through networking and advocacy, would be a turning point in

Maggie's growing sense of self-empowerment and her awareness of the power of activism.

Driven by an acute sensitivity to injustice and prepared to stand up and make a difference, she'd also become involved in local politics and had begun work on several political committees including the San Diego County Affirmative Action Advisory Board, and the County Animal Control Advisory Committee. In her spare time, when not teaching country and western dancing, she would assist the jobless and disadvantaged by helping them with their resumes or coaching them on personal presentation and how to conduct themselves during a job interview. Her activism and involvement with government committees had been quietly growing. One day, she could be found protesting in front of high-end department stores against their practice of selling fur, and the next, negotiating with Department of Fish and Game managers regarding the control of wildlife in the county. She would often come home after one of these meetings and complain about the number of hunters that made up such a high percentage of the commission. To her, the idea of hunters as policy advisors on issues related to fish and game was an arrangement that was tough to rationalize.

Later that year, my parents came to visit and during their stay, my mother was first invited, and then co-opted, into attending a protest outside the well-known aquatic park called Sea World. The focus of the demonstration was Sea World's exploitation of wild orca whales, which were the centerpiece of their entertainment. Alarmed by the isolation, these social animals suffered in the park, and the marked difference between their life spans in captivity versus in the wild. An activist group had formed, and it was determined to have its voice heard.

On a Saturday morning, the small band gathered on the road outside the entertainment complex and staked out a position close to the entrance. Waving their placards while withstanding the abuse and catcalls of the park's supporters, they stood defiant, secure in the justice of their demonstration and eager to educate the masses that poured into the park. Many of the visitors were only aware of the impressive sight of the animals and they were unwilling to recognize the cruel choreography behind the plunging bodies and colorful commentary that was the twice-daily orca show.

The media, having gotten wind of the demo, pulled up in vans emblazoned with their stations' logos, and camera crews spilled out into the street. A well-coiffed reporter stepped out of one of the vans and strode purposefully toward the group that was now positioned just beside a road that led into the sprawling parking lot. Raising his mic while addressing the camera, the reporter outlined the framework of the protest and then moved toward the group to get a statement from the protestors. He chose an older woman standing on the fringes who was energetically hoisting her sign while waving to the passers-by. "Hello, what does your group hope to achieve with its protest today?" he asked, turning his mic toward my mother as the cameraman zeroed in. Mother, of course, was the least qualified member of the group to deliver a thirty-second elevator pitch on man's exploitation of animals for entertainment purposes. Fortunately, a group organizer spotted what was going down and deftly stepped between the two, deflecting the question while saving my mother from her fifteen minutes of fame. During the evening news, however, it was still possible to pick her out in the crowd when the segment aired.

Shortly after my mother's brush with animal activism, a letter arrived in the mail with instructions and a date for Maggie and me to interview with the INS at the federal building in downtown San Diego. We didn't even rehearse how we would answer the expected questions. All those fears had vanished as a result of our new relationship, and the interviews were not the critical milestone they had once threatened to be.

On the morning of the appointment, we showered and put on our best attire. A couple of pairs of slacks and a jacket had made their way into my closet by now, and Maggie wore a conservative pantsuit. With our game faces on, we joined the hustle of the morning traffic and made our way downtown.

After signing in, we sat in a bland waiting room surrounded by two Hispanic couples and an Asian gentleman. The two couples either knew each other, or they had struck up a friendship that morning, brought together by the hope of a new opportunity in the U.S. They talked in Spanish with hushed tones, occasionally glancing at the two smartly dressed Caucasians who sat opposite—probably wondering what we were doing at an immigration interview.

After about an hour, an official-looking woman with a collection of manila folders under one arm called us into an adjoining room, which was equally as bland as the first. This one was empty except for the two of us. We sat thumbing through out-of-date magazines for another thirty minutes until a different woman, wearing an Immigration Service uniform, ushered us into a hallway. Here, we were separated, then we were directed into a long, narrow room that looked much like part of a bank.

A large glass partition with small openings similar to tellers' positions divided the room. With no chairs, the interviewees had to stand and answer questions from the officials who sat behind the partitions. Short glass dividers protruded from each of these openings so that any conversation would be limited to its two participants and prevent any eavesdropping by an attentive partner further down the line.

With much greater confidence than before in the validity of our answers, we were both ready for a relentless grilling. However, after a handful of reasonably superficial questions, we were ushered out into the lobby and sent on our way. I would receive notification of the outcome of the interviews within the next six weeks.

Three weeks later, I received written authorization to work while my application was being assessed. This news was timely, as my dream of becoming a globetrotting professional surfer was fading about as quickly as a winter sunset. And it was time to start pursuing more mainstream employment outside of the surfing industry.

As a foreigner with an accent who had traveled to a variety of countries, I decided that my next career move was to become a travel agent. I signed up for a crash course at a for-profit school. After graduating, I found a job in a local agency where I expected to share my international expertise by advising clients on how to make the most of their trips to exotic destinations. Instead, I found myself relegated to filing brochures and booking the occasional short-haul airline ticket to Mexico. After a few weeks of this grunt work and only seeing the owner of the business on rare occasions, I came to question the purpose of the operation. The owner was married to the president of the local BMW dealership, and the travel agency seemed to be a vanity project for her. After working at the business for a few months, I could see how poorly managed the operations were. It was time to look for employment elsewhere.

I soon found a position with a regional airline that crisscrossed the skies up and down the West Coast corridor, but, within months, the security of that job evaporated when I learned that the company was moving to Nevada. Not about to leave the coastal life that I had worked so hard to secure, I hit the job trail once again and found an opportunity at one of the international airlines. This time, however, the job was in LA at the international airport complex, which would mean finding accommodation in Los Angeles and staying up there five days a week. Neither Maggie nor I liked the idea of being separated. But in the interest of establishing a career and still living by the ocean, we agreed that I should take the position. I found a room to rent and started work. At the same time, back in San Diego, Maggie continued to uncover more challenges within the UCSD library system, where her abilities were about to be tested by a new assignment. The administration was becoming increasingly aware that many incoming students lacked the fundamental research skills necessary to take full advantage of their schooling. They didn't know how to use the immense computing power and access to world-class educational databases that the university provided. Realizing this shortfall, they asked the leaders of the library to work on a solution.

After scoping out the challenge, the head librarian and his staff concluded that the best course of action would be to create an outreach and instruction program. The classes would provide a focused environment for the students to learn about all the library's resources and how to use them. Now the only missing element was someone who knew the tools inside and out and who had the personality to engage students.

After assessing their staff for the necessary traits, they concluded that the extrovert, Maggie Houlihan, was best equipped to set up this new undergrad program, and they put a proposition in front of her. Eager for a new challenge, Maggie soon created a curriculum that went on to teach thousands of students how to parse Internet resources, while differentiating between popular material and scholarly writings. She taught them how to avoid the scourge of merely cutting and pasting from existing texts. Instead, she taught them how to use information that could be found online, in conjunction with their critical thinking, to build authentic research papers. The program was a success. And it achieved its goal of helping students become better researchers, thereby making them more competitive in the workforce they would soon be joining. The program would go on to become a standard part of the library's offerings.

One evening, as I was packing a few things for my weekly sojourn to LA, I was rummaging through a drawer where I came across an old newspaper article. It featured a picture of a younger Maggie staring up at the camera while she sat at a desk that was top-heavy with papers. The headline read, "FIREFIGHTER HOPEFULS WON'T GIVE UP DREAM." I pulled out the creased newsprint and started to read. The article, from 1982, recounted the experience of a group of applicants to the San Diego Fire Academy. The group had completed the pre-academy tests but had been denied the opportunity to enroll in the academy itself. What they had discovered was that certain applicants had received help from family members and friends who had contacts within the firefighting structure, and they had given those individuals the inside scoop on when and how to apply. They had also ensured that the applications from these chosen few conveniently found their way onto the right person's desk. As a result, that year's academy was already full, and there were no plans for another in the foreseeable future.

Outraged at such an inside job, ninety of the hopefuls camped out in San Diego's largest park, near the center of town. Here they held their daily protest to bring media attention to the cronyism and injustice they had experienced.

Curious, I asked her about the piece. "Oh yeah," she said, "that was a total jip. We went through all the qualification tests, written first and then the physical. They had us doing things like humping

85-pound bundles of hoses up a ladder with an oxygen tank strapped to our backs. Full gear! Then four of us at a time had to raise and lower 260-pound ladders. And that was just the warm-up. A lot of people dropped out or flunked because they couldn't do the tasks."

"And you guys protested?" I asked.

"Yep, when we heard we were being cheated, we decided to camp out and complain. We were pissed. I had Chris with me, he can tell you about it. He got really good at Frisbee during that time. I had fully qualified, and then they told us the academy was full and no more were scheduled. I went down and spoke before the San Diego Civil Service Commission and told 'em what I thought about the whole stinking process. I could've waited another year or two for another academy, but it would have taken too much time, so I moved on."

I could sense the bad taste that had been left by the injustice. "How many women were in your group?" I asked.

"Only me" was her reply.

"You wanted to be a firefighter!" I exclaimed, not bothering to cover my surprise. Here was a woman laying siege to the male bastion of the heroic firefighter, fully aware of the dangers not only from fire but also from her male peers, many of who would be sure to view her as a weak link in any life-threatening situation.

Undeterred, she'd thrown herself into the throng of applicants and by all accounts had come out with results that were easily strong enough to qualify her for the academy. Her subsequent resistance to yet another case of foul play by insider networks further solidified her willingness to fight for fair treatment, whether for humans or animals.

The following morning, I left for LA and in time we settled into our new routine. I was away for most of the week, and Maggie was in San Diego as we slowly nudged our careers in the right direction.

It wasn't long before Maggie received the UCSD Outstanding Employee of the Year award for revitalizing the university's Staff Association. The school's newspaper credited her with contributing countless hours working for the association and improving its structure. They said that she'd strengthened the association's image on campus and across the university among administrators and staff alike. Her award was delivered later that year by the chancellor in a special ceremony on campus.

While this was going on in San Diego, fate had presented me with a good news/bad news situation further north. Since joining the airline, I'd received a promotion to a supervisor position. Now I was getting the wink to apply for a manager role at the company's headquarters in Houston, Texas. Good news, promotion; bad news, Texas, and away from the coast. No contest. It was a simple decision, but one that held some downsides for my career. There is an understanding in the larger corporate world that if an employee doesn't apply for appropriate promotions, even if they involve a transfer, it will probably kill off any hopes of upward mobility in the future. Flexibility, especially when it came to relocation, was a must for any ambitious candidate looking to burnish their credentials with an international company, and this fact that wasn't lost on me. So, after almost three years with the airline, I declined the opportunity to apply. The next day I began looking for a job back in San Diego, preferably with a company headquartered in the area. I assumed that this would minimize any need to relocate for career advancement. After a search stretching over a couple of months, I found a family-owned catalog sales firm that was growing by leaps and bounds. It was well managed, and they needed a supervisor. Following a couple of interviews, I was offered the job. Now I could move back to San Diego.

While the excitement and energy of LA were intoxicating, its blanket of endless concrete and the accompanying crush of traffic had turned out to be a way station and not a destination. I welcomed a return to the quieter confines of Encinitas and proximity to a family for which I'd become the de facto patriarch.

PART 5
Entering the Machine

CHAPTER 14

Another Life-Altering Decision

Our house is a very, very, very fine house
With two cats in the yard
Life used to be so hard
Now everything is easy 'cause of you
Crosby Stills and Nash – "Our House"

As a paperwork marriage evolved into a relationship based on respect and growing affection, the alliance with our landlady took a turn for the worse. It all began with a stale smell of mold coming from the bathroom. The odor had become so strong that it was apparent there was a leak behind the wall. The tools and the know-how to rip out a complete shower and replace it were, at that time, beyond my rudimentary do-it-yourself skills, which maxed out if the project was more than replacing a faucet or fixing a hole in some damaged drywall. For that reason, a repair was requested. This simple request broke the unwritten rule in the rental agreement, which implied, "Don't even think of bugging me if you have any problems." Nevertheless, after much grumbling, she accepted the repair request. After a delay, and then an attempt to lay the blame for the leak at our feet, two workers arrived and spent a month ripping the room apart. These two maintained a hit-or-miss schedule that was about as predictable as a Big Foot sighting. Their work was substandard, even to a layperson. "Cheap and cheerful" would be a flattering description. Copious amounts of dirt from the demolition was tracked from the back of the house to the front. Pictures came crashing down from walls on the reverse side of the demolition while dust collected on furniture and countertops in all of the other rooms.

During this upheaval, when the house had taken on the appearance of a home in a Middle East conflict zone, a flyer arrived announcing that the residence on the opposite side of the street was up for sale. The ad referred to it as a cactus ranch. Since it was a convenient stroll to the property and the ask price wasn't outrageous, we decided to take a look and contacted the realtor.

He showed up a few days later dressed in a snazzy blue blazer with gray slacks and one of those garishly colored power ties that were fashionable at the time. It didn't take long to realize that this was a self-anointed deal-maker with enough blarney that he could easily have sold fire starters to the devil. We walked over to the house, a 1950s ranch design that was in bad shape. It had experienced a couple of fires due to the smoking and drinking habits of the owners, who had cut corners with the insurance settlements by repairing the damage as inexpensively as possible. We learned that during one of these fires, the husband, a stoutly built man rarely seen without a cigarette dangling from his hand, had, upon smelling smoke, jumped out of the bedroom window. Leaving his wife, who was still in bed, to fend for herself.

The house reeked of nicotine infused with dog urine, the result of the occupants using the dining room as a whelping area for their part-time dog-breeding business. The most ominous feature of the property, however, was a block of five chain-link kennels that sat on a concrete slab at the front of the plot. These spelled trouble. It wasn't hard to imagine that with Maggie's passion for animals, it wouldn't be long before the enclosures were teeming with abandoned dogs, cats, rabbits, and any other furry or feathered creature that had been mistreated or abandoned.

I made a mental note that this was a definite downside and that it would be at the top of my list of cons should we seriously consider purchasing the place. Later I learned that the property also had a kennel license. The prospect of a purchase with this double whammy quickly began to vaporize. Five kennels and a license spelled danger, and I needed to be ready. There was no way I was going to agree to a situation that provided such a tailor-made opportunity for a spouse who was known to stop the car in a torrential downpour to corral a stray dog or scoop up a bird with a damaged wing. Heck, the animals she already had—two dogs, a bird, a rabbit, and two cats—were all rescues or cast-offs. The cat, Barry, only had three legs, having been found by Chris and his mom in a ditch near their favorite restaurant after they had just finished one of their weekly dinner specials. These critters were certainly no fashion accessories. I could easily put two and two together and see this property becoming an unofficial animal rescue hub for the county, which was not going to happen on my watch.

Two months later, we moved into the property. My counter-arguments, honed by a few years of exposure to negotiation techniques in the business world, had been laid to waste in a torrent of rose-tinted appeals that promoted the advantages of owning our own castle.

And how it wouldn't really need years of hard labor and a bleeding checkbook to make the place presentable. The one victory I did secure, however, was an agreement that any new animal coming onto the property could only be a replacement for one that was adopted out or moved on to that big kennel in the sky. In short, no net new additions.

With these restrictions established, my attention turned to renovating the house in an attempt to bring it up to a reasonable standard of livability. My weekends and days off were now dedicated to the new house. The first steps were to fight through the dark-brown layers of nicotine on the window frames and throw out every square inch of fabric that could hold the smell of smoke or urine. Maggie helped when she wasn't out working with animal groups or meeting with the government boards she served on, which meant not very often.

As her political exposure had begun to grow, demands on her time had increased. It became routine in the evenings for the phone to ring. On the other end would be a local activist or someone from an organization who was a party to the workings of city government. And it wasn't long before I started to detect a vein of discontent in her descriptions of the happenings of the political arena in Encinitas.

Maggie's attention had begun to focus on the evolution of the city, and it didn't meet her vision for the town she'd adopted. Poorly designed buildings were popping up at an alarming rate, often cheap construction that was in conflict with the surrounding architecture. Cookie-cutter blocks of shopping malls and tacky condo developments started to overshadow the older beach cottages and ranch houses that were part of the original character of the city, a character that was now under siege.

"This county doesn't give a damn about us," I would hear. Have you seen that monstrosity they're building down on the corner? It's a piece of junk and doesn't even try to fit in with the surrounding buildings."

It wasn't long before Maggie was talking with a handful of people who would fight to incorporate Encinitas as a city. And while she wouldn't play a role in the initiative, her proximity to this grassroots fight, contacts with key community influencers, and education in the workings of county government provided an initiation that would later lead to a deeper involvement in the leadership of the town.

After the battle to incorporate was completed in 1986, Encinitas, as a city, was, for the most part, outside the control of county government. The town was now able to elect its own government and determine its future. Many of the hard-working activists who had orchestrated the split ended up on the first City Council, and as time went by, these councilors were replaced by new individuals with fresh ideas and perspectives. It was an evolution that left the door open for a darker element to join the City's leadership, notably those with ties to the development community. And it was just a matter of time before council members were elected who supported the agenda of those with wealth and power, above the wishes of the majority of residents, so they could enjoy the quid pro quo of strong financial support when it was time for their re-election campaigns.

Many of these subsequent councils began to allow development that was not aligned with the City's general plan. And they regularly consented to requests for increases in density and height that were granted through the issuance of what are called variances. Other giveaways and a lack of adherence to the general plan saw well-heeled development companies, both local and from as far away as Texas, making profits at the expense of the character of the city. And it began to chafe at Maggie's sense of injustice.

Some of the town's original activists organized and tried to stop particular projects that threatened areas of natural beauty or a neighborhood's character. But they were typically defeated. And, as an added insult, they were often treated with disdain by individual council members whose list of campaign donors underscored their links to the development community.

Maggie wanted to take action. It was too much for her to see this corruption of the ideals fostered by the city's founders as the city started to fall prey to the profit margins of out-of-town companies. Her conversations began to hint at a more formal role in the management of the City. And finally, one day, she said that she wanted to run for a seat on the next City Council.

It wasn't as if she needed my permission to do practically anything she wanted, but in this case, the stakes were higher than usual. This alteration in her career path would mean resigning from UCSD in order to mount an effective campaign. And if she were to be elected, the position would require hours of work on commissions and subcommittees, meetings with constituents, and reading documents, along with the day-to-day routine of City government. This change would put the primary burden for our financial security in my hands since compensation for a seated council member was less than $1,000 a month.

By now, Chris had finished college and had made a couple of visits to see his half-brother Ronnie in Idaho, finally deciding that his future lay in the mountains and not on the coast. It was with a heavy heart that he loaded up his car, bade farewell to his mother and me, and started the two-day drive to Sun Valley to begin his new life. I had seen Chris grow from a thirteen-year-old child into a man. During that time, he never voiced any resentment about having a stranger step into the role of being his father, and that was something I had always appreciated. Our relationship had evolved from my physically looking down at him with instructions that he needed to do his homework, to gradually having to look up to someone who, as a youth, grew to be a towering six foot eight. At which point I began asking him politely if he wouldn't mind completing his homework.

Over the past few years, my career had taken off. I'd entered the technology sector and had progressed through a couple of companies, rising to the ranks of upper management as a vice president. I figured that financially, we would be OK if Maggie changed her vocation. And since I was only a bystander to the world of City politics and naïve to its darker side, I wasn't opposed to her ambition.

"Is this what you really want?" I asked.

"I feel I've got no other option," she replied. "Someone has to stand up and stop what's happening. I think I know what I'm getting into, and yes, this is what I want to do."

The situation presented a recurring opportunity for me, which hinged on the agreement we had struck a few years earlier involving our animal population and the five chain-link kennels located at the front of the yard. At that time, beneath an arched eyebrow, and with the gravitas of a judge dishing out a life sentence, I had delivered an edict restricting the count of fauna to a replacement-only cycle. Within weeks of the establishment of this new Maginot Line, however, the first crumpled bird had arrived in a shoebox, peering watery-eyed over wads of toilet tissue at its rescuers, and I'd caved. The bird became a net addition, and Norm the Labrador mix followed. Then came Neville and Millie, then Bridie and Cody, all dogs. Then the rabbits took up residence, followed by rats, more birds, a chinchilla called Stanley, Donovan the iguana, and a revolving door of cats, both domestic and feral. Many needing to be nursed back to health from wounds such as a missing eye or gashed front leg, and all of them undergoing a mandatory spay or neuter procedure as soon as they were healthy enough for the surgery.

Spitting and hissing, and with no insignificant loss of human blood (principally mine), they would all be cared for until they could be released, adopted, or—yes, as was the case with many of them—they got to stay. My multiple attempts to lay down the law and maintain any semblance of population control had been trampled underfoot by a succession of furry vagrants. All of them were in need of care, or so vulnerable that to turn them away, when we had the facilities to provide shelter, would in itself have been an act of cruelty.

This time, however, things were going to be different. I would dictate new terms so that there could be no mistake as to my requirements. So it was with an even more emphatic dose of gravitas and an eyebrow arched even further skyward that I said, "If you're going to be a councilor then no more animals, and you cook the dinner every evening." Of course, there was an instant agreement with our covenant, an understanding that I knew would only provide a fragile foundation for any future attempts to stem the arrival of the next batch of displaced critters.

This lifelong quest to come to the rescue of mistreated animals led Maggie to realize that preventing the never-ending queue of unwanted pets was probably better than dealing with the anguish of seeing so many of them end up as discarded afterthoughts. The simple solution was having the animals spayed and neutered at an early age. Maggie picked up on the importance of this procedure and joined with a group of women who had recently created an organization called the Spay Neuter Action Project, or SNAP. Over the following months, the group raised enough money to invest in a mobile clinic, which was an old school bus converted into a rolling surgery that they aptly christened the Neuter Scooter. The scooter would be dispatched, along with its team of veterinary surgeons and support staff, into low-income neighborhoods where inexpensive spay and neuter surgeries would be performed for people who couldn't afford a regular veterinarian's rates.

Maggie's advocacy for prevention rather than cure didn't stop with SNAP. It was often the sighting of an intact pit bull, accompanying its unwitting owner down the path to the local beach, that led to a masterful, if unscripted, interaction.

"Ohh what a nice looking dog, is he good with strangers?"

Typically, the reply would be in the affirmative.

"Can I pet him?"

"Sure."

After some small talk about the breed and how handsome his dog was, and with the owner sufficiently softened up, Maggie would move in for the kill. "I see he's not neutered. Did you know neutering reduces the risk of them getting cancer and prevents them from roaming? They're generally better with other dogs than if they're left intact, and they're easier to train. You end up with a healthier pet."

With the element of surprise in her favor, it was rare that an owner, often sporting tattoos and a reversed baseball cap, would come back with anything other than an agreeable response. These ranged from the begrudging to the curious. The enlightened owner would then leave, equipped with phone numbers and instructions to call the Spay Neuter Action Project if they couldn't afford a visit to a regular vet.

While these interactions were playing out, I would hover nervously nearby. Ready to step in should the owner, or the dog for that matter, become aggressive toward the supplier of what could easily be considered unwelcome advice.

It wasn't long before Maggie sought to raise the profile of spaying and neutering animals. She met with council members and propositioned the City to issue a proclamation declaring February 29 as Spay Day, which they agreed to.

As a result of these animal causes, Maggie developed a background as a tireless activist. And it was this advocacy, along with her political assignments, excellent reputation from the University of California, and growing network of supporters in the community, that gave her the credibility she needed to create a viable campaign for the 2000 election. She pulled candidate papers and, with an announcement to the press, took her place in the race for one of the three vacant seats on the City Council.

Over the next few weeks, a team of well-qualified and determined people volunteered to become members of the campaign team. These included Bruce, an engineer and master strategist who would be the campaign manager; an attorney from the largest tech company in the county; a scientist; a skilled web designer; an environmental engineer; and a local activist. All felt disenfranchised by the direction successive City Councils were pursuing, and each was drawn to the beliefs and energy of a candidate who was gaining a reputation as a champion of the people. They wanted to win one of the three seats that were up for grabs in the election, and they were willing to fight to the last vote to secure it.

CHAPTER 15

"Hot Lips" Joins the Race

Face to face, out in the heat
Hangin' tough, stayin' hungry
They stack the odds till we take to the street
Survivor - "Eye of the Tiger"

Serendipity provided the campaign with a marketing hook that was plucked from M*A*S*H, a TV series that ran from the early seventies to the beginning of the eighties and was set during the Korean war. The episodes featured an outspoken female major called Margaret Houlihan. And although the spelling of the first name was different from Margret's, the link was strong enough that it inspired the campaign to print olive drab T-shirts featuring military stars, while promotional booths at street fairs and civic events were adorned with military camouflage netting. The public saw the connection right away. Some curious residents even saluted before questioning the candidate about her stand on various issues.

The campaign, built around slow growth and the preservation of the city's remaining open space and environmental stewardship, put candidate Houlihan squarely in the crosshairs of the building industry. Her vision meant that development trade groups, the real estate business, and its consultants provided early and ongoing support to the opposition—contenders who they could influence to their advantage. The development lobby's strategy was simple: undermine those who sought to temper, in any way, their business goals and profit margins, even if the majority of residents were in support of a slow-growth platform, while actively extolling the virtues of their carefully selected representatives. It was a strategy that required financial resources, and they were prepared to loosen the purse strings to secure victory.

It wasn't long before money came pouring into the coffers of the pro-growth candidates. These were rivals who claimed to respect individual property rights, which equated to supporting an owner's freedom to do pretty much whatever they wanted with their house or land. Also in this pro-development mix were the industries' sycophants who, eager to associate themselves with wealth and power, lined up in support.

Every Tuesday evening, the Houlihan campaign team gathered in the cramped dining space adjacent to our kitchen, which soon became ground zero for the operation. Team members would filter in, and the first few minutes of every meeting were filled with participants sharing what they had seen and heard over the past week. There were gasps of disbelief at reports of operatives spreading misinformation and expressions of disappointment at news that some desirable endorsement had gone to the opposition. Exclamations of astonishment were punctuated with disdain as each person became privy to the ups, downs, and dirty dealings of the opposing camps.

With everyone up to speed on recent events, voices would once again rise, and chairs would slide closer to the dining table as ideas were championed and fleshed out or rebutted, each suggestion receiving a thorough vetting before the successful proposals were merged into the campaign plan.

At some meetings, a group would break away and dissect content for mailers, viewing different options with the precision of brain surgeons huddled around a set of x-rays. In a separate corner, two tech-savvy members shared ideas for the digital side of the campaign. Back and forth they would go while outstretched arms would occasionally reach for the pile of chocolate chip cookies that always held a coveted spot in the center of the table.

While this activity was going on, the candidate would flit between the various projects like a facilitator at a speed chess event. She would ask questions and offer ideas, eager to ensure that any product the team put in front of the voters would have maximum impact while holding firm to the principles of her candidacy.

As the campaign wore on, it became apparent that outside this group, many in the community didn't believe their grassroots movement could actually win a seat. With only $16,000 in the bank, they were up against experienced contenders who had seasoned campaign teams, generous supporters, and consultants. Some even enjoyed the support of political action committees. What these observers failed to notice, however, was that most of Houlihan's donations came directly from residents and not from business interests. This would prove to be a vital differentiator in the fight for an open seat.

The opposition's support from the building industry came in a variety of forms. The usual campaign donations, not always within the limits set by campaign finance law, were offered up by several entities, some from outside the city and others from outside the county and even state. Tacked onto this revenue came the expensive glossy mailers touting the excellence of their candidates. Some of these were paid for by political action committees, or PAC's, which were often nothing more than fronts for development interests. Next came a tool that has become a standard weapon in both local and national elections, one that has left a permanent scar on our system of selecting civic leaders: the political hit piece.

Often funded by soft or dark money, these mailers typically masqueraded under names that suggested they were in support of the environment or acting on behalf of the residents. Either way, they ripped into candidate Houlihan's platform with constant scathing attacks aimed at scaring people away from her slow growth vision for the city. Scenarios depicting plummeting house values or homeowners restricted from adding a spare bedroom for a child returning from college or for an aging parent flooded mailboxes. Their attack strategy was surgical and ongoing.

Another tool in their kit involved the activities of the sycophants, individuals who the building industry and their candidates knew they could direct to create whisper campaigns, write letters, or submit op-ed pieces to the local press. Some even had electronic mailing lists, which they would use to blast out messages, designed to denigrate the opposition in the same vein as the content used in the mailers. Except these were often far more personal in nature.

Encinitas had a master of this genre in its midst, a gentleman by the name of Mike Andreen. Mike was a one-time journalist who presented his political and sometimes personal attacks using his "Wire Fire" email tirades and op-ed pieces. He even produced a vanity tabloid called the *Surf City Times,* which was largely funded by real estate advertising. The cadence of Andreen's activities increased and typically became more strident as Election Day drew near. And his crusades had successfully darkened the hopes and reputations of more than one hopeful candidate. And he was set to be unleashed in this fight.

With all political campaigns come oddities, revelations, and accusations of bad behavior, and this one was no different. The city's fire chief decided to step out from the crowd and stand up for his chosen candidate by creating what was a one-person non-profit organization under the name of the "Golden State Firefighters." This shell entity proceeded to pump out mailers featuring a picture of a rugged firefighter heroically carrying a hose while surrounded by fire, staunchly supporting a new entrant in the election called Jerome Stocks. No one knew for sure if the Chief was, in fact, the only member of this group as it had mysteriously sprung up during the campaign and was never heard of once the final ballots had been counted.

As election season rolled into its final weeks, many residents became aware of the David and Goliath struggle that Maggie and her team were waging. Volunteers from across the community signed up to walk neighborhoods or join phone banks. The goal was to call and educate wavering and, in many cases, uneducated voters. The candidate joined the volunteers, going door to door to introduce herself and present her positions on all the issues that confronted the future of the city.

On occasional dark and very early Sunday mornings, I would accompany Maggie through the deserted streets of nearby housing developments. In the darkness, we would slip campaign flyers under people's weekend newspapers, sometimes happening across an early riser, in dressing gown and slippers, reaching for their paper. They would be startled by the sound of a cheerful "Good morning," followed by, "I'd just like to introduce myself. I'm Maggie Houlihan, and I'm running for City Council." It was apparent that this shock at 5:30 on a Sunday morning jolted the casually dressed weekenders. Taking a moment to collect themselves through a post-sleep fog, they would often struggle to make sense of the onslaught of political rhetoric that came thick and fast. Some made the mistake of replying with a trigger phrase such as, "Yes, I've heard of you," or "Yes, I plan to vote," hoping to fob off this political interloper and return to their cocoons. Any hope of a swift exit, however, quickly disappeared as they stared, glassy-eyed, trying to focus on the person silhouetted against the beams of light spilling down from the streetlamps. A figure that was asking them about their concerns for the city while they were more concerned about what was for breakfast. Some recipients would genuinely engage in the dialogue, and when this was the case, I would sneak off and cover the rest of the houses on the block.

On other occasions, I would get up at 4 a.m., pull on some old work clothes, and take to the streets with a tool belt, hammer, and stack of campaign signs. Under cover of darkness, the signs would be hammered into the ground at busy intersections or threaded between the chain-link at suitably visible construction sites. It wasn't unusual at such an early hour for a black-and-white police cruiser to drive by. The officer would cast a suspicious eye in the direction of the shadowy figure clasping a hammer as he patrolled the sleepy neighborhoods in the early morning. Realizing that I was just another political fanatic out to get a jump on the competition for the most visible sign locations, and not a hardened criminal sizing up his next heist, they would hover for a moment and then move on—only for our paths to cross later on as I travelled to other locations within their jurisdiction.

My contributions paled beside the core campaign team who were relentless and calculating in their strategy to conquer the city. On weekend mornings toward the final run-up, a group of volunteers would congregate in Bruce's garage. This location served as the war room, where documents and handouts revealed a map of the city carved into neighborhoods. Each volunteer would choose a neighborhood or two to cover and then leave with pamphlets and instructions to knock on doors and talk to residents. At these gatherings, polling information was shared. Maggie was doing surprisingly well for a first-timer. But the last weeks of campaigning would be critical in deciding the final result. And it was during these weeks that the opposition was likely to roll out their most damaging attacks.

Election day finally arrived, and that night, the team and supporters gathered in the sitting room of a small hotel where they could track the latest results as they appeared on TV. This was the moment when they would find out if all of their hard work, planning, and execution would be enough to pull off an upset for their first-time candidate.

The group settled in and as the evening wore on the returns started to post. Early results showed an eight-year incumbent, James Bond, in the lead. Mr. Bond only used the first name James during the election season. Outside of this temporary campaign persona, he referred to himself as Jim. James was an alter ego that had served him well in the past as a vote-gathering tool, and he wasn't about to mess with a good thing.

The results also showed that Maggie was in second place. Upon seeing her position, the team leaped out of their seats and let out a cheer. In third place was Jerome Stocks, a local insurance broker and advocate for increased recreational facilities. Early in the campaign, Jerome had come across as a fresh-faced idealist eager to enhance the community through his chosen initiatives. This initial impression, however, had been dashed by the actions of special interests working on his behalf. Interests that took great pains to discredit Maggie and her positions. If elected, he would be the second freshman on the dais. The remainder of the field lagged in the early numbers, and with three seats up for grabs it was now up to the leaders to see if they could hold or even improve upon their positions.

The evening wore on, with each new count greeted with oohs and aahs as Maggie maintained her position in second place. When it was time to leave, her seat on the council had been secured. The grassroots strategy of connecting directly with residents through face-to-face interactions had been a successful one. The only question left was, would she move into the coveted first position? Either way, this was a win that would endorse her platform of maintaining the town's character and protecting the environment while also providing support for a healthy business community.

Considering the current first and third placeholders were the beneficiaries of well-funded operations, Maggie's selection was going to be an upset victory. A victory accented by her campaign slogan, "of the people by the people for the people."

The next day the official tally showed 007 had held onto first place with 9,946 votes. Houlihan was second with 9,414. Only 532 votes separated the first-time progressive activist from the eight-year conservative incumbent and first place.

CHAPTER 16

The First Signs of Trouble

I smell a rat babe
Something funny's going on
Since that other man moved next door
I've a funny feeling in my bones
Howlin' Wolf - "I Smell a Rat"

Maggie, along with fellow freshman Jerome Stocks, joined a council broadly divided along progressive and conservative lines. Along with her on the political left sat the current Mayor, Dennis Holtz, a smart and charismatic attorney. In the more conservative faction were Jim Bond, fiscally prudent and cautious, and former police officer Christie Guerin, who at the time was often the swing vote. Guerin had cut her activist teeth supporting a school bond initiative and would later align with the pro-development majority. Because of this balance, it was a council that would coexist in relative harmony until the election cycle came along two years later, at which time a change in its membership would shift the balance, leaving Maggie isolated and sorely unprepared for what was to come.

Her first year was spent lobbying her peers to form an environmental review committee, designate a dog-friendly beach, implement a trails plan for walkers and horse riders, and help get a new city park off the ground. The council majority voted against approving the dog beach, while the trails plan was approved, although with a much smaller scope. The environmental review committee and the new park also won sufficient votes to move forward, and with these successes, her agenda had started to create real change. Later on, her activism on behalf of animals would resurface when she added to an earlier victory by persuading the city to support the spaying and neutering of pets. This time she had the council consent to a proclamation announcing April as "Prevent a Litter Month."

While enjoying this early success, she reintroduced a controversial discussion that dealt with defining, and in her mind preserving, the inherent character of the city. And it came from a fear she and others had that the town was becoming smothered in the McMansion and shopping mall mania that was sweeping the coast.

Landowners in the city had recognized the growing value of their properties and the wealth that the beach area attracted. Lots with modest bungalows and single-story homes were being cleared to make way for large, and in some cases, multi-story residences, while greenhouse spaces presented the opportunity to build entire subdivisions. New homes were popping up that filled plots almost from lot line to lot line, and these projects would often attract the ire of neighbors as they blocked views and sunlight while also providing a stark contrast to the predominant, more modest residential architecture of the neighborhood.

This endeavor pitted her squarely against Stocks, Bond, and now Guerin, who was beginning to see that influence and power rested with the developers and landowners, not with the residents, who would regularly appeal to the council to stop what they saw as an insidious erosion of the look and feel of the city.

As this schedule of political issues took center stage in Maggie's life, at home, we began to notice an alarming change in the environment around our house. Rats, both dead and alive, had started to show up along the southern edge of the property, and whenever the wind blew from the south, the toxic stench of putrefied animal waste filled the air. This pungent odor continued for a few months, with the only conclusion being that there was a food source within the neighbor's property that was attracting the rats. Poison must have been laid down to control the problem, because the rats were crawling into our yard and expiring under the effects of a toxin.

With the combination of the stench and the bodies that appeared almost daily, it seemed reasonable to contact the City's code enforcement division and ask them to investigate, so Maggie submitted her request. It was this seemingly simple act that revealed the new political culture at City Hall and the influence the majority-voting bloc of Stocks, Bond, and Guerin had on the town's operations.

After receiving the request, the City stalled and did nothing for weeks. Despite repeated overtures, not a single staff person was dispatched. This was a sitting council member who had made the request. Had it been a resident, it was safe to assume that in a week or so, the department would have investigated the issue or escalated the matter to another authority. This, however, was not the case for Maggie, who soon realized that she was being marginalized by the council majority due to their opposing agendas. And she was now pitted against three of her four peers, all of whom supported personal property rights and, by default, most of the requests for development that came their way.

The influence of this bloc was evident to the city manager, who, at the time, was a man called Kerry Miller. It was Miller's job to work with the heads of each department on deciding what projects to take on. And it was apparent that heeding the request of a minority council member was not going to be a priority. Maggie reflected on her time spent working at the Bank of America when she first came to town all those years ago. Female staff members had been treated like second-class citizens with their wishes and input typically ignored by their supervisors. With those experiences fresh in her mind, she vowed that this time she was going to fight back.

Realizing that she had little influence within the City's operations, Maggie wasn't about to be discounted. She looked for another way to trigger action. Over the years, she had developed a friendship with a former Mayor Pam Slater, who had advanced in her career and was now a county supervisor. It was under Slater that Maggie had worked on the City's homeless task force, during which time they had developed a mutual respect. This relationship had grown stronger through shared beliefs about many of the problems facing the county and a similar philosophy regarding animal welfare.

Slater saw the scope of the problem immediately, including the threat to public health that the City was curiously unwilling to address. Within a couple of weeks, and much to the embarrassment of local officials, the county sent in animal control officers to investigate. What they found was appalling. In a barn on the neighbor's property, owned and operated by Pete Springer and his partner Robert Turner, 35,000 rats were being bred in squalor, some destined to be sold live, or frozen, for a dollar each to pet stores and zoos for reptile food. Others were destined for pharmaceutical labs to be used for research. Fifty to sixty rats per cage crawled over each other in a cocoon of filth, whereas the number of rats that veterinarians recommend per pen is ten to fifteen. Hundreds of dead bodies littered the floor of the barn. And the level of ammonia in the air was so strong that the animal control officers had to use a specialized breathing apparatus to conduct the investigation. Outside the barn, hidden by buildings and mature trees, lay a large pool of rat excrement. It was the only evidence of any attempt at clean up that the business conducted, and it was the source of the odor that permeated the neighborhood whenever the wind blew from the south. The reason we were seeing dead rats in our yard was because Springer dusted the floor of the barn with rat poison so that any rats bent on escaping would be killed by this toxic trap.

The owner of the business, which he called "Rats R Us," was eventually arraigned, on September 7, 2003, on a felony count of animal neglect and faced up to three years in prison. He was quoted in the press as saying, "[Animal control officers] don't understand the rat business. We attempt to care for them, but some will die."

Back at the City, there was no evidence of contrition. And the months ahead would show that the council was becoming more entrenched along political and personal lines. The majority was now deliberately working to block the upstart who was finding ways to work around the obstacles they placed in front of her. Their methods of suppression, however, were rarely on public view. They were often the result of members of the majority exerting influence over the city manager, leverage that was often the result of an inferred philosophy or a direct instruction by the current Mayor. And with the bloc playing a significant role in the city manager's employment and future compensation, it was not difficult to understand how compliant he could become. The City staff, in turn, were obligated to follow the direction they received from their chain of command.

The business of managing the town continued, with ongoing challenges confronting the council. These ranged from keeping sand on the beaches to protecting local watersheds that were suffering from pollution brought on by the ever-expanding development in the area. Simmering beneath the surface, however, was a growing animosity from the pro-development bloc toward the more resident-oriented Maggie Houlihan. A dislike that was becoming increasingly evident during the closed session meetings that were held outside of public view and attended only by the council, the city manager, and the city attorney.

At this juncture, Encinitas still had flower-growing at its agricultural core. The competition introduced after the signing of the North America Free Trade Agreement (NAFTA), however, allowed foreign companies with their lower costs of production to move into the market, and they were threatening the local business. This change, coupled with an ever-increasing appetite for land to be used for residential development, was putting pressure on the local floriculture industry. Growers, who owned large swaths of property, were well aware of the pot of gold that beckoned at the end of the development rainbow. And now, since they were land rich but cash poor, they made it clear that any political opposition to such an opportunity would be an unwelcome intrusion upon their rights as landowners.

The various aspects of the building industry in Encinitas, from the property owners to the developers, recognized the clout they would have if they joined together to fight against any resistance that threatened their business goals. So they formed a political action committee, or PAC, intending to persuade the community that if the growers couldn't develop their land, the flower business would be forced out of town.

A key player in this PAC was a development consultant called David C. Meyer. Meyer had married into what was the largest land-owning and flower-growing family in the city, the Eckes. Albert Ecke, a German immigrant, had started growing flowers in the LA area in 1909, moving to Encinitas to establish the Ecke Poinsettia Ranch in 1923. Since then, the ranch had been handed down through genera-tions and had become the largest grower of poinsettias in the world, with additional facilities located in Guatemala.

During their time in the U.S, the Eckes had purchased multiple parcels of land in Southern California and were no strangers to real estate development. They had created a development arm called the Carltas Company, in 1987, which went on to develop over 1,000 acres of coastal real estate. The name Carltas was a portmanteau of Carlsbad and Encinitas, two of the areas in which they operated. Meyer, for his part, had played a role shepherding a number of these projects from concept through to completion before going out on his own.

Meyer was a vital member of the PAC, for which one priority was to spend no small amount of money ensuring that the 2002 mid-term elections would produce a council majority that they could rely upon to support their cause. The candidate they brought forward was a local boy called Dan Dalager. Dan's father had started a tool-sharpening shop in the city in 1947, and Dan began working for him at the age of nine, finally taking over the business when his father retired. With its worn wooden floors, walls hung with agricultural tools and parts, and strong smell of used oil and grass clippings, the small shop was Dan's domain. It was here that he would hold court with many a customer by discussing the early days or the current goings-on in the city. These conversations were typically punctuated with heavy doses of nostalgia for the way it used to be. Around town, Dan was a well-known character, and he had relationships with many of the local flower growers and long-time residents, as he had spent his youth lifeguarding or playing little league with many of them. As someone who projected a country boy persona and reveled in the attention he was getting from the town's power brokers, Dan was a perfect asset for the PAC's goals. And it was instrumental in getting him elected in the 2002 race. They facilitated his ascendency by blanketing the community with mailers containing pictures of Dan having just emerged from the surf while heralding his long-term residence in the city. The majority on the council had also jumped on the Dalager bandwagon. And Dan, in return, slotted seamlessly into the power bloc following his election. His boast to anyone who would listen was that he didn't even need to campaign to get elected. This braggadocio, along with a misdirected belief that he'd evolved from local good-ol'-boy to untouchable elected official, would prove to be a character flaw that would result in his undoing further down the road. With Dan in place, however, there was now a supermajority in which four of the five council members supported if not development itself, then certainly the power and wealth that underpinned it.

One of Dan's early forays into setting the tone for the city was to change the name of the annual winter parade. This event was always well-attended, and it was welcomed as the unofficial kick-off for the holidays. The main street would be ablaze with lights as families, with cheeks reddened by the crisp winter air, would line the sidewalks, taking up prime positions in their beach chairs. Or they would lie on blankets bundled up in winter jackets and hats, eager for the procession to begin. Finally, a voice would ring out over the PA system and the parade would commence. Floats from the Girl Scouts, high school marching bands, the local surf club, and classic car groups would fill the street, while dignitaries sat atop a fire truck waving as it moved slowly past the crowds accompanied by blasts of its siren.

This annual shindig was known as the holiday parade. However, Dan wanted to bring back what he felt was a sense of tradition, so he decided to rename the event and call it the Christmas parade. There were a number of people in and out of town who supported the switch, as did the council majority. However, they wanted to complete the shift without presenting the idea to the public for comment. Maggie pushed back, arguing that the name change would be divisive and that it disrespected the other religions supported within the cosmopolitan makeup of the city. Although she stuck to her position that the residents had a right to weigh in on the decision, she was overruled.

The name change for the parade was soon announced to the city, where the backlash was swift and forthright. Religious leaders, including those from the local Jewish community, civic movers and shakers, the Girl Scouts, a dog club, and one of the city's business groups from the Leucadia section of town, all complained and threatened not to attend the event. Dan, despite the response, stood by his decision and was quoted as saying that he was just changing the name back to what it originally had been. Even though the outrage persisted, his reversal persevered, and it was the Christmas parade that took place that year. The new moniker, while under constant attack from residents and prominent citizens, lasted precisely one year. By the following winter order was restored, and the name was switched back.

It was during this period that the City received a communication from the American Humane Society. They wanted to present Maggie with an award for her work on behalf of animals by making a special presentation at an upcoming council meeting. The city manager heard of the request, and his decision was swift. Realizing that the remaining four council members would be incensed at this recognition and that they would categorize it as political grandstanding, he quashed the request. And in the interest of picking more meaningful battles, Maggie consented and declined the award.

As the council settled in and responsibilities were divided up, Maggie was assigned to work on the board of a local wastewater authority. And it was here, through her involvement in a land leasing proposal, that her relationship with development consultant David C. Meyer would be forged. A relationship triggered by self-interest that would devolve into an ongoing spectacle of public shaming and criticism the likes of which had never been seen within the boundaries of the city.

The Encina Wastewater and Treatment Plant's board would meet regularly to discuss service issues, investment, and operations. And it was at one of these meetings that an agenda item came up regarding a vacant plot of land that the authority owned adjacent to its treatment plant. The property was attractive to local businesses. In particular, a group of car dealerships saw it as an opportunity for expansion.

The authority's staff lacked the expertise needed to create a land-use plan. So they turned to someone who had a history of working with the City of Carlsbad, where the treatment plant was located. David Meyer had developed several parcels of land within the city, along with a number of commercial projects when he was a member of the Carltas Company. And he was considered by the plant's management to be qualified for the project.

As the board discussed the land use agenda topic, there was an assumption by the authority's staff that Meyer's company, DCM

Properties Inc., would be the expert who would guide them through the leasing process. As Maggie listened to the discussion, it occurred to her that having just one known entity as the assumptive consultant wasn't necessarily in the taxpayers' best interest. The project was not a no-bid situation, and other qualified companies may have been willing to compete for the business. She concluded that, at a minimum, the project should go out for bid. That way, the best value for money could be realized on behalf of the taxpayers, the people who would ultimately be shouldering the tab. The other board members, who had been going along with the Meyer recommendation, saw the logic in her proposal and voted for a bidding process.

Meyer, when he heard of this change, didn't see it the way the board did, and his subsequent action revealed his frustration at not being granted the contract. he was incensed. He saw himself as the incumbent for these projects. It was he who had spent years cultivating the right relationships within the City's staff to ensure that decisions like this went his way. It was his adopted family that had owned and developed many acres of land in Carlsbad. And it was he who had worked with the City over the years on many developments. This project was his, and he felt entitled to it.

Lacking sufficient clout with the plant's management to get them to change the decision, and unable to influence the board, Meyer couldn't avoid the perceived indignity of having to compete for the taxpayer's dollar. And he was forced to join the bidding process.

Two proposals were submitted, one from DCM Properties and one from Keyser Marston Associates, both companies located in the county of San Diego. The Meyer proposal came in at four pages in length. It provided generalities on how DCM would interface with the authority's staff to complete the work, and it only approximated the acreage of the project. With a grammatical error on page four, the bid went on to offer an open-ended hourly rate for its services—a fundamental flaw when dealing with the financial constraints of a municipality that answers to its residents.

The Keyser Marston proposal came in at fourteen pages in length. It contained a full introduction to the history and expertise of the organization, an understanding of the exact acreage of the property, and explanations of how they would analyze the project, make preparations to solicit potential lessees, and assist with the subsequent negotiations. A full, closed-ended budget, with the hourly pay of each person involved in the work, was included. The bid also contained the maximum cost for the project, a list of general provisions, details of insurance, and steps to be taken should a conflict of interest arise. Rounding out the proposal was a list of the principles assigned to the project, along with their resumes and examples of comparable assignments the company had previously completed.

When faced with the two proposals, the authority made a unanimous decision, and Meyer was left out in the cold. His loss was the result of a lackluster bid that suggested a misplaced confidence in his longstanding relationships and the influence of his wife's powerful family.

Meyer's initial chagrin at having to compete for the work deepened with his loss of the work. And this change in his fortunes turned into a simmering rage. But instead of employing the prudent introspection of a high-caliber organization by reviewing the performance of his company, he chose instead to pursue a path of retribution, and for that, he needed a target.

It didn't take long before his conversations with confidants and insiders turned up the information he was seeking. He discovered that his proposal had been on track for approval, like so many in the past, but that a procedural switch introduced at the last minute by the Encinitas council member Maggie Houlihan had derailed it. It was Houlihan who had come up with the idea of releasing the project into the perilous waters of a commercial bidding process. A contract that he viewed as a right, hard-earned over many years of relationship-building. This was the same Houlihan who had been actively working on the community character guidelines initiative in Encinitas. An effort that threatened to put unwanted constraints on future development in the city. And if it proved successful, it would be a change that could quickly threaten the profit margins of his company. Meyer had found his mark.

Brimming with anger and carrying all the spite of a jilted lover, he first went to the city of Encinitas with a written complaint, then to the media so he could inform the public of his series of accusations. The next day the newspaper read, "Something stinks at Encina Wastewater Authority, and critics say it isn't sewage." Meyer's version of events painted Houlihan as a political backstabber using her influence to orchestrate a Machiavellian scheme solely designed to obstruct his company from being awarded the consulting contract. All because he was politically opposed to her slow-growth development agenda.

Meyer's complaint read, "It is my belief that an honest, objective analysis should be the basis for all decisions made by public officials, not vindictive motivations to punish political rivals." Strangely enough, it was this same type of "objective analysis" that Maggie had proposed to the board and that, after some debate, had been approved.

The media ate up the controversy. Here was a juicy scenario pitting a wealthy and well-connected development consultant against a City bureaucrat. Meyer went further and demanded that the City discipline Houlihan while failing to provide any specifics as to just what kind of disciplinary action he was seeking; he was not content with outlining a simple complaint. His accusation then broadened as he attempted to encapsulate what, in his view, was wrong with politics in the state, by assuming the role of spokesperson for all of California's residents. His email read, "Encinitas deserves better. The people of this state are sick and tired of the backroom dealing, the fraud, the political blood sport."

It was ironic that a businessperson who often engaged in ex parte meetings with select members of the City Council, and who was an influential member of the Flower PAC, had become the embittered "victim" of a taxpayer-sanctioned board that was doing the right thing on behalf of its constituents.

"Most people really do have a problem with public officials abusing their power. Vendettas embarrass the city and its citizens, and it has to stop," continued Meyer while providing no proof to validate his ever-expanding litany of accusations. The last of his contrived motives for her supposed skullduggery was that he had supported a pro–property rights candidate during the 2002 election cycle—and that the contender, Dan Dalager, had captured one of the two vacant seats.

With such a catalog of misdeeds, it seemed only logical that the next step would be litigation to put things back in their proper order. But Meyer, no stranger to suing the City for other building industry–related issues, took no such action. He had the deep pockets to go the legal route and an ample supply of moral outrage. Still, he stopped short, perhaps satisfied for the moment that the smearing of a local politician's character in the press would suffice.

Maggie was shocked at such a petulant display of outrage against what Meyer viewed as a heinous injustice perpetrated by a politico who was out to get him. She had only proposed a logical course of action that the other members of the board had endorsed. Meyer's reaction came as a complete surprise. The city manager took the complaint and forwarded it to the city attorney, who found no cause for any action to be taken.

While all this was taking place in plain sight, council members Bond, Stocks and Dalager, recipients of election campaign contributions from Meyer, declined to comment and watched the proceedings from afar. The newspapers, seeing that the City was not going to take any action, realized that there was no evidence of any ethical violations and wrapped up their coverage. With that, the matter slipped off everyone's radar, only to appear a year later in a more destructive form.

PART 6

The Power of Compassion

CHAPTER 17

The Old and the Young

Your poverty you declare
The paint blisters on your stairs
The dampness in your bones is always there
The Tiger Lillies – "Nightingale"

C rises like these didn't have long to simmer around our household. A cavalcade of animal issues, social causes, and regular City business soon pushed the Meyer episode into the background. And it wasn't long before Maggie arrived home one evening with news of an elderly Hispanic woman who lived a couple of miles away and was in distress. People in her neighborhood had gotten word that she was an animal lover who would do anything to help an injured or unwanted pet, and this benevolence had resulted in unknown individuals dumping the occasional animal in her fenced front yard, under cover of darkness. Now of advancing years, she'd become unable to care for these animals. However, they continued to appear on her property. A neighbor had heard about her predicament and took steps to help her out by adopting one of the abandoned dogs. In the process of collecting her new pet, she was shocked to see the woman's living conditions. As she was over eighty years of age, infirm and with failing eyesight, the maintenance of her household had become a daunting responsibility, one at which she was failing badly. And it was through the neighbor who attended the old woman's church, that word reached Maggie.

"We have to go over there and see if we can help," she said, wrapping a coat around her shoulders as she looked appealingly at me. "If we don't go around to see what we can do, who will?" I whined about not having had dinner, fully aware that any appeals to my creature comforts rarely carried any leverage when there was a higher cause at stake. Knowing that a refusal to accompany her wouldn't have stopped the visit, and that she was stepping into unknown territory, I sacrificed my visions of an evening meal and agreed to join her. After a quick debrief on what scant information she had, we were in the car, weaving our way under the streetlamps, to an address that Maggie had jotted down on an old shopping receipt.

The house was a small, dilapidated pale-blue shack that would have gone unnoticed had it been in a Brazilian favela. Perched as it was amongst the high-end residences of this affluent neighborhood, the shack stuck out like a Toyota in a showroom full of Ferraris. The paint was peeling, roof shingles were missing, and Mother Nature had blanketed the yard in a thick carpet of weeds. In the half-light I could see the backyard, where the margins were marked by a rickety lodge pole fence that had weathered into a dark gray color. Within the fence stood an orchard populated by a collection of dead or dying trees that were a testament to the effects of California's long hot summers and a lack of attention.

The porch creaked with every step we took toward an entrance that was fronted by a ripped screen door hanging at an angle. Looking at the damage and judging from the chorus of barking that was coming from inside, I guessed that the damage had been inflicted by one of the dogs.

After we knocked on the door, a timid voice from inside provided our first indication of the frail condition of the occupant. "Who is it?"

Maggie launched into the logistics of who and what had led us to her porch that evening. When she was halfway through her explanation, the door scraped open just enough to give us a glimpse of a woman who was little more than five feet tall. She was clad in an aging housecoat that bore the stains of years of wear, the kind of stains that no amount of washing could ever erase. At one time, it must have matched the pale-blue color of the house, but now, its glory days long gone, it had taken on a greeny-brown hue. Above the housecoat appeared the leathery skin of someone who herself had seen better days. She wore a pair of thick glasses, the lenses tinted to protect the wearer from bright light, a filter that we would later learn was needed to provide some comfort against the chronic dry eye syndrome from which she suffered. A scarf, equally as ratty as the housecoat, adorned her head, while a pair of tattered gray slippers completed her outfit. Seeing that the visitors didn't appear to present any immediate threat, she invited us into the dank and dimly lit interior of the house, where the smell of animal urine immediately clogged our senses.

The main room contained an unmade bed, a couple of rickety wooden chairs, and a bedside table complete with a small lamp that illuminated a faded picture of the Madonna. The threadbare curtains that covered the windows were drawn, and, we learned, remained that way even during daylight hours because of the challenges bright light presented to the occupant's vision.

Mary Reyes was her name. She'd grown up in Los Angeles, and her story, which we discovered over time, was a sad one. In her childhood, her mother had been the only buffer against an abusive father who, while limiting his treatment of Mary to verbal and emotional abuse, would regularly beat her brother with his belt. Her mother had passed away when Mary was young, and her father had gone on to remarry. Upon joining the family, her new stepmother immediately saw Mary as competition for her father's affection, and she took out her resentment through a variety of cruel methods that included preventing Mary from eating. She would stand behind Mary's father while wagging her finger in front of her mouth, daring the child to raise a forkful of food. It was only a matter of time before Mary was shoved out of the picture and dumped in a sanitarium where, although by no means enjoying a comfortable lifestyle, she was fed and sheltered. And it was here that she acquired a deep and lasting faith in God, an anchor that she would cling to for the rest of her life.

Upon entering adulthood, she had left the confines of the sanatorium and met a man named Teddy who would turn out to be the love of her life. Their relationship had blossomed, culminating in marriage. Teddy was reasonably astute in business, and it wasn't long before they started to live a comfortable life with the kinds of amenities Mary had been privy to only through the conversations of others. They had their own house, a regular supply of food, and, most important of all, Mary received unquestioning love that awakened her spirit and fed her soul.

After years of loving marriage, Teddy had died of a heart attack while he was still quite young. Judging from a couple of old black-and-white photographs, it looked like he'd been around fifty when he passed, and he'd made no arrangements for the support of his wife.

We never learned how Mary had come to move to Encinitas. But all the signs suggested that since Teddy's passing, she'd been on a gradual decline, both physically and financially, to the point where she was now getting by on a small social security income. We also learned that she'd given most of the resources leftover from her marriage to animal causes. That philanthropy, coupled with a pronounced inability to manage her money, had resulted in her straddling the line between being poor and being outright destitute. Unable to drive, because of her failing eyesight, she had developed a sizable past due account with the local cab company, which had become her only means of transportation to the grocery store and her beloved St John the Evangelist Church, a sanctuary where she attended morning and evening service every weekend.

After the three of us spent a couple of hours deep in conversation, I asked Mary if I could look around the house, and she agreed. As she and Maggie discussed animal cruelty and flipped through some of her mail, I stepped into the back of the house. As I had expected, it wasn't a pretty picture. Newspaper covered part of the floor in an area just off the kitchen, and it was here that the dogs were encouraged to pee and poop. Mary considered this to be acceptable behavior as she had never house-trained the two aging pets and didn't think she could at this stage of their lives.

In the kitchen, I opened a couple of the grimy wooden cabinets that hung precariously over the countertop and looked inside. There was a tin of refried beans and a half-eaten box of crackers sitting beside just enough crockery to support two people. I closed the doors and continued my tour. The house was filthy. As I made my way out to the backyard, I looked up and, in the half-light, noticed a blue tarp covering a quarter of the roof.

The backyard, lined with the skeletons of dead trees, stretched back to a broken fence some distance away. At one time, this must have been a lush and productive orchard. Guessing that what I saw was probably over an acre of land, I realized that although Mary may have been cash poor, the property itself was worth a significant amount of money.

After nosing around, I made a mental inventory of the leaking faucets, a shower that lacked a curtain, sagging door hinges, and the kind of layers of dirt and grime that build up when something has not been cleaned in months, maybe even years.

I strolled back into the house, where the two ladies were finishing up their conversation, and we soon bade Mary farewell, Maggie promising that we would return. We creaked our way across the porch, wrestled the side gate open by lifting it up on its sunken supports, and made our way out to the parked car.

No sooner were we out of earshot than plans were delivered with the rhythm of machine gun fire. "We have to bring Mary food, did you see the state of the kitchen, the stink. I've got to get her to understand that those dogs can poop outside. Let's go and get some food and come back; she can't go on living like this."

I started the car and pulled away from the dusty sidewalk as options ranging from calling social services to contacting the church rattled around inside the vehicle. It was evident that something needed to be done, and food was the immediate concern. I now realized why Maggie had been so adamant that I accompany her on this reconnaissance mission. She'd known the squalor in advance. And, based on the reports, she understood that it would take more than one person, perhaps even a team, to provide any kind of improvement to the old gal's environment.

We went home and emptied our cabinets of canned and dry food along with some milk, bread, and dog food and headed back to Mary's. It was now after 10 p.m. We brought the food in and dropped it on a countertop in the kitchen, and it was immediately refused. As a result of her upbringing, Mary never felt deserving of any form of charity. And she didn't know how to deal with simple acts of generosity other than to decline them.

I stood back and waited, fully aware that Mary had no idea what she was up against. And sure enough, it was only a matter of seconds before her plaintive refusals were drowned out in a barrage of counter-arguments from Maggie, delivered with the assurance of an experienced defense attorney. The cans and packages were then stacked on empty cupboard shelves. And, after a brief stay, we again wrestled our way out of the front yard and drove home, busily planning a weekend visit where we would return with cleaning equipment, more food, and some cash, which would be tucked inside a half-empty cereal box.

That Saturday, we arrived on Mary's porch dressed in work clothes and tooled up with bleach, scouring powder, rags, and disinfectant, ready to attack the layers of grunge that lay in wait beyond the screen door. Mary again resisted our help, but once again, she fell victim to the bulldozer of goodwill who deftly sidestepped her protests as we made our way into the house and began our projects.

After four hours of work, the odor of dog urine was overpowered by the thick smell of disinfectant. The kitchen was clean and orderly, and the bathroom was spotless. The only ill effects of all this work were a couple of minor dog bites inflicted by Mary's collie mix, who, we later learned, had been abused by a previous owner. In all the excitement, Mary had forgotten to warn us, and it had taken a couple of timely nips before we established our respective comfort zones. Mary was thankful for the deep clean, but I could see that she harbored some resentment at this invasion of her personal space. There was no question, however, that the house was now a more sanitary environment in which to live, and we left that day with promises to return.

The following weekend, I went to Mary's alone because Maggie had a commitment. There was almost always a cause or meeting that consumed most of her waking hours.

After fixing a leak under the sink, I asked Mary if she had enough food. As I opened one of the kitchen cabinets where we had stocked the cans and boxes from our earlier visit, I saw that there was only a can of chili and a packet of spaghetti on the shelves. "Have you eaten all that food?" I asked, realizing that a single person of such small stature couldn't possibly have got through what amounted to two weeks of groceries in only a matter of days. "Not all of it, she answered demurely. "I gave some of it to friends who need it. They have children, and I just couldn't let them go hungry." I stopped for a moment. Here was this destitute woman giving much of her newfound bounty to others despite her own desperate need for adequate nutrition. I didn't say anything but realized that Maggie and I were probably not going to become the food bank for an unknown network of needy folks. And if we were to keep Mary fed, we would need to change our strategy and bring around cooked meals. That way, it would be more difficult for her to give the food away.

Over the ensuing weeks, we developed a routine of cooking enough of an evening meal that it would feed three people. And on Monday, Wednesday, and Saturday we would take a hot dinner over to Mary, collecting the containers from the previous deliveries while we were there. This new system seemed to work splendidly. Maggie was dropping by from time to time to check on her health while I continued to fix broken or worn items on the weekends. And it wasn't long before we could see that Mary was growing stronger. Emerging was a person frail and retiring on the outside, but with a stubborn streak that had begun to reveal itself when it suited her or, as we would later learn, when it came to an important issue regarding the management of her house. There was no doubt, however, as to her weakness when it came to financial matters. This aspect of her behavior had surfaced on our initial visit while discussing the pile of charitable solicitation letters that lay stacked up on her bedside table. Mary had little willpower to decline requests for money when it came to animals subjected to any kind of suffering. Needless to say, regular donations to various causes continued to deplete her meager income. Realizing the full extent of her vulnerability, we continued to maintain a routine of weekly visits in order to monitor both her health and her financial stability.

As if keeping an eye on Mary, managing a small animal kingdom, and governing a small city weren't enough to fill an eighty-hour week, I arrived home one day to another set of requests. Only this time, they involved the other side of the world.

Maggie had discovered an organization that provided summer stays in the U.S. for children who had been exposed to the aftereffects of the Chernobyl nuclear power plant meltdown in Ukraine. Children, that is, who were strong enough to travel. The program brought kids over to the U.S., where they stayed with host families. They would then undergo a series of social, medical, and recreational events designed to fortify their health against the long-term effects of the radiation-tainted environment they lived in. The program included visits to doctors and dentists where they underwent physicals and received primary medical care, as well as a collection of vitamin supplements. These visits, coupled with good food and fresh water, might give their young immune systems a boost as they fought to resist the cancers and heart disease that lay in wait for many of them.

I was familiar with the events of April 26, 1986, when, during a routine test, reactor number 4 at the Chernobyl nuclear power plant had exploded, releasing a radioactive debris cloud containing Cesium-137 over Northern Ukraine, Belarus, and Russia. The fallout was 400 times greater than the atom bomb used at Hiroshima, and one million people were directly affected. Since the disaster, congenital heart defects and cancer had increased 250 percent, and the infant mortality rate in Belarus alone grew to 300 percent higher than the rest of Europe's. The area, to this day, is still polluted with Cesium-137, Strontium-90, and Plutonium-239, resulting in alarming congenital disabilities and heart conditions so common that the local medical community calls the ailment Chernobyl heart.

This time, I didn't make my usual arguments against taking in sick and injured beings. And in October of 2002, we welcomed a pale and matchstick-thin thirteen-year-old Ukrainian called Alena Dzmetrienka into our home. Her story was probably not unique within the group. One of the organizers told us that her home life was austere. Her mother had died when she was young, and her father was a truck driver, when he could find work. He was also an alcoholic who rarely had enough food in the house for both of them. For the most part, it was her grandmother who shouldered the parenting responsibilities.

Alena didn't speak a lick of English, and neither of us spoke Russian. But it didn't matter, as we quickly settled into a summer of pointing, drawing, and gesturing to communicate. Pool parties, dental fillings, and medical evaluations took up the first two weeks, and it was only a matter of days before we noticed a change starting to come over the youngster. Exposed to the California sun and receiving the type of nutrition that she had never experienced in her devastated homeland, she began to flourish. More color came to her cheeks. She stood erect rather than hunched over, and, while she gained in confidence due to a feeling of well-being, her personality started to reveal itself. Maggie would pull out her jewelry box of an afternoon, and the two of them would spend hours inspecting every piece, with Alena skipping off to the bathroom to try on her favorites. She would stare into the mirror to see how the sparkling silver or marbled turquoise looked around her neck or draped around her slender wrists, returning to the front room to model her accessories in front of an appreciative audience.

By the time the six-week stay was complete, Alena looked just like any other California kid. Sneakers on and wearing a T-shirt advertising the Hello Kitty clothing brand, she looked healthy and tanned as she boarded the bus to LA with the other children. Stocked up with vitamins, enough toothbrushes to last until she was thirty, and sporting a pink backpack, she made her way down the bus to a window seat where we could see her. Many members of the host families, along with their children, were in floods of tears as they shared copious hugs and commitments flew about repeating the visit next year. Alena waved to us from the window as the bus pulled out of the parking lot and left for the airport, where she would board a flight back to an uncertain future. Standing next to a teary-eyed Maggie, I pictured the desolation and deprivation that awaited the children upon their return to a polluted homeland. How different our two worlds must have seemed to them.

During her stay, we had contemplated adopting her, even broaching the subject with one of the organizers. She told us that the Russian authorities frowned on any action that would result in a child not returning to Ukraine. And that if such an event occurred, it would inevitably jeopardize the future of the program. She then went on to tell us about Alena's position in Ukrainian society, where it was not unusual for a girl like her to have to marry an older man to gain any financial security for her adult life. I shuddered at the prospect. That afternoon we returned to our home with a commitment that we would host Alena again the following year.

CHAPTER 18

No Good Deed Goes Unpunished

If there's a bustle in your hedgerow,
don't be alarmed now...
Led Zeppelin – "Stairway to Heaven"

After Alena had departed, and a few months after meeting Mary for the first time, an opportunity arose to visit Encinitas's sister city, Amakusa, in Kumamoto prefecture, Japan. It was an annual event when either the Japanese made the trip to Encinitas or vice versa, and this year a contingent from Encinitas would be heading east. Meetings between city officials had resulted in a full itinerary of site visits and social events with every minute detail attended to by the Japanese hosts.

It was now 2004, and at this point in the council's cycle, Maggie had assumed the rotating position of Mayor. She reached out to her counterpart in Amakusa with a proposal that Encinitas enter a recreational team in their annual triathlon, since the competition happened to coincide with the visit. The legend was that Amakusa held brag-ging rights for establishing the distances for each leg of the Olympic triathlon. Maggie's counterpart in Amakusa, Mayor Yasuda, thought this would be a great idea. So it was agreed that a local team would join the competition. After some discussions, the U.S. competitors consisted of Councilman Jerome Stocks, who would enter the swim leg of the race. He would hand off to Maggie for the bicycle segment, and she would then tag Mayor Yasuda for the final run to the finish line. There was also a space for a recreational triathlete from the City to be included. I had the good fortune to be invited as the token entrant who, along with the other contestants, would compete over the entire course.

The visit turned out to be an illuminating cultural experience with trips to local shrines, temples, and city facilities. Our hosts were hospitable to a fault, providing chaperones and transportation while joining us at site visits and social events. A dark cloud, however, over-shadowed the tour, growing from the political divisions that existed on home turf. This pervasive animosity had come along for the ride. And it wasn't long before councilperson Christie Guerin began criticizing Maggie's handling of her role as Mayor, quietly supported by council member Stocks, who was keeping a calculating eye on the proceedings.

Guerin's criticism sunk to an all-time low when the Mayor's attire and the content of her speeches fell between her crosshairs. And it wasn't long before other members of the party became aware of the bad blood that the politicians couldn't leave behind. Later that week, the triathlon would provide all the fuel that was needed to inflame this criticism. And it would transcend borders, making its way back to the U.S. and into the regional newspapers.

The evening before the triathlon, participants, locals and visitors alike, gathered in the town center for a briefing on the logistics of the event. Earlier in the day, our hosts had driven Maggie and me along the bicycle course so we could familiarize ourselves with the route and its topography. We had passed by Japanese architecture in small seaside villages, scaled hills with sweeping views of the ocean, and cruised alongside bright-green rice paddies as we took in each grade, curve, and straightaway. Since we didn't ship our own bikes to Japan, generous local athletes loaned them to us. And during the afternoon, we had the bikes adjusted to suit our physical frames.

Later that evening, we had dinner with the Mayor and his staff, and the festivities progressed far into the night. The next day we assembled on the beach below our hotel, which was becoming crowded with athletes, support staff, and onlookers. It was a hot and particularly humid day typical for the area, but not the perfect conditions for a triathlon. However, the scenery was unique and dramatic. And it wouldn't be long before the course would take us through the emerald green fields and out along the ocean road that we had traveled the previous day.

The clock wound down, and the starting pistol echoed across the beach. Jerome took to the water and swam a respectable leg, sprinting up the beach to hand off to Maggie for the bike segment. Maggie took off with Parks and Recreation Director Chris Hazeltine from the city of Encinitas cycling alongside as chaperone, just in case any unforeseen incident occurred that might interrupt her progress.

I'd completed the swim and was on the return leg of the bike segment when I spotted Maggie and Chris huddled near a hedge by the side of the road. They were surrounded by a few of the local townspeople who had assembled earlier to cheer the competitors along. I slowed down, wondering if there had been an accident. When I came level with the group, I heard Maggie shout, "Ian. Come and look at this!" I could see that she wasn't in any kind of physical distress, so I replied that I happened to be in the middle of a race and couldn't stop just at that moment. As I continued to pedal down the road, I wondered what could have caused her to interrupt her cycling. And why a crowd of local people seemed to be involved.

Back at the beach, I parked the bike in the staging area and started a sultry slog on foot through the streets of Amakusa, finally making my way into the local sports stadium and toward the relief of the finish line. By the time I got there, the elite athletes had all finished and the amateurs were filtering in, jogging around a stadium track that comprised the last 400 meters of the race. Crossing the line, I walked over and got water and a hose down from one of the aid stations as relief from the conditions.

Looking around, I spotted members of the Encinitas contingent milling around the center of the track, but there was no sign of Maggie. I walked up to the group and asked if anyone had seen her and was informed that she'd gone to the athletes' luncheon with one of the event's attendants. No surprise there. However, a member of the group told me that she'd pulled up during the race when she'd heard a kitten meowing from a hedge along the route. She had insisted on stopping and, along with the parks and rec director, had gone to investigate. What they had found was a starving kitten, covered in fleas and trapped in the brambles. With help from the local townsfolk, they had freed the kitten, given it food and water, and brought it back to town. Now Maggie was trying to figure out if she could find someone who would give it a home.

This course of events was no surprise to me. After all, we had a house full of rescued animals and would frequently stop for injured critters struck by cars, or for dogs that were wandering in the street with no collar on. The circumstances surrounding this incident, however, were a little more complicated. Maggie was in a race, and when she completed her bike leg, she was supposed to hand off to Mayor Yasuda. He would then complete the event by running the final distance. What had happened as a result of Maggie's dropping out was currently a mystery. How this departure from protocol was going to be viewed by our Japanese hosts was yet to be seen.

I stayed with the group and watched as the last of the competitors struggled across the finish line. By now, the sun was at its zenith and, coupled with the humidity, the heat felt strong enough to melt the composite running track that circled the infield of the stadium. The red faces worn by the last of the athletes revealed competitors who had forced tired limbs and flagging psyches through the final few miles so they would at least be able to claim a personal victory after completing the 31.93-mile distance.

The last item on the event agenda was to recognize the winners. The crowd gathered around the podium, clapping with gusto, as the Mayor draped medallions around the necks of the top three finishers in each age and gender category.

The awards ceremony now complete, the group made its way downtown to a community building where a reception and lunch were in full swing. It was there that I finally caught sight of Maggie, still cradling the kitten, which was looking up at her with sleepy eyes as it pumped its claws into the soft flesh of her rescuer's forearm.

"What happened?" I asked.

"We were cycling, and I heard this kitten meowing. It was stuck in brambles in the hedge, so I asked Chris to stop so I could take a closer look. It's so small and emaciated. And when we got it down, it had a ribbon tied around its neck, which was so tight, it was going to strangle it. I got it out of the brambles, and we took it into one of the stores there. The owners were great! They brought out a box and some water, and they had some cat food, so I had someone radio ahead to tell them what was going on so the Mayor wouldn't be kept waiting. I think I've found a home for her." She beamed. "One of our chaperones has talked to someone who knows a lady who lives in Fukuoka who might take her. She's calling her now."

"Great, so the Mayor just took off when he realized you were going to be delayed?"

"Yes. He didn't want to be late for the awards ceremony, so he took off. I spoke with him just now, and he said it wasn't a big deal and not to worry about it." I breathed a sigh of relief, realizing that her stopping had not interrupted the surgical planning that had gone into a flawlessly executed event.

As we were talking, a woman approached Maggie. After a short conversation, they headed off toward the other side of the hall. I grabbed lunch and sat down with some of the organizers of the program from the Encinitas contingent. After listening to their conversations, I began to realize that the other members of the City Council viewed this incident with the kitten in a starkly different light than Mayor Yasuda. In their eyes, the rescue was not a spontaneous act of compassion, but behavior that belied such a monumental error of judgment that the whole affair had escalated and was now an international incident. It had become an episode that threatened to derail the entire sister city program and ruin a relationship that countless people had worked hard for years to build. They considered it a slap in the face to the Mayor of Amakusa and an embarrassment to the City of Encinitas and Americans in general.

While their reactions seemed to be excessive, I could see both sides of the argument. Yes, it probably wasn't the best protocol to stop during the race. But if you knew Maggie, then you also knew that she would never turn her back on an injured or distressed animal, no matter the circumstance. The competition had continued. And it wasn't as if anyone expected our dual city team of social athletes to win the race. I began to wonder if our hosts were as dismayed as the rhetoric was making them out to be. I hadn't heard any feedback from them firsthand as to their take on the severity of this rapidly developing issue, not to mention the whole international incident thing. So I waited to see how the Japanese, and their culture, would view this apparent breach of protocol.

As lunch continued, I could see Maggie deep in a conversation that was alternating between a chaperone, who was acting as translator, and a young Japanese woman. Finally, Maggie came over without the kitten. "Guess what, I think I've found a home for her," she said, a broad smile spreading across her face. "That was the woman's daughter. She's on the triathlon organizing committee, her mom is sixty, and she just completed the race. She thinks she'll take the cat. She's got it, and she's calling her, but her mom's not home at the moment. I'm so glad; I didn't know what to do. Here I am in a foreign country, and I don't even speak the language. How am I going to take care of this kitten? I was panicked."

Phew, I thought to myself, fully aware that if she couldn't get the cat adopted in Amakusa, that the next step would be finding out how she could get it back to the U.S. (an option that Maggie later confirmed had crossed her mind.)

That night we were hosted at a local watering hole, and the extent of the outrage felt by the other side of the Encinitas political spectrum was on full display. Guerin was outraged and, at one point, dramatically broke into tears, ashamed and spitting angry both at the same time. Stocks was more reserved. But based on the serious faces of the two during their more private conversations, this incident had become the topic of some intense discussion throughout the evening.

When it came to our hosts, there was little mention of the kitten. Whether this was the stoic graciousness of a culture disciplined to respect foreign visitors, I couldn't determine. However, during the evening, they focused on the race, our times for each leg, and the history of triathlon in Amakusa. The kitten incident, when mentioned at all, was gently brushed aside as just something that happened but had not marred the day or disrupted the Mayor's schedule.

Guerin's actions, conversely, went from being personally angry to sharing her outrage with our hosts while apologizing profusely for Maggie's behavior on multiple occasions. When not talking with the Japanese, she spent the rest of the evening bending the ears of members of our contingent, stating how outraged she was, what an atrocious error of judgment this had been, and how it endangered our sister city relationship. I didn't get any hint of that type of reaction while talking with our hosts, and we enjoyed a pleasant evening of drinks and tales from the day.

The next morning, we were scheduled to go sightseeing in Nagasaki. The trip was to include a visit to the site of the World War II nuclear bomb blast, along with the various memorials and museums that had been erected following the tragedy. The bus ride there set the tone for the rest of the trip. Guerin spent much of her time once again bending ears and making loud remarks about how poorly Maggie had behaved and how outraged our hosts had been. And this undercurrent of criticism was evident during the remaining events on the calendar, creating an atmosphere of contempt until, finally, we bade our hosts farewell and boarded the first of our flights back to the American mainland.

At home, the press had already picked up the story, and it was a field day for the outlets. Splashed all over city- and countywide newspapers were front pages proclaiming, "Encinitas drops out of Japan triathlon," "What happened in Japan?" or "Mayor's detour in Japan a cat-astrophe." The question created by this general awareness amongst the media was, how could all of these publications have picked up on the story before we had even set foot on American soil? It wasn't long before a journalist for the *San Diego Union-Tribune*, a long-time critic of Maggie's, disclosed in print that it had been Jerome Stocks who had supplied him with all the details—details embellished by a remarkably skewed assessment of the impact of the incident and the reaction of our hosts. While quietly watching what was unfolding in Japan, Stocks had been determining how he could use the information to undermine Maggie. And how best to present the story for maximum effect, especially since later that year, both of them were up for re-election.

The articles featured Maggie as an irresponsible, insensitive, and incompetent buffoon. Not only that, but they portrayed her as a sorely inadequate representative of the city of Encinitas, of San Diego, and of America in general. Of course, the articles were not unexpected. But the extent of the coverage and the pillorying of the perpetrator went beyond what had occurred, and it didn't accurately portray how our Japanese hosts had reacted. One of Guerin's quotes described the incident as "mortifying," claiming that Maggie's reaction after the event "had complete disregard for our feelings." Logan Jenkins, an acerbic columnist for the *San Diego Union,* opened his first piece on the topic with the line: "The following article is not a joke." He continued, "It is not an outlandish situation for an Encinitas-based comedy troupe called Maggie Python and the Humane Circus. No, what you're about to peruse is a straightforward discussion of a diplomatic gaffe so goofy that it may set a world record for clueless American insensitivity." He continued in bold upper case font, "IN THE MIDDLE OF A TRIATHLON FOR WHICH HER TEAMMATES HAD TRAINED LIKE SPARTANS THE MAYOR STOPPED TO COMFORT A HOMELESS KITTY, her act of charity conveys a condescending message: Japan is a Third World nation that does not care properly for its cats." His final slap to close out the column read, "As for Houlihan, if she's to finish in the top three in an upcoming competition (the November council race), she'll have to pedal like crazy against a wind of incredulous laughter."

Back home, our house sank beneath a dark cloud. I could tell that the onslaught of bad press was taking its toll, even upon someone strong enough to have negotiated a difficult childhood, an abusive first marriage, and a struggle to get by—all the while protecting a son and her omnipresent entourage of animals. The difference between her earlier challenges and this one, however, was that the previous tests of her resilience were private. This one was available to anybody who bothered to pick up a newspaper or explore the local headlines online. Maggie started staying up much later than usual and would return from City business with tales of who had told who about her disgraceful behavior. It was a depressing time, and the follow-up articles continued to rub yet more salt into an open wound.

After a couple of weeks of this treatment, and at a point where it didn't seem as if it could get any worse, an unexpected wind started to blow through the community. Letter after letter submitted by private citizens began to appear in the media criticizing the negative reporting surrounding the incident, while proceeding to recognize the compassionate nature of her act. Regular Joes began writing in saying things like they were "proud of their mayor" and that "Small acts of kindness should be a normal part of one's life and not something we have to apologize for." A weekly editorial column that awarded "Roses and Raspberries" backpedaled from its former and more critical stance and delivered a rose to Mayor Houlihan. It said that Masao Nakayama, Chairman of the international committee of the Japan Triathlon Union, the organizers of the event, had written to them stating, "People around were much moved by her tenderness to the tiny animal," and that a photograph of the kitten in its new home was on its way to the city of Encinitas.

A cartoon appeared in the local newspaper depicting an older couple in their front room surrounded by dozens of cats. On the wall above the fireplace hung a poster of the D.C. Comics character Catwoman. They were looking at a newspaper headline criticizing the Encinitas Mayor, and the punch line, delivered by the husband, read, "She's got my vote." Even Logan Jenkins, who had gone to great lengths to demean Maggie, and not for the first time, was shamed into publishing a letter from Alexis Coxon, a reader who resided outside the state. It read, "As a fellow journalist, I have to say that your July column deriding Maggie Houlihan is the most insensitive piece of writing I have ever read. I don't live in Encinitas, or even in California, but I am extremely proud of Ms. Houlihan's actions. Her compassion is something to be applauded, not something to be condemned as causing an international incident. Do you really think the Japanese were that insulted? Would YOU be insulted if a Japanese person cared for a homeless kitten they found on an American street? Because I certainly wouldn't be. I would think that that person was a kind-hearted individual and not worry so much about how a single feral kitten made my country look. Frankly, I am shocked at how many people seem to be making such a huge deal over this. I don't know what sort of values you Californians have, but here in the Midwest, we would be proud of our Mayor for demonstrating such regard for God's creatures."

Another letter read, "That this incident has been negatively inflated to attack her character indicates how far some Americans have drifted from genuine values. This country was founded on Judeo-Christian values (not religion but values), and these stipulate that an enhancement, not a curtailment, of charity is a good thing. Remember that a bicycle race is fleeting, whereas a being's life (even a kitten's life) is something that persists, in suffering or in health."

One of the last articles to be written before the press, and Jerome Stocks, moved on, gave an update on the status of the kitten and the family who had adopted it. It informed the readers that the cat had been named Amakusa by its new family, the Yoshimuras from Fukuoka City. The article quoted Mrs. Yoshimura as saying that she and her daughter were "so much moved by Encinitas city Mayor's kindest attitude to tiny animals and them as well."

While there were still those who clung to their choice of vilifying the Mayor's actions as disrespectful and insensitive, it had become overwhelmingly evident that a host of people from inside and outside the country chose to view her actions through a more compassionate lens.

CHAPTER 19

Another Clown

Work it harder, make it better, do it faster…
That that don't kill me will only make me stronger
Kanye West – "Stronger"

Councilperson Houlihan had been in office for almost four years and had held the position of Mayor for one of those years. It was now 2004, and another election season was upon the city. This time, her seat was up for grabs. The landowners and developers from inside and outside the region had taken notice of the controlled growth approach that she championed through her Community Character Development Plan. And, reinforced by the actions of local operatives, these special interests were determined to remove her and install a replacement who would align with their vision for the city. Encinitas had continued to attract development, with many of the flower growers, recognizing that their industry was in decline, now eager to sell their land. And there was no shortage of builders and speculators keen to snap up acreage for residential development, with many applying for density increases and variances to the City's general plan. The very idea of not being able to build multi-story McMansions irritated the building community. In this election, they were coordinated and would come out in force, turning a small town ballot into a blood bath of misinformation, character assassination, and lies, all of which was handsomely funded by the deep pockets of real estate interests, business owners, and consultants. These benefactors would benefit from City leaders who had a history of allowing buildings with higher density, height, and mass than the general plan allowed.

As election season opened, the attacks came thick and fast, typically presenting a deft manipulation of the facts. An early example appeared in the mailboxes of voters addressed to "Dear unsuspecting homeowner." It came from a wealthy real estate broker named Douglas Harwood and his wife, Orva, who resided not in Encinitas but in one of the most affluent and private rural communities in the nation, Rancho Santa Fe, California, which was home to the likes of business elites, successful entertainers, and professional athletes. It was a community sheltered by a protective covenant that stringently dictated the style of any development,

The full-color letter, printed on glossy stock and containing pictures of before and after home remodels, warned recipients that the equity in their real estate was under threat and their right to improve their homes was going to be taken away by the City Council. The final comment named Maggie and her former campaign manager Bruce Ehlers, who was also running for one of the open seats, as the culprits who were about to impose these restrictions. It also claimed that voters should vote for the building industry's candidates Stocks, Bond and, new candidate Alice Jacobsen.

A second letter from the same duo appeared a few weeks later. It falsely inferred that if Houlihan and Ehlers were elected, the City would pass regulations that would restrict a homeowner's ability to improve their property—resulting in a loss of equity equal to as much as $270,000. An elaborate calculation in the body of the letter arrogantly assumed that everyone aspired to own a McMansion, with their analysis highlighting a residence with a substantial volume of square footage in an attempt to validate their exaggerated claim.

As the misinformation pipeline grew, Mike Andreen, the bearded and corpulent member of the board of the Encinitas Chamber of Commerce, was once again dispatched to join the election fray. Andreen, an adversary of anyone who promoted controlled growth, which was contrary to the vision of his handlers, elevated his game. He'd played a small role in unseating a past councilperson in an earlier election by spreading misinformation using his vitriolic email newsletter the *Wire Fire*. In these emails, he typically demeaned his chosen adversary by starting out giving them and their followers nicknames. Former Mayor Sheila Cameron became the head of the anti–property rights "Cameronistas." Maggie Houlihan became "Moolihan," and so on. He typically laced his inflammatory emails with colorful attacks and the occasional profanity in order to add impact to his arguments. Andreen also had at his disposal his developer-funded vanity tabloid the *Surf City Times*, a publication that he employed to bolster his tireless support of the latest iteration of the pro-development majority bloc on the council.

Andreen often appeared at restaurants, bars, and City events with councilperson Stocks and didn't hide his allegiance, regularly referring to Stocks in the *Surf City Times* as his "homie." He went on to make this reference numerous times during the election season. All Stocks had to do was show up at a pancake breakfast, and the *Surf City*

Times would herald the sighting with flattering pictures and gushing observations of his culinary expertise.

When it came to "Moolihan," it was a different matter. There was little chance of Andreen writing anything positive about her activities. If there was a reference at all, it typically came as a warning to voters summed up in the paper's recommendations on which candidates to vote for in the upcoming election. These might say that no additions would be allowed to resident's houses or that the council would be adopting a "Big Brother" approach to any real estate improvements. Manufactured ethical violations regarding loans made to her campaign also appeared along with promises that city parks would shut down under her watch.

One issue he chose to focus on was Houlihan's initiative to outlaw helium balloons, the type that can be purchased from any party store. These are typically released at festive events where they can float off and disrupt city power lines. Others end up on the beaches, eventually drifting out into the ocean where their shiny exteriors and brightly colored streamers disintegrate over time, only to be mistaken as food by unsuspecting fish destined to choke on the plastic that strangles their digestive systems or disrupts their ability to reproduce. Andreen's message to the public was that this fight was an example of pettiness pushed forward by a candidate who was out of step with the majority of her constituents.

Andreen also took his attacks on the road to candidate forums, where the contenders would sit side by side at a long table and field questions from an audience of residents. It was at these forums that one particular candidate provided him with an irresistible target.

Acting under cover of his *Surf City Times* press credential, Andreen would crouch just in front of the candidates' table, directly in front of

Maggie, and proceed to shoot picture after picture of the candidate, accenting each of her responses to the audience's questions with the constant click, click, click of the camera's shutter. It was an activity designed to put Maggie off her game. None of the other contenders received this kind of attention, and strangely enough, the only evidence of these "shoots" to show up in his tabloid were photos of Homie and the other candidates.

While this activity was taking place, a sticker campaign sprung up around the city. Mylar labels appeared on cars and were illegally posted on road signs and utility boxes, announcing that residents should "Save Encinitas, Vote No on Houlihan." Going out to collect the mail one day, I came across one of these stickers strategically planted on our mailbox. It was evident that even personal residential space was fair game in this pool of dirty dealings.

In concert with Andreen's activities, David Meyer was about to reveal his partnership in the orchestrated effort to unseat their target. And he came out with a series of glossy mailers warning voters to vote "No on Houlihan," a serendipitous co-branding of the anti-Houlihan campaign.

It was Maggie, however, who would have the last laugh. After the election season was over, when Andreen had finished his work as an enforcer, he would become the target of an unrelated investigation into the finances of the Downtown Main Street Association.

David Meyer, for his part, continued his vendetta against Maggie, and a stream of hit pieces started to appear in the mailboxes of city residents: "Newspapers Blast Maggie Houlihan," "Encinitas Can Do Better than [Maggie Houlihan]," "Information Maggie Houlihan Doesn't Want You to Know," "Maggie Houlihan's Hidden Agenda," and so on. Still harboring animosity from his failed real estate bid with the wastewater authority, he decided that the mail alone would not achieve the result he desired. He needed something that would bring more attention to his target. Something that would embarrass her and make her appear incompetent. Something that would generate publicity, resonate with the voters, and be a vehicle that he could use again and again to keep his attacks relevant until Election Day.

His answer came in the creation of a clown whose activities he could direct. He soon found a local dancer who would don costume and makeup for a fee. Meyer liked what he saw. The dancer appeared clad in a bright-red wig, a black-and-white box-pleated skirt, hooped socks, and a red nose along with a black mask over her eyes to disguise her identity. Meyer unleashed the clown on the community, paying her to show up at civic events where the candidates would be working the crowds seeking votes. Prancing, pirouetting, and bowing amongst the surprised onlookers, the clown would mock Maggie by holding up signs that read "It's Not About the CAT" on one side and on the other side, "It's About Poor Judgment." Meyer had picked up on the kitten incident in Japan and proceeded to weaponize it in the hope of persuading voters that councilperson Houlihan was irresponsible and unfit for public office.

Maggie would dread showing up at gatherings such as the local sundowner meetings where businesspeople networked. She would spy the clown lying in wait, warming up the crowd, skirt twirling and head bowing as she danced amongst the attendees—all the while operating behind the protection of free speech rights.

At one of these events, a supporter of candidate Houlihan could contain herself no longer and reached for the clown's wig and nose, lifting them deftly from the startled dancer's head and, with a flourish, tossing them unceremoniously into a nearby fountain. So much for free speech rights. The clown, in the true spirit of the profession, rescued the dripping articles from the water and, after a quick shake, returned them to their rightful locations before twirling away into the crowd.

The Downtown Main Street Association, fearing that their annual dinner might become the center of an election-season spectacle, asked Meyer not to bring his clown. Despite their solicitations, he dispatched her to the venue. The press picked up on this new sideshow, and pictures and articles started to show up in the media. Meyer's clown was proving to be a very worthwhile investment; the plan was working. At one event at the community center complex Meyer showed up and was seen off to one side as his clown executed her performance. Beside Meyer, and reveling in the spectacle, stood Mike Andreen.

As election day neared, the attacks continued. Andreen used his vanity press to proclaim that Maggie would turn the city into a vast homeowner's association, with all of its suffocating rules and restrictions. Meyer meanwhile continued to dispatch his jester to selected community events.

One day a greeting card arrived in our mailbox, and Maggie opened it. Inside, the card read, "Mayor of Encinitas, when it gets closer to election time, you need to be euthanized." It went on to reference her "jackass" incident in Japan when she came to the aid of the emaciated kitten. The envelope contained no return address. Maggie contacted the police, who seemed wholly uninterested in the whole thing. This lack of concern by the police would become a pattern of behavior under the leadership of their Captain, a man by the name of Fowler.

Shortly after the card incident, a large four-feet-by-six-feet sheet of packing box appeared nailed eight feet above the ground on a telephone pole at the end of our street, where it was visible to the traffic passing below. The sign was crudely painted in multiple colors and read, "Save a Cat! Go to Iraq, and don't come back!" Again, the inference was to have Maggie eliminated one way or another.

I climbed the post and removed the sign, flipping it over for clues as to its origin. On the reverse side, there was a commercial logo referencing a horticultural company that specialized in plant-rooting products. Maggie called the 800 number, and they confirmed that they were a vendor who supplied products to the Ecke Ranch.

Maggie contacted Paul Ecke III, the current CEO of the business, and the titular head of the Ecke family, although he seemed to be firmly under the control of his mother, sister, and brother-in-law. She asked him about the box and also about the activities of David Meyer. Paul was genuinely taken aback by the sign and didn't seem to know anything about it. And without directly condemning Meyer, it was apparent that his brother-in-law's activities with the clown were also an embarrassment to him. He apologized for the harlequin's presence in the community and Maggie, sensing an opportunity, pushed further. She asked him to reign in his brother-in-law. Nothing came of the request, however, and Meyer continued with his program of denigration.

While this was going on, the source of the information on the kitten incident, and the object of Mike Andreen's adulation, delivered a hypocritical statement of marvelous proportion. Stocks was quoted in the press as saying there would be "no negative comments from my campaign." It was a campaign supported by the Eckes, Andreen, Meyer, the Harwoods, and others, who apparently didn't share in this newfound restraint. The puppet master was disingenuously attempting to place himself above the destructive elements that he'd provided with the very ammunition they needed for their ongoing attacks.

A new entrant into the proceedings, a local columnist called J. Stryker Meyer, no relation to David C., had also picked up on Stocks's information about the cat incident. He proceeded to refresh the voter's memory, just in time for the election, by writing in a regional newspaper, "Here [is an] easy prediction. On November 2, voters will reject Encinitas Mayor Maggie Houlihan. Houlihan lacks the common sense to apologize for her recent cat debacle in Japan, and apparently cares more about catering to animal lovers than being a diplomat."

The battle for the vacant council positions had now reached its apex. Volunteers from Houlihan's low-budget campaign were knocking on doors and standing outside grocery stores behind tables filled with literature, busily handing out leaflets to anyone who passed by. Side by side with the volunteers, Maggie addressed questions from voters who were curious enough to engage the councilor and find out more about a person who was proving to be a lightning rod in their community.

On the opposition front, both paper and digital disinformation continued to spew forth to a city now jaded by the mudslinging and the hit pieces that clogged their mailboxes. The estimate for Meyer and Harwood's activities alone was over $80,000 spent on mailers, robocalls, and other election weaponry.

The day for vote-casting rolled around, and the polling stations opened, accompanied by a final salvo of accusations that campaign signs had been removed or damaged by the other side. Now it was time for the candidates, handlers, marketers, clowns, and journalists to take a back seat to the voters who turned out to determine the makeup of their City Council for the next two years.

That night, a spacious Italian restaurant became election central for Maggie's campaign. Pino, the owner, had become a firm friend and was happy to hook up a TV behind the bar to tune in to the election results.

The campaign team, supporters, and friends huddled nervously under the bright lights of the bar sipping an occasional cocktail or supporting saucers that held steaming cups of coffee. All the while, they hoped that in the voters' minds, their candidate's platform would beat out the hate and manipulation that the other side had paid to have sloshed around the town.

Conversations were muted, as some attendees harbored uncertainties about the outcome, afraid that what should be an evening of hope would become a wake for the crushed political vision of their embattled candidate.

A ripple went through the group as three figures strode into the lobby of the restaurant. They displayed all the swagger of a cowboy posse that had just captured a fugitive that they were preparing to drag in to face justice. It was the troika of David Meyer, Douglas Harwood, and Michael Andreen. The results of their earlier phone surveys must have suggested that their attacks had worked and that they were now on track for the outcome they had paid so handsomely to secure. Smelling blood in the water, they had tracked down where Maggie's campaign team was assembling. And they had come to revel in the results of their work, eager to celebrate over the ragtag band of insurgents who had dared to champion a vision for the city that contradicted their own.

The results ticker came up on the TV and showed zero for all the Encinitas candidates; it was approaching 9 p.m. All the polling stations had closed, and the early count would soon be showing up. The three interlopers settled into a comfortable booth where they could maintain a clear line of sight to the campaign team. They ordered drinks and glanced at menus, laughing from time to time, presumably at the team's expense.

Just before 9:30, the TV screen went through its changes, and the initial national and state results posted. After an agonizing wait, regional counts started to appear. Finally, the Encinitas numbers came up for the first time. Houlihan in first place, Bond second, Stocks third. The cheers rang out as the threat of a thrashing, always a possibility, had been lifted. While these were early numbers, which could easily change, they were typically a good indicator of how the race would end.

The trio at the rear of the restaurant began to fidget in their upholstered seats as a more serious conversation filled the booth, replacing the mocking laughter that had once permeated the air. A fresh set of updates cascaded down the screen, national first, then state, and once again local. Maggie was pulling further ahead! Not only was she beating Bond this time around, but Stocks was trailing a distant third. And the developer's choice, Alice Jacobsen, was so severely in arrears it was apparent that a chunk of special interest funds had been wagered on the wrong horse.

After a couple more screen changes confirmed Maggie's commanding position at the head of the pack, Meyer, Harwood, and Andreen got up to leave. Chastened by a defeat that was rapidly turning into a rout, they rose to exit the restaurant but not before facing a gauntlet of the very people they had come to mock. All eyes at the bar focused on the three who had now shed the swagger they exuded when they entered the lobby. And a parting barb from the candidate herself hung in the air as the three made their way through the door: "That was a waste of $80,000!"

The party continued into the night as the returns trickled in. The following morning's tally had Houlihan at 13,129 votes with a firm grasp on first place. Second, with 12,701 votes, was James Bond. Maggie had turned the tables and had now beaten 007 by 428 votes, or 6 percent of the total. Stocks trailed with 11,770. The voters had evaluated the platforms and the characters of the candidates, and they had made their choice.

One last irregularity occurred soon after the election was in the books. During the campaign, a complaint had been lodged with the Fair Political Practices Commission (FPPC) regarding a loan that Maggie had received from her campaign manager. Opponents claimed it was a loan that didn't comply with campaign finance law. The FPPC had taken the complaint and investigated it, returning with a determination that it fell within the guidelines of the law, and Maggie was exonerated. However, financial questions connected with the campaign didn't stop there. A local news reporter had decided to look beneath the covers at the contributions each candidate had received. What he discovered was damning, but not to the Houlihan campaign. The press published its findings under the headline of Jerome Stocks being "caught with a whopper of an illegal contribution from a developer." Barratt America, the developer in question, had put on a fundraiser for Stocks at one of their subdivisions. Part of the event included the company footing the bill for $2,603 in catering services. This payment, under campaign finance law, fell into the category of a contribution, for which the limit was $250, an amount that Barratt had already provided. Coincidentally, the article went on, days before the election, seven employees of Barratt had contributed $1,250 to Stocks's efforts. This activity was on behalf of Barratt, who not only had business in front of the City, but was also suing Encinitas in a case that was currently in front of the state's supreme court.

Shortly after this news hit, Stocks reported that he'd returned the money along with the donations from seven individuals that were over the $250 limit. On top of that, he'd returned illegal contributions to four companies, three of which were real estate businesses, including Barratt America. Stocks's excuse was that he'd acted as his own treasurer and that he was "not a very good bookkeeper." The FPPC took no action.

Maggie, meanwhile, eager to move on with her agenda, threw herself into a fight to have leg-hold animal traps outlawed in the city. Leg-hold trapping is an inherently violent practice that uses traps with spiked teeth designed to clamp down on a limb and hold a wild animal in place, while still alive, until the hunter arrives to dispatch them. As a result, many animals die trying to free themselves or from dehydration, blood loss, or, in certain climates, hypothermia. Many animals become so desperate they resort to chewing through or wringing off their trapped limb to escape, breaking teeth and bones in the process. Animal groups and speakers addressed the City and wrote to their elected officials. Finally, in October, the City introduced a ban against the traps. Despite the rancor of election season, Maggie was back pushing her agenda through City Hall as far as public opinion and her council peers would allow.

Despite the renewed surge of City issues and the demands of my career, we'd never lost contact with Mary Reyes. However, it came as a surprise when one day, we discovered that she'd taken in a couple and their child as tenants. She was introduced to the family by some friends and described them as "nice folk who needed a place to stay." We never actually met them as they always seemed to be holed up in a single room. But nevertheless, we were concerned about her decision. Mary had displayed a propensity to be overly trusting when it came to people. The arrangement, however, was in place, and there was nothing to be done. We didn't visit as often after that, and our contributions of food dwindled as we knew she was receiving more income than before, but also, because we realized that as soon as we dropped off meals, she would be sure to share them with her new tenants.

Later that year, during one of our infrequent visits, Mary surprised us with a decision she was mulling over. It was at the request of her tenants and amounted to their committing to taking care of her until she passed away if she would sign the deed to her house over to them, making the couple the owners of the property.

When we heard this, our jaws dropped. It reeked of being an elder scam, and we immediately told Mary she shouldn't do it while peppering her with a myriad of reasons why this deal favored the tenants' interests above hers, and that it could quickly go off the rails, leaving her without a roof over her head. We left with an uneasy feeling about the intentions of her lodgers, but confident that we had scared Mary sufficiently that she wouldn't take any further action. At least not without consulting us first.

About a month later, we dropped by Mary's house on the way back from LA, just to check in on her. The news was not good. Despite our protests against signing her home over to her tenants, she'd gone ahead and done exactly that. What's more, within the contract, no legally binding language would hold the tenants liable for Mary's care and feeding up to her day of passing. She'd permanently signed her house over to the tenants, no strings attached.

We considered going to an attorney for some advice but realized that any intervention on our part would be undermined by Mary having willingly, while in control of her faculties and without duress, signed the deed. What's more, she was comfortable with her decision. Maggie and I both saw the folly in the deal, but it was complete, so we left Mary's house that day harboring grave misgivings about her future.

It was only a few weeks later that we heard from Mary and she was in a panic. What we picked up from the conversation, amongst the ramblings and other indications of distress, was that the tenants had told her she needed to move out of the house as they planned to sell it and move back to Mexico. This change in her affairs was no surprise to either of us, and, as we were well aware, Mary now had no place to go. Here was an eighty-something-year-old woman about to be tossed out onto the street. A stark and testing environment, even in California, and one that with her health problems, she would be hard-pressed to survive.

Outraged at such a callous act, but powerless to change a legally binding decision, we left Mary's house upset both with the tenants, who were absent at the time, and Mary's abject trust in human nature. Her naivety and faith in others were on their way to providing the foundation for her obituary.

It wasn't more than seconds after the phone call that Maggie started to work on solutions to keep her off the street. Solutions that contained a single recurring thread. "We could have her stay with us until we figure out what to do. We could fix up that basement room. It has a stove and a sink; it wouldn't take much to make it comfortable." I'd heard these overtures many times in the past, although they had never involved a human being, and I balked. "How can we take care of an eighty-year-old senior citizen with health problems when we're both working?" I replied. And the negotiations ground slowly to a halt, for that day at least.

The following week I realized that my arguments had received their customary lip service when I heard that work had already started on Maggie's vision to house Mary and to keep her and her two dogs off the streets.

She arrived home one evening with news that several people in the community had become familiar with Mary Reyes because of their attendance at the same church. Upon hearing of this twist in her circumstances, they had all pledged to help fix up the downstairs room in our house. One of them was Jack Good, the owner of a midsize commercial building company. Jack and his wife, Betty, knew all about Mary, and Jack was ready to put in flooring and cabinets and fix the kitchen area all free of charge.

Reflecting upon this rapid escalation of events, I was amazed and somewhat piqued at how little weight my arguments carried. We shared an equal partnership when it came to our affairs in general, but when the issue was compassion, not only was Maggie a relentless negotiator, but I found that my rebuttals were often tinged with guilt and a measure of insincerity. Each animal, and now person, in need resulted in no material gain. She just wanted to help. And so it was with Mary. I repeated my earlier arguments, knowing that I was now up against not only my wife but also a group of empathetic residents, tools in hand, ready to descend on our house and turn it into an episode of a home improvement show. I'd been painted into a corner and sensed defeat in the air. Once again, I folded and promptly joined the ranks of volunteers who would turn the downstairs room into habitable quarters for our new octogenarian roommate. At least we wouldn't have to worry about wild parties or late-night escapades.

Within weeks the room was transformed from a tatty downstairs storage area to a cheerful studio with bright white cabinets, linoleum flooring, and new paint. Everything was ready for move-in. And Maggie had arranged a surprise party. Not only for Mary, who, by the way, was terrified of being the center of attention, but also for the volunteers who had made the whole rescue mission possible.

The big day arrived, and Mary walked into her worst nightmare, a room full of people all focused on her. She was fussed over, complimented, fed, and, much to her chagrin, photographed, until finally the partygoers drifted away, and Mary began to settle into her new home. Naturally, she brought her two dogs, Kelly and Bianca. Kelly was the collie and the one who seemed to take great delight in biting me without provocation. And I resigned myself to co-exist at arm's length with this aggressor, hoping that in time she would realize that I was just another non-threatening fixture in the house, along with the bedside table and kitchen cabinets.

Six months passed, and Mary seemed satisfied with her new living conditions. However, I could tell she missed the independence of having her own home. During her stay, she experienced a couple of health scares that saw paramedics hustle her off to the local hospital, until one day she fell ill with a cold, and the cold went to her chest, eventually turning into pneumonia. Paramedics rushed her to the local hospital, where she was tubed up and medicated. I visited her the next day on the way back from work, and all she wanted to do was come home. I sat with her, and we talked about how she was feeling and how her two dogs, Kelly and Bianca, were faring without her, while touching on subjects related to her life, religion, and the state of the world. When I got up to leave, I realized how frail she'd become judging from her sunken eyes, the color of her skin, and the deep grooves the tubes had formed in the delicate skin of her lips. Although she could probably fight through this illness, she was somehow depressed from being in a hospital environment. And I was concerned that she was preparing to choose this time to stop fighting for her life.

Mary had tremendous faith and did not doubt that she would end up in heaven reunited with Teddy and all the animals she'd saved. As

I got up to leave, I told her that I loved her, not realizing what effect such a simple gesture of affection would have. Her eyes quickly turned in my direction, and she caught me silently in her gaze. I could see that she was tearing up. I had no idea the power those few words would hold for her even though I knew that Mary had not experienced a lot of love in her life, at least not before or after her marriage to her beloved Teddy. And those three words meant something far more than I could imagine from my fortunate vantage point of a happy and comfortable life underpinned by a supportive family.

Less than an hour after I left, Mary passed away. Maggie was on her way to the hospital when it happened and was saddened both by her passing and by the fact that she couldn't be by her side when the end came.

CHAPTER 20

An Unwelcome Visitor Arrives

'Cause it makes me that much stronger
Makes me work a little bit harder
It makes me that much wiser
So thanks for making me a fighter
Christina Aguilera – "Fighter"

Now that the most recent election cycle was in the rearview mirror, it was time to settle back into managing the affairs of the City. An early initiative was a clean water fee that Maggie championed, designed to keep the area's beaches, lagoons, and watersheds protected from the effects of stormwater runoff. Following a court ruling, the decision had to be made by the voters, and a ballot date was under discussion. Meanwhile, Maggie turned her attention to starting a pet health expo using the City Hall parking lot as the venue. Microchipping, spay and neuter services, rescue groups, pet supply vendors, and the Department of Animal Control fleshed out a rich complement of animal-related service providers, with the first expo scheduled for June.

As the pet fair was taking shape, she was also completing work with a partner to create a small animal-rescue organization called Wee Companions whose focus was on saving and adopting out smaller varieties of household pets. I started to wonder how much sleep a person could be getting with this type of schedule. She almost always stayed up way beyond when I made the trek to bed, reading City documents or talking on the phone. And I was typically gone when she would get up in the morning. I spoke with her about reducing her schedule. However, I could tell how hard it was for her to turn down a meeting with a resident, decline an invitation to talk to kids about local government, or attend the myriad of other commitments a hard-working councilperson can find themselves tackling. Sure enough, only a couple of days later, a casual chat about the city's heritage of flower-growing sparked an idea and prompted her to approach a local gardening expert about starting a public tour of many of the city's elaborate and unique residential gardens. Within weeks, the two had put together a committee of twelve people to kick-start the event. And after several meetings, with Maggie leading the way on obtaining the necessary city permits, all systems were go for the launch of the city's first garden tour.

That same year would also mark the twentieth anniversary of the incorporation of Encinitas as a city, a change that involved the town's split from the county of San Diego in 1986. Nobody on the council seemed to be interested in recognizing the milestone since many of the original activists who had championed the cause, and who wanted the anniversary celebrated, were out of sync with the current council majority's agenda and often criticized their decisions. For that reason, negotiations regarding a community celebration were stonewalled.

Some of the original members of the incorporation team approached Maggie. This group had fought hard to separate the town from county government, mainly due to the bureaucrats in San Diego approving development that didn't suit the community while keeping residents out of the conversation. Because of their focus on controlled growth, this group was shunned and sometimes even disrespected by the council majority at City meetings.

They saw the year of incorporation as a special event in the city's history and a time for celebration. Maggie agreed and jumped in to help by finding people who would sponsor the design and manufacture of memorial banners. The plan was to feature the banners on lampposts throughout the city. And it wasn't long before sponsors began to step forward while artists submitted drafts of their ideas for review.

News of this effort soon made its way back to City Hall, where the council majority was incensed that she was once again going it alone. They quickly demanded that the city manager and city attorney investigate where the funds for this initiative were coming from and how they were being spent—going so far as to accuse her of blatantly attempting to promote her political career.

In due course, all receipts were submitted to the city attorney, who, in turn, contacted the fair political practices commission for judgment on the complaint. The FPPC came back with an all clear, and the city attorney's report read that no misconduct had occurred. Yet another attempt by the power bloc to subdue the slow-growth advocate failed, and the banners were soon displayed in front of businesses and shopping malls along the city's downtown thoroughfare.

With a full calendar of city responsibilities, voluntary initiatives, and activist events, it was hard to keep a handle on what meeting, ceremony, or coffee with a constituent would hit the calendar next. Controversy, however, was always lurking nearby. And it wasn't long before another clash with David Meyer would erupt, this time over what the state called the development density bonus law.

In a nutshell, this clause allowed a developer to increase the number of housing units in a residential development by up to 35 percent as long as one unit out of each block of ten was affordable. At the end of the thirty years, if the affordable units were rented, the ownership reverted back to the developer. This accommodation was reasonable since, based on the high housing prices in the city, it was difficult for low-income families to live within the town's borders. And Maggie's early days of struggle as a struggling single mother gave her a unique insight into the challenges involved.

Residents, however, started complaining to Maggie about the developments. They seemed to be cramming in extra units to the point where the concentration of houses didn't fit with the general look and feel of their neighborhoods. People felt that they were being suffocated by development. They saw that the quaint neighborhoods that had initially attracted them to the city were slowly turning into the concentration and uniformity that they saw in areas to the north such as Orange County and Los Angeles.

The media picked up on the story, and in turn, Meyer went to great lengths to explain how unprofitable such a model was. The model would cut into developer margins due to the need for smaller lots and incurred additional fees. If this was such an untenable business model, however, something didn't ring true. Because, as he was making his case, there were already five proposals for density bonus projects sitting in the Planning Department of the City, each requesting the necessary up-zoning to accommodate additional units. These increases were legal by state law, and no amount of protesting at the City level would overcome that right.

Development was a constant issue throughout Maggie's tenure. And it wasn't long after the density bonus issue that another divisive real estate issue reared its head, pitting ordinary residents against the town's preeminent landowner.

Ten years prior, the Ecke family had turned 853 acres of their flower-growing ranch into housing, commercial space, and a golf course. Under this agreement they had also committed to leaving the remainder of their holdings as agriculture in perpetuity. However, they were back at the door of City Hall once again. This time they wanted to develop sixty-seven of their remaining eighty-seven acres by putting 201 housing units on the land, while donating a works yard and a park to the town as an incentive. This would leave a much smaller twenty acres in agriculture for perpetuity. If this second attempt to rezone the land were to prove successful, however, it would be reasonable to assume that another attempt to develop the remaining acres would be forthcoming.

The change from agricultural to residential would increase the value of an acre of land from around $70,000 to approximately $350,000 or more. Ecke's argument was that the business needed to upgrade its greenhouses, a familiar plea that had accompanied the original request to develop the ranch some years prior. However, there was no visible evidence that any of the millions of dollars generated from that initial development had ever been invested in their local operations.

The residents of the city weren't suffering from any long-term memory loss. They quickly recalled that this argument had surfaced ten years ago. What had happened to the millions of dollars earned from the first swath of development? They also remembered that the original deal committed the family to leave the last sixty-seven acres in agriculture in perpetuity. And they were keenly aware that it was they who had supported the original project and that this last slice of agricultural land was off limits for development. This time around a sufficient number of residents resented the family's ongoing push for financial gain and were not prepared to see their earlier accord cast aside.

The once-proud Ecke family, at one time a pillar of the city and the region, compromised itself by masquerading under the shadow of a business needing investment. In reality, they were positioning themselves to haul in substantial personal profit at the expense of the quality of life of the city's residents due to traffic, the loss of green space, and impacts on local services. The lure of financial gain had trumped any sense the family had of responsibility or obligation to the community.

Fortunately, with Maggie's reelection, the Eckes had failed to add to the development-friendly power bloc on the council, which would have given them a supermajority, thereby circumventing the need for a citizen's ballot. As a result, this latest quest for development profits would go before the voters.

The Eckes poured $168,000 into their initiative called proposition A, while opponents raised $14,000. The proposition was soundly defeated with a margin of 65 percent against the proposition to 35 percent for it.

It was now a year since the 2004 election, and the dividing line between the political camps on the council was as entrenched as ever. The power bloc, devoid of a significant event such as an election that would allow them to marginalize and attack their minority peer, resorted to more mundane methods.

Maggie started to discover that items such as invitations for council members to attend community events were failing to get delivered, and she would have to hunt them down within the administration. An additional insult arrived during the Downtown Main Street Association's annual dinner where City Council members were seated at a large table near the stage for the speeches and presentations. Except for Maggie and me. Strangely enough, we got sanctioned off to a dark corner at the very rear of the room. At the ceremony, where the installation of new association board members was the main event, Maggie had a proclamation to present. But her presentation didn't appear on the agenda, despite arrangements made earlier that month.

None of this came as a surprise and undeterred, she would not allow City business to be marginalized. Gritting her teeth, she picked a transition point in the speeches and made her way to the stage, where she drew the MC to one side for a few words. The microphone quickly changed hands. And after a brief introduction, the proclamation was delivered to resounding applause from the audience, who were completely unaware of the dynamics unfolding in front of them.

This culture of marginalization had become the unspoken protocol at the City, and while the power bloc perpetrated it, it was often executed by the compliant city managers of the day, initially Kerry Miller and later Phil Cotton, who had been appointed from his previous position as Director of Parks and Recreation. Both of these city managers took their lead from Jerome Stocks, who had become the dominant personality at City Hall.

These new attempts to bottleneck information, while irritating, didn't impede Maggie's agenda. However, the time spent managing her calendar did exacerbate an already demanding workload.

By typically opposing inappropriate development, and because of the methods used by her opponents to distort her record and attack her motives, the pressure continued to grow. I wondered how long she could continue to operate in such a toxic climate before something had to change.

On a warm spring evening in 2007, after the emails had been read and the first round of phone calls returned, Maggie shared a concern that had been bothering her for a few days. She was experiencing signs of blood where, in a fifty-nine-year old post-menopausal woman, that cycle should have ended some time ago. I asked her how she was feeling, and she responded that there were no other symptoms or any discomfort, and she couldn't find an explanation for the blood. We talked about what it might mean and decided that a visit to the doctor was in order. But, with the pressures of city business, and the animal and social activism that filled her days, what we thought was an anomaly was put on the back burner to make way for more pressing issues. A few weeks later the signs reoccurred and a precautionary visit to her doctor was finally squeezed into her schedule.

To a lay person, the symptoms didn't indicate that anything was seriously wrong, so on the day of the appointment, I left for work. At the same time, Maggie made her way down to the UCSD medical campus on the university grounds. There, the doctor administered a series of investigative measures starting with a simple Q&A and progressing to physical assessments, followed by a computerized tomography (CT) scan. A few days later, the doctor called her back to go over the results.

The medical version of the findings was that there was some upper peritoneal thickening and nodularity, accompanied by abnormal findings on the CT scan. This analysis suggested the presence of a pelvic mass and a possible adrenal nodule. The use of Latin in medical language makes the delivery of exam results akin to a computer scientist explaining to a four-year-old how the serial processing of data by a supercomputer differs from the parallel techniques executed by an ordinary laptop. It's a foreign language. And one that without translation can evoke the darkest of expectations. Anyone hearing news that they had peritoneal thickening and multiple nodules on this and that, with a pelvic mass thrown into the mix, could well jump to the conclusion that they'd better get their affairs in order as they have just received an invitation for the next flight to nirvana.

After the oncologist had delivered an analysis that suggested a grim future, the conversation took on a new direction as the doctor reeled off a list of caveats and waivers that, in their sum, painted a far more benign outcome, one that would leave any patient with the impression that there was nothing particularly serious going on.

The presentation concluded with a wave of the hand and a recommendation for removal of all reproductive organs by way of a hysterectomy. This procedure would also facilitate a more in-depth evaluation of what was going on with Maggie's reproductive system. The hysterectomy came with a bonus of a bilateral salpingo-oopho-rectomy, meaning the removal of both fallopian tubes and ovaries. In sum, it was a decision not to be taken lightly.

After a couple of days of thought and discussion, and with some time spent researching the pros and cons of the surgery, Maggie placed her trust in Western medicine and made an appointment to go under the knife. The surgery was termed a hysterectomy with pathological diagnosis, which meant that first the reproductive organs would be removed. Then a pathologist would take a look at selected tissue samples under a microscope to see if there was any cancer lurking amongst the cells.

The day of the surgery arrived, and we returned to UCSD. After our final farewells and Maggie's repeated requests that I take care of all the animals should something terrible happen during the procedure, she was wheeled away by a team of medical personnel.

Some hours later, the surgeon arrived in the waiting room and informed me that all had gone well and that he'd removed thirty lymph nodes from the right side of the pelvis, twenty-five from the left, and eighteen from the periaortic region in front of the lumbar vertebrae. All of which he would be including with the tissue samples that were to go to the pathologist. Two days after the surgery, I returned to the hospital to pick her up. On the way home, I could sense that something was different. It was a quiet and somber person who sat gazing out the window in the seat beside me, and I could see she was lost in thought. While I tried to attribute the moment to the lingering effects of the anesthesia, I knew that the idea of a serious diagnosis was weighing heavily on her mind.

A few days later, we made the trip back to the hospital to find out the results of the pathologist's analysis. Upon arrival, a receptionist ushered us into one of the many uniform rooms that lay behind the ranks of administrative personnel who sat busy entering patient co-pays and making appointments. In the room, an industrial-looking bed sheathed in paper lay beside a half-closed curtain. Two chairs sat adjacent to a cabinet that supported a stainless-steel sink and the standard swan-necked faucet, while a dispenser of hand sanitizer hung conveniently below a trio of white cupboards.

After a brief wait, a rap on the door announced the arrival of the oncologist, who greeted us as he reached for a low stool that sat on wheels in the corner of the room. Deftly scooting across the shiny floor, he came to rest in front of where we were seated and opened his manila folder. We listened to him sift through the whats and wherefores of the diagnostic procedure and endured the technicalities of what the unknown pathologist had discovered under their microscope until he finished talking. What he left us with was summed up in one unforgettable statement that stood out from all the rest. The medical team had identified the cause for our concern, and its name was endometrial adenocarcinoma. Or, in layman's terms, cancer.

It was one of those moments when time stands still. We looked at each other, neither of us saying a word, while the doctor continued his presentation. By now, we were familiar with some of the key terms likely to be used during the diagnostic process, and the doctor had come up with the most undesirable ones. There was no time for reflection; however, he played up the positives, educating us on survival rates, how the disease had been caught early in its development, and how the chances were reasonably good for a full recovery. We probed for what the next steps would be, eager to find out what could eliminate this unwelcome invader from her body. A course of chemotherapy was the recommended treatment.

Chemo's possible side effects read like a menu from a medieval torture manual. The list started with some benign inconveniences, like nausea and headaches. From there, it took a more sinister turn with peripheral neuropathy resulting in pain in the hands and feet. Hair loss came next along with the news that the patient would be susceptible to most airborne diseases due to a compromised immune system. All of this was trumped by the fact that the medicine itself might cause death. Chemo would introduce an indiscriminate poison into the body that would kill a wide range of cells, both cancerous and healthy. The treatment, even if it was to prove successful, could have long-term effects. We left the hospital with another difficult decision to ponder.

Back at home, politics, animal initiatives, the environment, and city residents still tugged at Maggie's sleeve. And she persisted with her role as council member and animal advocate, choosing to keep the announcement of her diagnosis to a time when she had come to terms with it.

CHAPTER 21

An Unexpected Champion

It's against the law, it was against the law…
what your mama saw…it was against the law
Paul Simon – "Me and Julio Down by the School Yard"

A s she contemplated the next steps in her treatment and continued to recover from the hysterectomy, a series of events began to unfold related to a landscaping business that occupied part of a property directly across the street from our house. The City had received a complaint from nearby residents regarding the intensity of operations on the land that the landscaping company was using as their headquarters. Running a landscaping business from this location ran afoul of City zoning laws, regulations that had changed after the incorporation of the city. And the only way it could now pass as being legal, or legal non-conforming as defined under the law, would be to prove that a landscaping business had existed on the property before

Encinitas separated itself from the county of San Diego some twenty years earlier. That way, the company could claim that it had a right to be grandfathered in as a legitimate business. The Planning Department had researched the operation, determining that it was, in fact, illegal as there was no evidence to suggest that there had been an unbroken and ongoing existence of such an entity. Also, the existing business had gone so far as to intensify its operations by adding additional trucks and employees, which was also contrary to the City's municipal code.

The proprietor of American Landscape was Russell Bowman, who promptly appealed the Planning Department's decision that he had to cease all operations and embarked on a process to build a case that would prove that there had been an unbroken chain of landscaping businesses on the land before and after the city's incorporation.

The first step in his strategy was to appear on the doorstep of every residence in the neighborhood, accompanied by what looked like his three- or four-year-old daughter to solicit support for his livelihood. Some homeowners, surprised by his direct solicitation, signed a letter that he would later submit to the City in support of his case. Many who had tired of the speeding trucks, spilled loads, and a general increase in traffic declined his request.

Our home was probably the one most impacted by the trash, employee off-street parking, and the thunderous morning and after-noon chorus of trucks and trailers that came roaring up and down the narrow street. There was no support coming from our house, and we gave Bowman our answer. When he realized we were not in favor, he gathered up his child and stalked off the property, casting a threatening gaze my way. This display of irritation was an omen of a series of incidents that would darken the political landscape of the city for months and push the council into unethical and, arguably, illegal action.

Two hearings took place before the City. And it wasn't long before Bowman discovered that Maggie Houlihan was a member of the council, albeit one who had to recuse herself from his agenda item because she lived in close proximity to the property in question. Protocol dictated that because of the possibility of bias regarding a vote, any council member with a vested interest in the outcome of an agenda item must not take part in the council's proceedings or the vote itself. I, on the other hand, as a private citizen, was not constrained by the same rules.

Bowman, through his attorney, submitted a blizzard of paperwork to defend his side of the argument: letters and testimony from owners of landscaping businesses that had operated on the lot, letters from employees of those businesses, contractor license numbers linked to these operations, and receipts from companies that had supplied them with parts and service. Bowman's evidence was overwhelming and buttoned-down tight. But by the very nature of its almost perfect dovetailing of business to business and signed statement to signed statement, the body of work looked suspicious, an observation made both by the Planning Department and by council member Houlihan, who, although recused, could still view the proceedings from afar. And whose suspicions warranted a closer look.

The first crack in Bowman's appeal came from an unexpected source during the first hearing. Unable to resist the opportunity to display his hometown knowledge, council member Dan Dalager, whose tool repair and sharpening business catered to many of the local landscaping operations, took exception to one of the letters it had received in support of Bowman's appeal by Sean Rowe, an employee of Robert Rowe Tree Services, one of the businesses listed by Bowman as operating from the property. The letter was odd in that it was on business letterhead but lacked any address or phone number. During the council discussion, Dalager lowered his glasses onto the front of his nose, leaned toward his microphone, and stated that he knew the Rowe family and that there was no member of the Rowe family with the name of Sean. The statement was a bombshell from Dan who, in his eagerness to appear in the know, had cast a pall of doubt over the entire body of work submitted by Bowman and his legal team.

Maggie, in the meantime, had harbored similar suspicions about the documentation and set about contacting every owner, employee, and retailer whose evidence of business operations had been submitted to the City as evidence. For my part, I researched the contractor license numbers with the state licensing board to determine their real ownership.

Maggie's research soon revealed a complete and absolute pattern of fraud and deception. Every single one of the submitted documents had used either a copied letterhead, fake lease agreements, forged signatures, or poached contractor license numbers. Her research showed that the appeal was a scam, cooked up to secure a lucrative land designation that would protect an intensive landscaping operation that was in violation of the city's zoning.

By this time, Bowman, well aware of Maggie's role on the council and her proximity to his project, had gleaned from his earlier visit to our house that she was not in sync with his cause. He took this disapproval as a de facto endorsement to embark on a campaign of intimidation against her.

The motivation behind his actions was unclear. Maggie could not vote on the appeal. And the other council members would not be influenced by her arguments even if she were to act illegally and try to sway them. She provided no threat to his goals. Nevertheless, he put into play a number of actions designed to coerce, bully, and intimidate her. And his methods carried about as much sophistication as a rusty cudgel. At the same time other attacks against our property occurred although with these there was no direct proof that they were of Bowman's doing.

His reign of intimidation started subtly. One morning, as we drove out of the driveway, we were greeted by two large American Landscape trucks, which had been strategically parked inches away from each side of the entrance to our driveway. The goal, aside from making the point that he was not happy with Maggie's lack of support, was to make exiting our property as awkward and dangerous as possible by eliminating visibility both up and down the street. The trucks would stay parked in this fashion for days on end.

Step two saw the trucks deliberately, and on multiple occasions, parked with our empty trash cans knocked over beside them, as they assumed their positions astride the driveway. Then other attacks started to occur where an unknown perpetrator operated under the cover of darkness to avoid being recognized. One morning, as I left to go to work, I saw scattered along the driveway the entire compliment of our weekly trash and recycling. Grass clippings mingled chaotically with junk mail. Old shopping lists and paper towels were impaled on the nearby shrubs where they flapped in the breeze, while used food containers spilled the last of their contents onto the asphalt. I reversed and spent the next fifteen minutes rounding up the debris and placing the trashcans in their rightful place for collection, assuming that the perpetrator wouldn't be so brazen as to return during full daylight to repeat their work.

Days later, the small palm trees that lined one side of the driveway began to show signs of burns on their fronds. These burns became more defined with time, and it turned out that some form of acid had been tossed onto them, presumably in the dead of night. Over time the toxin continued its work until some of the trees looked like they had suffered through an extended drought. What was left of the foliage was yellowed and draped downwards from the main trunk toward the ground below.

The series of attacks, up to this point material in nature, became personal when later that week, Maggie was out at the front of the house collecting the mail. Bowman emerged from the property across the street to get something from one of the two trucks that had become almost permanent fixtures on either side of our driveway. I'd come to refer to them as the stone lions, the kind you might find on pillars at the front of the driveway leading to an English stately home. Maggie decided to grasp the moment and address her concerns directly. They met in the middle of the street, where she politely asked if he could park his trucks in a less intrusive fashion so we could get out of the driveway without the risk of a collision. This simple request precipitated a reaction you might expect if you had struck a bee's nest with a pole.

Bowman, already filled with resentment, realized she was defenseless and verbally tore into her, in the process threatening to kill not only her but also her husband and all of her animals. Realizing that Bowman was unstable, and fearing for her safety, Maggie retreated to the house, where, after taking a few minutes to collect herself, she called the sheriffs. It wasn't long into the call that the officer informed her that they had only just received a similar call from a Russell Bowman. He had reported to them that Maggie Houlihan had just come out of her house and threatened to kill him.

She argued her case with the officer, who informed her that since it was a "he said she said" situation, an investigation would not take place. As it turned out, the sheriff also failed to write a report on the incident. And only after Maggie pursued it with several members of the police department over a period of months did she finally approach the San Diego Police Department, where a sympathetic officer filled out the paperwork. The anomaly was that this was a civic leader whose life had been threatened. And I was left to wonder if there would have been a different approach from the police if one of the other council members had had their lives jeopardized in the same manner.

Bowman, seemingly emboldened by the ongoing success of his strategy, engaged in two additional attacks, both of which caught the attention of the media while tipping public opinion firmly against him. And these last steps triggered the entry of an unexpected champion into the mix.

I wandered down the driveway one weekend morning to check on any damage or obstacles that Mr. Bowman may have set up the previous night. What I saw confirmed that he would stop at nothing to make his point, only this time he'd decided to appeal to a broader audience. On a large five-foot-by-five-foot sign prominently displayed at the entrance to his property were painted the words "HOULIHAN IS A WHORE!"

After taking in the scenario, I walked back to the house, where Maggie was still sleeping. I struggled with how to soften the blow regarding this latest act in Bowman's reign of terror, as she was still recovering from the effects of her recent surgery and cancer diagnosis. She finally awoke, and after giving her time to adjust to the day, I started dropping pieces of information about the sign. Finally, I described its contents, and I could see a look of horror and disbelief spread across her face. Even with Bowman's penchant for intimidating and threatening behavior, this one had hit a new low.

After wrapping herself in some clothes, Maggie made her way to the street to assess the damage. As she looked at the sign, I could see the shock in her face. But only minutes after the emotional impact had settled, her survival instincts kicked in and she started to evaluate her options for fighting back.

As we returned to the house, we questioned the legality of Bowman's behavior, and Maggie decided to call the City Attorney to find out if his actions fell into the category of libel. Over the next couple of days, while the city attorney looked into her request, Maggie conducted her own research. What she discovered was that, as a public official, she was more exposed to public criticism than an average resident, and it began to look as if Bowman might be within his rights. She made calls to friends who were attorneys and asked them what their opinion was. They didn't have immediate answers but promised to get back to her after consulting with others more expert in that specific area of the law.

While this was going on, Bowman had not been idle. One morning a neighbor, out walking her dog, spotted me in the driveway and waved me over. "Have you seen what's at the front of the property over there?" she said, pointing to Bowman's greenhouses that looked out over the freeway. "You'd better go and have a look." She stood waiting while I strolled to the end of the road, where I could see the entire frontal sweep of the property.

When I reached the end of the cul de sac, I looked up. Staring back at me, nailed to a full-size cross, was the effigy of a woman in the act of being crucified. With a mop of red hair trailing in the wind, there was no doubt as to whom the figure represented. The diorama of the crucifixion also contained two other effigies of unknown personalities impaled on smaller crosses behind the main event. Completing the spectacle was a statement painted in large letters down the side of the greenhouse most visible to the freeway, which again read, "HOULIHAN IS A WHORE."

For those nearby drivers, familiar with local City leadership or not, Bowman had left nothing to the imagination, and it wasn't long before the media jumped on his latest attack. Within hours his handiwork was on TV and in the newspapers.

The following morning, I went to work at the technology company where I was a vice president. Shortly after entering my office, an employee came in with several sheets of paper under his arm. "I took these off the fax machine," he said. "I thought you should see them first." He handed me the papers, and on each one was a stick figure that represented a woman committing various sexual acts. Someone had discovered where I worked and had decided to broadened their attack. I glanced through the childish drawings before taking a stroll down to the HR department to explain what was going on in case there were any more incidents in the future. Walking back to my office, I set about analyzing each of the documents for any identifying numbers or addresses that might provide a lead. The only identification of note was that of the local FedEx store. The perpetrator had been smart enough to cover their tracks, but I had my suspicions as to where the crude images had originated.

One evening Maggie returned from work, and she was elated, which under the circumstances was odd, as recent events had once again dampened spirits around our house. She was maintaining a cheerful persona when it came to activities outside the home, and she was undoubtedly a strong individual. Still, Bowman's assaults were a form of public and private bullying that took their toll and she was still learning how to deal with the stress that came with each devious blow.

The reason for her delight was that she had met one of the partners of a law firm by the name of Worden Williams, located in the neighboring city of Solana Beach. They had been following Bowman's activities and during the conversation agreed to sue him for libel with Maggie only on the hook for direct costs, as they would forgo their legal fees. Maggie, of course, jumped at the chance and arranged a consultation for later that week. The firm asked that both of us attend, which made sense as I'd been a co-victim of the attacks and had received some questionable faxes at work.

We were interviewed and provided the attorney with photographs, faxes, and notes from each event that had taken place. Two weeks later, the law firm filed a brief with the court, and the case was officially underway. Bowman prepared his defense and, in the process, burned through legal firms at a breakneck pace. These unwitting professionals typically lasted only a few weeks before they realized they weren't getting paid on time, or for other unknown reasons.

The core argument that surfaced in Bowman's defense was that, as Maggie was a public figure, he had the right to criticize her. And that he'd done so under the guise of her being a "political whore" based upon her vision for the city. In my estimation, it was a contrived and somewhat fragile defense. And one that Worden Williams attorney Tracy Richmond exploited—arguing that advertising derogatory statements to passing motorists, most of whom lived outside the city and knew nothing of local issues, did not come under the protection of political free speech.

After a few appearances in front of the judge, with different attorneys, Bowman settled out of court for a sum of which Maggie's share ended up being $12,000. The greater satisfaction, however, came from a requirement that he take down or cover up all the libelous graffiti and signage that he'd assembled on his property. Maggie and her attorney immediately held a press conference in front of City Hall to express their satisfaction that the case had concluded in her favor—and to express that although political figures are subject to greater scrutiny and criticism than regular citizens, such criticism cannot rise to the level of hateful insults displayed in the public domain.

In September of that same year, Russell Bowman's appeal appeared on the council's agenda for a second time so that a decision could be reached. With Maggie recused, I would present our arguments. Between us, we had gathered up a substantial body of information and put together a presentation that would bring each fraudulent document to the council's attention. With every minute detail highlighted, there could be no doubt that all of Bowman's documentation was perjured and fallacious, and we were confident of victory.

Since members of the public who address the council on an agenda item are only afforded three minutes to speak, I solicited time donations from supportive members of the audience and cobbled together the maximum allotment of nine minutes to state our case. And after some standard City business issues, the appeal came up as the next agenda item. With a slide presentation on video screens for the public to see, I displayed receipts from a rental company that had been out of business for eight years; the letter from Sean Rowe, allegedly an employee of Robert Rowe Tree Services, who council member Dan Dalager had called out as not being a real person; numerous faked letters that used the names of unsuspecting landscaping businesses; written statements that Maggie had obtained from each of the legitimate business owners affirming that they had never operated a landscaping business from the property in question; and print-outs from the State of California's licensing board clearly showing that while a number of the contractor licenses were legitimate numbers, they belonged to different businesses than the ones submitted by Russell Bowman.

One example was for a company called Isberg and Sons. The license in fact belonged to Artistry Tree Services, whose sole owner was Clifford Lee Pratt. Mr. Pratt faxed a letter stating that he lived outside of the city and had never had a business in Encinitas. Marvin Gunn of Gunn's Landscaping wrote in as the legitimate owner of one of the misused licensed numbers and stated the locations of his company's outlets, none of which were in Encinitas. There were misspellings of the fraudulently used names of the legitimate business owners. Bowman even recruited his father, or at least his father's name and signature, when he included two letters under someone else's license number. Strangely enough, his father, Neville Harold Taffe of Las Vegas, had spelled his name differently on each of the letters.

Not content to stop at family members, Bowman also exploited his brother's ex-girlfriend, Deborah Powell, by persuading her to perjure herself and say that she and her parents owned El Rancho Greenhouses and Gardening. This was a business that did exist on the property; however, she had nothing to do with the company, which was wholly owned by the original owner of the land on which it stood. When he was questioned, he stated for the record that he didn't know anyone with the name Deborah Powell. The city's fire marshal was included in my arguments as he was prepared to testify that greenhouses and not landscaping businesses had occupied the property for years. Past clean water inspections by City staff had also referred to the operations on the site as greenhouses and growing operations, not landscaping. And the head of the local clean water program had stated his willingness to testify to that fact. A relatively recent request from one of the tenants who rented a greenhouse on the property was for a minor use permit to retail plants on the site. His application also referred only to greenhouse operations and not to landscaping businesses, and the chairperson of the City's planning commission was prepared to verify his statement, having reviewed the original permit request.

The presentation had laid out a compelling set of data from which a reasonable person couldn't fail to conclude that Bowman was lying to the council, and, therefore, should not be granted the opportunity to continue his non-conforming use of the property. Arguably, he could be referred to the authorities for further investigation under California penal code 115 PC, which makes it a felony to knowingly file a false or forged document with a government in the state.

My closing remarks reiterated the fact that the records I'd presented from the City's staff, the State of California, and the signed statements from the legal owners of the relevant licenses, showed that Mr. Bowman, and the people who were involved in his arguments, committed fraudulent acts in presenting these materials as factual.

I sat down and awaited the deliberations of the council now that they were fully aware of all of the evidence. In the meantime, the attorney for American Landscape, Larry Marshall from the law firm of Wertz, McDade, Wallace, Moot, and Brower, had seen the writing on the wall. And in his rebuttal to my arguments, he spent his entire time trying to extricate first himself, and then his law firm, from representing what he now realized was an appeal based on fraudulent information. Coincidentally, the law firm of Wertz, McDade, Wallace, Moot, and Brower was the same law firm that David Meyer used to file an unrelated complaint with the press some time later regarding the accuracy of some quotes they had used in an article about him.

With Mr. Marshall's closing remarks, the item went back to the council. What happened next was a combination of amateur theater and pure, unvarnished malignance, as the clumsy manipulation of procedural precedence and manufactured sympathy for Russell Bowman revealed the entrenched bias of the council majority toward Maggie Houlihan.

Councilmember Dalager, once again lowering his glasses below the bridge of his nose, symbolically beat his chest by stating, "I was the one who brought [these issues] into our staff and said a bunch of this stuff is bogus…These letters are phony; these are bad signatures…I know these players…I did my own research. [The] evidence that was presented to us wasn't worth the paper it was written on…but I was convinced of the continuity."

The public in attendance looked at each other in disbelief. Had Dan just confirmed that all the documentation was fraudulent but that due to the knowledge that he possessed it was he alone who knew that an unbroken line of landscaping businesses had used the land? Jerome Stock's statement on the matter was more obtuse as he punted and claimed that he wished the council had received my information earlier, as though some procedural timeline had expired, and the evidence presented was no longer valid. Stocks then asked the city attorney what options the council had at their disposal. The city attorney advised that they could pull the issue back for further discussion based upon this new information. Stocks, Bond, Guerin, and Dalager, however, were in no mood to prolong a situation. And with that, a motion was presented, and the four members of the council voted.

All four voted to approve the appeal and not only to permit the business to continue but to allow Bowman to intensify his operations by a factor of six. Jerome Stocks then summed up the affair by stating that "Some of the evidence was bogus. We had to make a decision whether to eliminate a man's business or not...A tough decision. We made the right decision." These proceedings had taken place in front of the media, residents, and those watching the streamed content on TV. And the public was left wondering in whose hands the leadership of their city lay.

That night Maggie and I replayed the meeting, appalled at how such a decision could be made in public view and in the face of such overwhelming evidence of fraud. Both of us came to the obvious conclusion. The property was directly opposite where we lived. A residence that belonged to the one person on the City Council who had proved to be a foil to the majority's pro-development agenda and who would be directly impacted by their decision. A decision for which the council bloc was willing to compromise their integrity in front of the entire city. Not to mention favoring the landscaping business over the ability of the residents on the street to enjoy their homes unaffected by increased traffic, trash, and on-street parking. After many replays and analysis, we concluded that their action could very well be illegal. So we started to develop a plan to take the issue to the San Diego Grand Jury, since it was the body that had the necessary oversight authority to review city or county government behavior.

While Maggie buried herself in researching the Grand Jury's procedures, work on the house had stalled. In contrast, the march of animals onto the property had only accelerated, this time under more clandestine rules of engagement.

That fall I took a surfing trip to the Maldives, in the Indian Ocean, without Maggie, who was tied up with City issues. I returned two weeks later, tired from the flight, and fell into bed. The next morning, I got up and with a steaming cup of coffee in hand strolled out into the front yard, eager to check on the progress of a couple of aging avocado trees that I'd trimmed just before I left. As I walked down the steps from the house and crossed the driveway, I felt the sun, which filtered through a row of fir trees lining an easement beside the house. As I enjoyed the warmth of the summer sunshine, I began to realize that something had changed. Adorning the fence line on the eastern side of the yard, and standing like a bulwark against an invading army, lay not one, not two, but six brand new eight-feet-wide by twelve-feet-long and two-feet-high concrete enclosures.

I stared for a moment at the uniformity of this new construction rising from the ground, neatly stacked and cemented into separated stockades. But for what purpose? Still struggling to absorb the magnitude of this new addition, I strolled over to take a closer look, fully expecting that there would be some form of wildlife hopping, stepping, or slithering amongst the trampled remains of plants that had once proudly reached up to the heavens.

Carefully placing my coffee on one of the flat capstones that topped the walls, I peered into the first structure and saw the flattened grass and exposed dirt that made up the floor of the enclosure. From amongst the blades of grass, the small head of a box turtle stared back up at me. Close by was another. In the dirt, partially buried, was a third, while a fourth stopped its aquatic pursuits and peered up from a large, shallow container of water, which served as a hydration station as well as a venue for recreation.

In the corner of the enclosure stood a three-foot square box with a small opening cut into its side. I lifted the lid, and lo and behold, inside lay six more of the gang huddled beneath a heat lamp and blinking slowly, surprised by the sudden burst of sunlight from above.

I walked back to the house and waited for Maggie to wake up. When she did, I was waiting in the kitchen.

"What's the story behind those enclosures in the front?" I asked.

"Oh," she said. "I paid for those with the settlement from the Bowman case."

"That part's fine," I replied. "But what if I don't want them there?"

Needless to say, the heated argument that followed had little impact on the future of the enclosures. And as the weeks went by, they became further colonized by a growing population of lost, injured, or abandoned diapsids.

PART 7

The Biggest Struggle of All

CHAPTER 22

The Gathering Clouds

I want a new drug, one that won't spill
One that don't cost too much
Or come in a pill
Huey Lewis and the News – "I Want a New Drug"

A few weeks had passed since the council granted Russell Bowman and American Landscape the right to continue and to intensify operations across the road from our front door. Maggie had been busy contacting confidants about how to approach the San Diego Grand Jury with her concerns regarding the council's willingness to accept fraudulent information.

A complaint seemed to be the best way of obtaining a reversal of the council's decision, and, as a bonus, a black eye for the council majority might be in the offing. Maggie constructed the documentation, and we both agreed that I should submit it as a resident rather than have it come from a peer of the other sitting council members.

Maggie had done a stellar job. The complaint mapped out the agenda item and each of the fraudulent instruments that Russell Bowman had submitted in support of his appeal. Records of staff visits to the site, signed statements from the actual business owners, and the actions and comments made by the council members were all meticulously dated, documented, and serialized along with the recorded video of the council meeting. Maggie's background as a cataloger came in handy as the package looked like a well-constructed research paper.

The complaint was submitted, and we waited to see if the Grand Jury would see merit in its contents. Two weeks later I received a letter with a notice to appear at the courthouse in downtown San Diego. We drove down to the meeting where, after a short wait, we were ushered into a room with a large conference table that was surrounded by the members of the Grand Jury—all casually dressed and looking very informal, which was not what I'd expected. The group drilled us with questions for about an hour. And at the end of the meeting they told us we would be notified of their assessment.

We waited for five months with no word until Maggie finally contacted the jury foreperson and was told that the complaint had been handed over to the District Attorney's office, and that he could provide no further information at this time. Maggie then contacted the DA's office and was again told that they were not at liberty to give out any information. A month later, and only through Maggie's constant pursuit and contact with the DA's administrative staff, we managed to get a meeting with the lead investigator on the complaint.

Once again, we drove downtown, this time to the DA's office, where we were to meet with the investigator, and it wasn't long before a middle-aged man in shirt sleeves arrived. After the perfunctory greetings, he started to give us a broad overview of the lines of investigation he was pursuing. As he began to explain, it dawned on us that he was only talking about Russell Bowman and had wholly ignored the actions of the City Council. When we protested his lines of inquiry as being misplaced, he told us that if the behavior of the council was our concern, then that was an issue for the Grand Jury, not the DA's office. We looked at each other in amazement. Did the DA think we were that stupid? The Grand Jury's obligation was to look into the alleged wrongdoing of the City Council, and nothing they had said during our meeting with them indicated otherwise. To suggest for an instant that we had directed our complaint at Russell Bowman was a glaring deflection of the issue. We had just run full speed into the incompetence and bureaucracy of the county's legal system at its highest level. Or was there another reason?

Not one, but two of the most powerful entities within the legal community charged with protecting citizens from aberrant government behavior, had failed to do their jobs. Then it dawned on us. There was no question that our complaint to the Grand Jury explicitly focused on the City Council. Was the DA's office truly this inept, or was this a clumsy attempt to avoid holding the Encinitas City Council to account? We speculated about a connection involving the influence of Christie Guerin and her husband, a police captain, within the legal community. Still, without any substantiation, it just made for interesting conversation. The DA at the time, Bonnie Dumanis, had her sights set on higher civic office. And perhaps ruffling the feathers of some fellow politicians was an endeavor that she didn't want to touch for fear it would have repercussions on her campaign for county supervisor.

I resubmitted the same complaint to the Grand Jury, who replied that the last sitting jury had evaluated the issue and that as new members, they would not be reviewing the claim for a second time. Our fight, not only for us but for the right of due process for the residents of the city, had come to a screeching halt, evaporating through a fog of incompetence and finger-pointing, or perhaps something more sinister.

While the Grand Jury issue was in progress, a decision still had to be made about addressing Maggie's recent diagnosis of endometrial cancer. Chemo was the standard procedure, according to the oncologist. But, of course, there were no guarantees of a cure. And the side effects were potentially devastating and affected multiple functions of the body. We knew one potential side effect was a compromised immune system due to neutropenia, a situation where white blood cells are dramatically reduced, leading to an increased vulnerability to contracting a separate disease. The promise of joint pain and tinnitus, a constant ringing in the ears, were additional intimidating aspects of the treatment. Having no real experience with alternative therapies, it was with some reluctance that Maggie decided to go ahead with the chemo.

Our first visit to the infusion center at UCSD was like stepping into an alien holding tank where humans were the inventory. As we walked into the infusion area, we could see that some patients were gaunt and pale, having received their first treatment some time ago. Others looked robust and seemingly hearty. Many had their heads cloaked in beanies or scarves to cover up a lack of hair. A few individuals shuffled aimlessly around the room, simultaneously pushing on their chrome IV poles and using them for support. Each stand was topped with the omnipresent bag of poison that was slowly dripping into the patients' bloodstreams. Others sat alone in recliners, reading magazines or books as the drug cocktails bearing exotic names such as Paclitaxel and Carboplatin slipped effortlessly through the drip chambers, down the plastic tubing, and on through a needle inserted into a vein. Here it was introduced into the bloodstream, which allowed the heart to pump the toxic payload around the body.

As this was Maggie's first dose of chemo, the nurse led her to one of the rooms that contained a standard hospital bed. On the way, we passed other rooms where relatives hovered over prone patients. Next to where Maggie was to receive her first dose lay a pale-looking child who couldn't have been more than six years old. It was difficult to make out whether it was a boy or a girl. Below a bald head was a pair of sunken blue eyes in sockets ringed with gray, an indicator of the physical and mental stress of the whole ordeal. A young mother sat beside the bed reading from a book. As we passed, the child cast a weary glance our way, a look of fatigue coupled with resignation. Even the bright yellow pajamas adorned with cartoon characters failed to bring any joy into the room, and I realized that this was an equal opportunity disease that made no differentiation between the rich and the poor, black or white, young or old.

Maggie made herself comfortable on the bed while a cheery nurse bustled around preparing the patient for the chemicals that were to come. Administered first were the anti-nausea drugs. And after waiting an hour, the bag of fluid, which was the main event, arrived and was hooked to a pole beside the bed. With the insertion of a needle and a quick flick of the drip chamber, the chemo began its journey.

During the four-hour process, a series of visitors arrived to wish Maggie well. Some had unwittingly brought gifts of flowers that the receptionist swiftly intercepted at the check-in desk since they carry fungal spores that could impact immunocompromised patients.

After the visitors had departed, Maggie slipped into a shallow sleep until the procedure drew to a close. Before we left, the nurse delivered a series of dire warnings about avoiding fresh produce, nuts, flowers, and gatherings of people to minimize the chances of picking up an infection.

A few days later, back at the City wearing a protective mask, Maggie launched an initiative to protect the town's environment from non-native species with a proposal to list plants such as the castor bean, wild fennel, and acacia as unwelcome invaders who were not to be encouraged. At the same time, she joined a fight alongside the American Lung Association and a local group calling itself "Drug-Free Youth" to ban smoking from the beach's parks and trails within the city's boundaries. Stocks, Bond, and Dalager, meanwhile, were working on a pay raise for the newly appointed city manager, who would be a key player in the workings of the administration, and someone who could make life easy, or difficult, for any council member who lacked the backing of the majority bloc. This increase would not only raise the city manager's pay, but would also raise the hackles on the backs of several fiscal conservatives in the community. The new city manager had only been in the position for six months, and the proposed increase was a whopping 20 percent. The pay hike issue hit the next council meeting, where Stocks, Bond, and Dalager voted for its passage. Houlihan, and the newly elected Theresa Barth, who had claimed the seat vacated by Guerin in the 2006 midterm elections, voted against it.

A day or so later, I walked into the bathroom at home to find Maggie with a handful of her signature red hair sitting in the palm of her hand. I watched as she reached up and pulled out another clump. There was resignation in her face for a moment. But within minutes, she was talking about not trying to hide her baldness under a wig. She was going to wear a beanie hat.

An astute shopper and follower of fashion, she was also the most strategic and focused buyer I'd ever seen. A clothing purchase always had to be made during a sale and had to have the maximum markdown, even if it meant putting an article on layaway until the very last day of the offer. This approach had resulted in closets full of high-end clothing purchased at a fraction of their initial retail value. So the idea of picking up just one beanie hat was a non-starter. Sure enough, within weeks, there were patterned hats, single-color hats, hats with bobbles, hats with ears, and even a Hello Kitty hat that a friend had made by hand. There was a hat for every occasion—business, pleasure, fun, and formal—and the hats soon became a rotating fashion statement as she resumed a full workload.

A few weeks passed, and Maggie decided to contact the newspapers so they could inform the city's residents of her health situation. The next day the press came out with a front-page spread showing her wearing a beanie hat in the council chambers beneath a headline that read, "Thankful for the gift of life." In the interview, she warned her constituents that they had better get used to seeing the bald woman around town. Her feeling was that women shouldn't be so self-conscious that they have to wear wigs to conceal their disease. She went on to say that she would be prepared to step down if and when needed. Up to this point, however, she hadn't missed a council meeting, although she did attend a couple via conference call and two others while wearing a cotton mask to avoid infection. Maggie, grateful for all the support and well wishes she was receiving, chose this as her final quote in the article: "I could not have gotten through this without the support and love of my friends, family, and the community." After the article appeared, flowers and beanie hats started arriving in our mail or were hand-delivered by supportive friends and constituents.

Despite her illness, there was still the work of the City. Residents would bring their issues to specific council members who they thought would advocate for their causes. Maggie, of course, was the go-to person for anything animal related. And a new issue began to surface as complaints trickled in regarding the display and use of exotic species at civic events and street fairs. Coincidentally, the national news at the time was featuring clips of elephants becoming uncontrollable during circus events and at rides at fairs. Others showed chimpanzees attacking unwitting onlookers. And concerned citizens had been taking notice.

Frustrated at their lack of freedom and loss of connection to a family unit, while chained to posts, struck with bull hooks, or confined to cages, these wild animals were lashing out at their handlers, or, worse still, the audience that had come to see them perform. Customers of roadside zoos were also suffering injuries from monkeys, and scratches and bites from smaller mammals.

Maggie recognized the danger to human safety and the exploitation the animals were experiencing and she worked to ban the display of all exotic creatures at civic events. Since the council viewed the initiative as innocuous and a win for protecting residents, they voted to allow the ban to pass. The local paper ran a backhanded compliment in a cartoon, which showed an activist nailing a poster to a tree advertising the ban flanked by the cartoon characters Bambi, Thumper, and Smoky Bear. Above her head in a bubble were the words "Beat It!"

The 2008 election season was soon upon the city. And it arrived with its inevitable cast of indignant and maligned individuals dedicated to derailing the campaigns of their targeted candidates. As the season gathered momentum, a series of robocalls hit the community. One of them stood out. It was the work of Harry Eiler, who bore a grudge against Maggie for her supposed dismantling of a lecture series he had planned on city property. He was making it his mission to let the residents know how corrupt and evil candidate Houlihan truly was.

The unanswered question that always hung over these attempts to derail a campaign was, who was providing the money? Robocalls weren't cheap. In this case, was it Eiler himself, or had he been co-opted by one of the PAC's, or perhaps by a wealthy individual opposed to Maggie's agenda?

Eiler knew that the FPPC had issued the Houlihan campaign an earlier warning about inaccurate reporting of campaign contributions. Now he had what he considered to be the smoking gun necessary to remove her from office. On his robocalls he railed against Houlihan for failing to include the occupations of some of her donors in her financial disclosure forms and referenced an FPPC investigation that was "ongoing." He continued the call by saying that Houlihan had received a "troubling gift" in the form of a $1,000 cash payment, claiming the payment had been delivered in an unmarked envelope by Japanese officials during the sister city trip to Amakusa, Japan in 2004. As a parallel strategy, Eiler had taken this payment information and filed his own charge with the FPPC, saying that Houlihan had failed to disclose a gift.

Using information that was this specific—from an event that happened four years prior, at which he wasn't present—pointed to Eiler having acquired the details from another council member. Someone who had been on the same tour. How else could he have been privy to such detail? The other two council members on the trip were Guerin and Stocks. Both strongly opposed to any success Houlihan might attain, and both capable of seeding the election with information designed to denigrate their opponent and hopefully remove her from the council.

My suspicions led me to believe that the purveyor of the information was none other than Jerome Stocks, who had masterminded the media circus around the cat incident from the Japanese triathlon. He was probably seeking any avenue to paint his nemesis in a bad light. He even gave a quote to the newspapers saying, "There's no question, she took the money."

The reality was, of course, far different than the fabrications used to make the transaction look like payola. I was the one who had accepted the compensation. And yes, it had come in an envelope, which was indeed unusual. However, it was compensation arranged in advance to cover some of my expenses as the invited recreational athlete who would compete in the triathlon, as agreed before the trip. And our Japanese hosts had very thoughtfully taken the trouble to pay the amount in US dollars.

Maggie, once again, was forced to prove her innocence and took the issue to the city attorney, who, in turn, consulted with the FPPC. Following his communications with the commission, he delivered a statement that the FPPC had found "No impropriety." Eiler, of course, was not satisfied with this result and stepped up his fabrications claiming, "She gave the attorney false information, she is bad news."

Since the press was always interested in the wrinkles of election season, a reporter followed up with Eiler and dug deeper into his ongoing attacks. The reporter revealed that Eiler had executed the robocall using a professional agency. At the same time, he had placed an ad on the front page of a local publication touting the economic experience of his two favored members of the power bloc who were up for re-election, along with one other hand-picked member of the community who, if successfully elected, would create a new voting majority.

What Eiler had not bargained for were the very FPPC rules that he had used against Houlihan. They are very specific regarding contributions toward a political candidate's operations. And anyone who spends more than $1,000 on campaign activities, independent of the direct involvement of the candidate, must file a disclosure form with the commission.

When confronted with this requirement, Eiler said he'd yet to receive a bill for the robocall. Which by then had hit thousands of residents. And he said that the cost of the ad was under $600. Apparently, Eiler was sufficiently solvent that he didn't need to know the expense attached to the robocall, having given the agency carte blanche to call thousands of people, or his activities were being funded by another entity.

This latest barrage of misinformation fit into a strategy that the Stocks camp was executing, and they had chosen election season to strike. It was on the trip to Japan that Stocks had made a point of paying for his own airfare, an admirable and fiscally conservative act by any measure. However, he now spun this into a narrative and inferred that the airfares of other council members, specifically Maggie's, legitimately paid for as an approved expense, was, in fact, a dereliction of financial responsibility to the community. Painting himself as a prudent and conscientious servant of the residents, he inferred that Houlihan was exploiting taxpayer dollars—and once again used his cunning to portray her in an unfavorable light.

By now, the residents were starting to tire of the negativity emanating from City Hall. And a new school of activism was emerging from within the community with the mantra that fellow residents should not vote for the status quo of the incumbent majority. Instead, they should consider altering the makeup of the City Council. Slogans advising the community to vote against selected incumbents had an almost poetic ring, as signs appeared saying "No More Stocks and Bond." It was a typical election season, and it was coming down to the wire.

With a group of ten contenders for three seats, there was concern that such a broad field would split the vote and jeopardize the ability of the incumbents to get re-elected. By now, anyone following local politics knew the three candidates' platforms, not only as advertised, but also as revealed in their community involvement and as recorded in their votes on City issues.

As the mudslinging, misinformation, and complaints to the FPPC drew to a close, the polls opened. That evening, Maggie, along with her campaign team and supporters, gathered at a local restaurant to track the results as they trickled in. It was soon apparent that the residents approved of the quality of life and environmental focus of the two-term councilperson. And Maggie ended the evening in first place, garnering almost three percentage points more than Jerome Stocks. And nearly four percentage points over the third, and last, open seat–getter, James Bond. There would be no change in the division of power within the council for the next two years.

CHAPTER 23

High Crimes and Misdemeanors

All that money you made will never buy back your soul
Bob Dylan – "Masters of War"

It had been a couple of years since Maggie's initial diagnosis of cancer, but shortly after the results of the 2008 election were finalized, the same ominous symptoms of the disease began to reappear. She made an appointment to see the doctor, who promptly set about conducting a barrage of tests. The timing couldn't have been worse, as later that month she was on the council rotation to once again assume the position of mayor. Being next in line, however, didn't always guarantee appointment to the post. In the past, the council majority had shown a penchant for skipping unaligned councilors and randomly assigning the role to their more complementary colleagues. This made the passing of the gavel an annual crapshoot. The residents had seen this old routine enough times and showed up at the designated council meeting in droves to shame the council into doing the right thing. Maggie's supporters were a compelling sight, with their signs and speeches. The council majority, seeing that they would get a black eye if they didn't follow protocol, voted her in.

That same day, Maggie had gone down to the hospital to go over the results of her recent tests. Due to work commitments, I hadn't been able to attend the meeting. When we met that evening outside the council chambers, I could instantly tell by the expression on her face that her appointment had brought bad news. Her face was taut. And when she saw me, her attempt at a smile was overridden by the fear in her eyes. As we drew close amongst the crush of her supporters, she whispered, "The cancer's back." And I could see she was fighting back tears. Later that night, she gave me the stark details, malignant uterine neoplasm with peritoneal thickening along the surface of the liver. In short, the cancer had returned, and it was stronger than ever. By now, she had gone through chemo, her red hair had fallen out and regrown silver, and she was bearing the side effects of the treatment with neuropathic pain in her feet, sore joints, and the constant ringing of tinnitus in her ears.

The doctor's recommendation was to undergo another round of the same chemo, to which she reluctantly agreed. And so a rinse-and-repeat cycle of visits to the infusion center occurred. During the next few weeks, she suffered through a lack of appetite, hair loss, and having to be on guard for infectious carriers.

Throughout this second phase, as with the first, she continued her city functions and responsibilities, never missing a council meeting. She did whatever it took to maintain her perfect record, attending a couple over the telephone to avoid infection. For my part, I was promoted from part-time animal keeper to full time, cleaning cages, emptying cat litter trays, and picking up the dog poop. A few volunteers from the community would come by to help on their days off as we managed our way through her recovery from a second round of pharmaceuticals.

2008 had been a year of mixed fortunes, with cancer topping the list of negatives. Maggie and her campaign treasurer had also received a slap on the wrist from an earlier technicality; the professions of some of her donors had not been entered on the financial disclosure forms, a step required by the Fair Political Practices Commission.

One of the highlights was the opening of a brand-new city library. It was an event near and dear to Maggie's heart as she had worked in the UCSD library system for the first part of her career. The library was an initiative that had started before her time in office, but it was one that she embraced. She eagerly joined the fight to situate the building on its planned site overlooking the city and the Pacific Ocean, which was against the wishes of some dissenting groups who wanted it built inland and in a less scenic spot. This vantage point made it a landmark for residents and visitors alike. Here, people could study and conduct research or just relax with a book while enjoying a million-dollar view and a cup of coffee.

With 2008 now over, it was 2009 that saw an agenda item come in front of the council that would lead to one of Maggie's most committed adversaries receiving his day of reckoning. The local Chamber of Commerce had a contract with the City to operate a visitors' center, and the contract was up for renewal. Maggie, knowing the importance of visitors to the local economy, had become concerned about the operations of the center and she saw the need to raise these concerns during the renewal discussions.

The Chamber had violated its current contract by closing the center on weekends, arguably the most crucial time for it to be available to visitors. No one communicated this to the council. It had also failed to report a high staff turnover rate. And, into the bargain, the bureau was running a poorly maintained website while providing outdated promotional materials to anyone looking for city attractions.

Maggie lambasted Chamber officials for these and other deficiencies, which included the firing of all of their volunteers and publishing a politically biased Chamber newsletter. This last item was not surprising since the Chamber board member behind the publication was none other than Michael Andreen. "This is not what the taxpayers are paying for!" Maggie exclaimed to the Chamber officials.

Two months earlier, the group's executive director, Gary Tucker, had resigned four days before his scheduled performance review, citing differences with the board. It was a decision that would prove timely based upon what was to come. In a newspaper article, he claimed that he had been personally maligned by Houlihan's accusations, stating, "I put a lot of blood, sweat, and tears into that organization, and I really take offense to having it publicly knocked in a way that wasn't fair." These words would come back to haunt him when the council added a requirement to the new contract that would result in both Tucker and Andreen's undoing. They required the Chamber to conduct an audit of its finances using an objective and independent outside accounting firm.

The council then moved to renew the contract, and in due course the Chamber hired the independent CPA firm of CFO To-Go, which set about combing through the organization's books. A few weeks later, the Chamber released the results of the audit, and the press got a hold of it. The details were startling. The Chamber had closed the visitors' center on weekends due to a cash shortage. Again, no one had communicated to the council that taxpayer funds from a grant allocated to operate the visitors' center had been exhausted.

The report went on to reveal a pattern of co-mingling of funds, diversion of specific use funds, and the use of funds in such a way as to provide financial benefit to a board member. Specifically accused of the mismanagement of funds were former CEO Gary Tucker and Marketing Director Mike Andreen. People soon began to put two and two together and saw Tucker's resignation as a tacit admission of guilt. Andreen had also resigned shortly after Tucker left but had continued to work for the association as a contractor.

Damaging information in the financial review included evidence that $18,500 was designated to buy out an existing copier lease. However, the money had been used as "cash flow" during the last four months of Tucker's tenure. The report then called into question the financial benefit Andreen received from being a member of the board. He'd received $78,584 for "various business-related transactions." This amount included $1,200 a month in "draw against commission" for recruiting new members. However, no evidence existed to reconcile this amount with actual revenue from any new membership dues. The report concluded that Andreen had been paid 53 percent of all membership commissions from January through May of the year under review.

Now that the cat was out of the bag, other members of the board stepped forward claiming that Tucker and Andreen had acted like a two-person show in operating the organization, consistently disregarding the concerns and directives of the board. "They were bullies," one former member said. "It was a good old boy system, and you didn't want to get in their way." When asked why the board did not call for Tucker or Andreen to resign, one member cited fear of retribution.

All this talk of Andreen's bullying and intimidation came as no surprise to Maggie, or to the other politicians who had suffered through his attacks in the past. And it was only appropriate that by raising the issues surrounding the visitor center, she had inadvertently exposed a person who was misappropriating taxpayers' money.

Shortly after the report came out, Andreen cut ties with the Chamber and started a competing business organization on the other side of town, calling it the New Encinitas Network. Despite the press coverage that indicated he was not a person to be trusted, many business owners still signed up.

As a final slap on the way out of the Chamber's door, Andreen played the card he knew how to wield best and threatened to sue anyone who took the audit report any further, even suggesting a grand jury investigation. As a result, the fear and intimidation that Andreen was so adept at casting stifled any further steps to hold the duo accountable.

Maggie, typically not one to gloat over another person's misfortunes, took great delight in poring over all of the reporting surrounding the nefarious activities of her antagonist.

With a third election in the history books, we both turned our attention to cancer and its many causes and possible remedies. It became clear from my research that, although not actively promoted by Western medicine, diet could be a factor in surviving the disease. The question was, why hadn't Maggie's strict vegetarian regimen, a by-product of her devotion to animals and the environment, kept her from getting the disease in the first place? Further research into cures inevitably favored the pharmaceutical solutions of the day. And it took a deeper dive to discover alternatives to the conventional methods most commonly recommended by western medical doctors.

As my digging sidestepped the copious promotions for chemical or radioactive cures, I discovered that the advocates for alternative therapies promoted regimens that employed raw, fresh organic foods, juicing vegetables, and strict avoidance of sugar and the chemicals found in most processed foods, along with all animal protein. With this new information, both of us set about adhering to an even more rigorous regimen. The first thing to go was the sugary caramel coffee drinks from Starbucks, which Maggie loved. Instead, we relied on a more austere rotation of wheatgrass shots, salads, steamed vegetables, and vegetable juice, made possible by the purchase of a sizeable commercial juicer. This was an appliance that consumed most of the kitchen counter and looked more like a model of the Starship Enterprise than a kitchen appliance. When this beast was turned on, the whole house vibrated, and you could barely hold a conversation over the noise. The machine spat out juice by the quart in seconds, but there was one big downside. If the juicer's cargo was not correctly balanced, the entire mechanism would shake as if caught in a 6.0 earthquake and start to work its way off the counter, all the while spewing juice and vegetable particles all over the kitchen wall. The waste chute, directed toward a bucket placed on the floor, chucked out the after-products of the event like a bilge pump on a small fishing vessel. Woe betide the person who didn't ensure that the aim of the chute was directly into the bucket, or the next hour would be spent picking shredded vegetable matter from the floor and the walls, where it would lodge itself in the grout between the tiles.

Exercise was another recommendation, but with peripheral neuropathy and joint pain now firmly established, most forms of athletic endeavor were out of the question. Stress emerged as a co-conspirator in the genesis of the illness. But stress was unavoidable if Maggie were to continue her role on the City Council. We talked about her resigning. But she was adamant that her work on behalf of the residents would continue no matter the outcome of the disease. So we looked to identify other potential causes and remedies.

The location of our house, which stood within two hundred feet of a busy freeway, had always been a probable factor. Pollution, and exposure to the types of carcinogens that vehicle traffic kicks up, such as Benzene, were known causes of certain types of cancer. However, selling up and moving out was not realistic as a short-term goal. What would we do with the flocks, herds, packs, and swarms that made up our animal-scape, all of them happily munching through their lazy days spent in the front yard?

As we continued, I stumbled across several reminders of the importance of prostate cancer screening for men over fifty. And since I was in that age band and had not been tested, I reluctantly decided to make an appointment with my MD. Although I must confess that the prospect of another male evaluating any of my body's cavities using an outstretched finger did little to encourage the phone call.

While I was wrestling with the indignity of such an encounter, Maggie's usual hectic pace of attending civic events, ribbon cuttings, animal functions, and educational sessions slowed. But she still willed herself to participate in important occasions, even if it meant just showing up for the introductions before becoming exhausted and having to leave. When she couldn't drive, City staff members would drop by the house with documents for her to read and sign, and she would go over City emails, agenda items, and reports on her laptop while in bed. Friends would drop by to drive her on errands, or for fun local trips when time and her strength permitted as she was now starting to grow weak.

Looking to educate others on what she'd discovered during her experience with the disease, she created a series of lectures for presentation at the new city library. As she gathered leaders in the field of oncology, all from her alma mater of UCSD, her goal was to introduce residents to these local physicians and to enlighten them about early detection and treatment options. Over five months, she helped educate the community on breast, prostate, and lung cancer. She also took the lead in a session that showed attendees how to research information using the latest online databases, so that a committed researcher could delve into specialized medical resources from around the world all from the comfort of home.

For my part, my date with destiny arrived, and I showed up at the doctor's office for my prostate exam. During the typical extended stay in the waiting room, I picked up some of the same magazines that seemed to adorn each of the medical offices that I'd visited in recent months. I began to wonder if all doctors spent their spare time playing golf. My musings were interrupted as I was ushered into the examination room. The doctor arrived shortly after and fired off several questions related to whether I had any of the common symptoms that came with prostate problems. I answered each of his questions in the negative and quietly wondered if it would be possible to test out of the physical part of the exam that was now looming large. "Stand up and remove your trousers and lean on the bed," came the instructions. I considered concocting some excuse about needing to go to the bathroom so I could exit the room and make a break for the parking lot. But instead, I dutifully fumbled with my belt and carefully lowered my apparel while turning to lean on the bed.

As I was performing my part of the ritual, I caught the doctor out of the corner of my eye reaching for a box of beige-colored latex gloves. He removed a pair and expertly snapped them onto each hand before squeezing a copious amount of clear goop onto his right index finger. I pictured the scenario in my mind. Here I was, doubled over the bed like a Thanksgiving turkey, awaiting the advancing figure of the doctor who was brandishing his lubricant-swathed digit like a modern-day broadsword.

I tried not to pucker, but the urge was too great. This was the last bastion of privacy, and my derriere was not about to give in without a fight. "This might feel a bit cold," said the doctor. What I heard was that this was my last chance to duck the slippery offender heading in my direction. But alas, it was too late. He was right about the cold. After that, there was relatively little discomfort as he probed around in front of my bladder, eager to find any irregularities in the walnut-sized gland that is responsible for a diagnosis of cancer for one in nine males during their lifetimes.

After a few seconds, which felt more like minutes, the doctor withdrew his finger and snapped off the gloves while gathering up enough tissue paper to wrap Macy's entire inventory of Christmas gifts. I huddled by the wastebasket, rapidly trying to get rid of the oily goo that covered my rear end so I could once again feel the security of being fully clothed. "I can't find anything that seems out of the ordinary, no lumps, no hardening, it all seems to be fine." I breathed a sigh of relief. "I do think that at your age, it would be a good idea to have a blood test just to make sure," he added."

"OK," I replied, no big deal. Although at that point I would have agreed to wash his car just to get out of the office. He scribbled down a number on a pad of paper and told me to call and make an appointment. "I'll send in the order, so leave it a day before you contact them."

Dutifully agreeing to follow all of his instructions, I grabbed the piece of paper, thanked the doc, and made my way out through the waiting room, hoping that I'd removed all the goo before I'd put my pants back on. It must have been six weeks later that I finally decided to go and have a blood test. By that time, it was convenient, and I thought I might as well get a final confirmation that I was in the clear.

CHAPTER 24

Kitchengate

And if I claim to be a wise man,
then it surely means that I don't know.
Kansas – "Carry on my Wayward Son"

There was never any shortage of drama at City Hall, where the lines were drawn between the agenda of the special interests and the needs of the residents. And with election season over, the first contentious issue was the how to rotate the position of Mayor amongst the council members as Maggie's one-year term was expiring. The ploy of sidestepping the next logical person in the interests of political disagreement had by now become an occasional tool in the majority's back pocket.

Sure enough, this time around the bloc decided to skip Maggie's newly elected and left-leaning partner on the council, Teresa Barth, and instead appointed Dan Dalager to the role. One of the reasons given for this anomaly was that Maggie had cancer. No one I spoke to could quite wrap their heads around this rationalization, as it was Maggie who had the cancer, not Teresa. What wasn't mentioned was that there had been an earlier complaint of sexual harassment from Barth toward Jerome Stocks which may have influenced the snub However, it didn't deter the steamrolling majority from installing Dan as the new leader of the council.

Dan had always lived in the town and prided himself on his family's local roots and he enjoyed dispensing his hometown wisdom to anyone willing to listen. Dan's aw-shucks approach to his role as a council member included showing up to civic events with his work clothes on. These included a bowling shirt with his name embroidered on the breast and a soiled pair of work pants. It was all part of a presentation designed to show that he was just an ordinary guy unchanged by his new role as a civic leader.

Contrary to this persona, on the dais, he would often quote from the French diplomat, political scientist, and historian Alexis De Tocqueville, who had written the book *Democracy in America*. His quotes, plucked directly from the text, were typically injected into the discourse at council meetings to accentuate a point he was making. But the academic change of pace often seemed out of sync coming from someone who portrayed himself as a blue-collar worker. Three years earlier, Dan had hit the headlines by calling the annual holiday parade the Christmas parade. Now he hit the headlines again, but not for introducing controversial changes to the traditions of the city. This time it involved his financial dealings.

Following his election, Dan had accepted a loan from a friend and fellow longtime resident, Dan Shelley. To seal the deal, Dalager and his wife had put up their home as collateral. However, the loan was never disclosed, which was a requirement of state law: Dan's disclosure document, Form 700, a standard submission for all politicians, made no mention of the loan, even though the questionnaire included a section for divulging income, loans, and business positions.

Three months after borrowing the money, Dan cast the only vote on the council in favor of a builder's appeal to avoid $225,380 in development fees. It was Shelley who had previously owned the 5.25 acres on which the builder planned to build ten homes. And it was Shelley who supported the builder's position by petitioning the council to reduce the fees to $125,000 from $350,000. Even the pro-development majority couldn't stomach this giveaway of taxpayer funds and nixed the proposal. Dan's vote wafted through the council chambers like a bad smell. When questioned by a reporter about Shelley and his vote, he downplayed the situation. When the journalist tried to dig deeper, he quickly terminated the conversation.

While his vote was undergoing scrutiny, the press discovered another source of alleged aberrant behavior regarding Dan's work for a local bank. Following a public records request, a reporter identified several complaints filed with the FPPC, one of which claimed that "Dalager uses his position as Mayor to recruit customers for the bank by strong-arming people doing business with the City." Dalager, eager to cover his tracks, realized this side job was not on his disclosure form and quickly submitted an amended version. In it, he specified that he had a "consulting" business whose primary focus was public relations.

It's never a good thing, as a public figure, to garner the attention of the press when it comes to questionable activities. Investigative reporters tend to peel back the layers of the onion in their quest to find other mischiefs that might interest their readers, and so it was with Dan. It wasn't long before he gave them what they were looking for. In a conversation, he bragged to a reporter about a "free kitchen" he'd received for his home. Of course, this slip of the tongue was not missed by an alert journalist who immediately smelled a story and began to dig deeper.

The reporter's research linked Dan's off-the-cuff comment to an appliance store owner by the name of Mathew Gordon. Gordon lived in a multi-million-dollar house on the nearby bluffs that overlooked the ocean and had provided Dalager with a stovetop, wall oven, and range hood for $137.93. These were units that at full retail had a value of around $1,400. When the "gift" was exposed, the rationalizations for such a low price came thick and fast—both from the giver and from the recipient. Gordon described them as "scrap," older models with no value to him because they were damaged or returned. Dalager stated that it was all "old crap," but the reporter wasn't deterred.

The story hit the newspapers like another episode in an ongoing soap opera. Gordon, the owner of Aztec Appliance in San Diego, told the reporter it was Dalager who suggested the "$150" price tag. A separate reporter, who had visited Dan's home and had seen the new units, wrote, "The brushed-steel stove setup looked pretty sleek, modern, and functional to me. In short, this is the best cooking crap I've ever seen."

Dan, for his part, continued to claim that he'd not received any special treatment. He even produced an invoice for the three appliances he bought from Aztec. However, the document contained an anomaly: a pick-up date of August 18, two days after the reporter had started to ask questions about the transaction.

The newspapers, blogs, and social media piled in. "Dalager into the Frying Pan." "Encinitas Mayor Feels the Heat in His Kitchen." And the most damning of all, "Dalager: DA Is Probing Claims." What prompted this headline was a series of events that provided reasonable evidence of a quid pro quo arrangement between the two, although both parties vehemently denied it.

After the "Kitchengate" transaction had taken place, Mathew Gordon registered an appeal with the City against a demand that he remove a garden wall he'd constructed on his multi-million-dollar bluff-top property. The wall had encroached on the public's right of way and prevented them from parking in front of his house. It was, therefore, an illegal addition. The City had given him notice to remove the intrusion, and he had spent two years appealing the decision. When the council voted on the issue, it was a split decision of two versus two with Dalager being one of the votes in support of Gordon. Councilmember Stocks recused himself, as Gordon was a client of his insurance business. With no majority in favor of Gordon, the wall had to come down, but not before yet another bizarre twist in the story arrived in the form of a complaint presented by Gordon's wife, Robin.

Robin Gordon submitted a bizarre and rambling grievance to the city attorney in which she stated her goal of postponing the order to remove the wall until the council could evaluate the basis for her complaint. According to the letter, Robin Gordon had employed a "professional investigator" to look into the affairs of council member Maggie Houlihan. The accusation included two fuzzy black-and-white photographs of Houlihan, apparently taken one hour before she voted against Gordon's appeal. The first showed her exiting her parked vehicle in front of their house. The second was a grainy image of her leaving the residence after the visit. However, the second picture showed Maggie carrying a package, something that wasn't evident when she entered the home. After a strange and seemingly irrelevant disclosure that the house was in a trust where she was the trustee and her husband had no ownership in the property, she began the complaint.

She claimed that the photographs showed Maggie picking up gifts that Ms. Gordon had brought back from a recent trip to India. Gifts that Maggie had allegedly asked her to procure during a luncheon they had had back in December of the previous year. Based on this "friendship," and presumably the delivery of the gifts, she expressed her concern that Maggie had not recused herself from the vote on the notorious wall. She then went into medical details of how people who have undergone chemo can have memory lapses. She included references to the famous singer "Kelly Mingoue." I can only assume that Ms. Gordon meant Kylie Minogue, the Australian singer. Maybe the incorrect spelling was a lapse of memory. She also referenced skater Scott Hamilton and provided a link to some scholarly articles on post-chemo conditions.

The complaint continued with examples of Maggie allegedly not knowing what was behind the gate at the Gordons' home, and that she had to ask the Engineering Department at the City if they knew. Her point was that Maggie had been to her house and should have known what was behind the gate. However, the full context of councilperson Houlihan's inquiry to the engineering staff didn't appear in her letter.

Ms. Gordon then stated that Maggie had accused her, in the press, of bribery, an accusation that, strangely enough, had never appeared in print. The real intent of her complaint then came front and center, and it was in the form of a Hail Mary designed to secure the illegal wall for their property. She requested that Ms. Houlihan's vote be rescinded or canceled. This request, if granted, would, of course, change the two versus two votes, to two votes for and only one against, thereby nullifying the council's denial of her husband's appeal.

After giving examples of her social interactions with Maggie, she concluded with the statement, "My friendship is always open to her even if she has forgotten it." Maggie was astonished by the accusations, having been, at best, a passing acquaintance of the Gordons during the execution of her political duties. Needless to say, the City summarily dismissed the curious complaint. And the decision of the council remained intact.

Meanwhile, not deterred by the storm swirling around him, Dan Dalager employed the often-used political tool of engaging the media to fire back against his accusers. An article by Dan appeared in the Community Commentary section of the local press titled "Highlighting the Positive Amidst the Negative Council Campaigning." In it, he touted his and the council's achievements before launching an attack on his "political opponents, who were trying to tear me down right before the [upcoming] election." He went on to complain about the "nasty negative politics" at the national level coming to our small town. Hitting his stride, he then attempted to deflect all the damning information that was coming out about him in the press by pinning it all on his opponents—specifically, those who disagreed with his votes on a city park and a nearby hospital expansion. His final rallying call in the op-ed piece asked for the residents' "continued faith and support." And he concluded with the rallying cry, "Together we will make Encinitas an even better place to live." I was left to ponder his grasp on the seriousness of the legally suspect position he'd put himself in. And now here he was telling the residents that it was all the dirty work of his political opponents.

In another article regarding the state's investigation into his miscreant behavior, he stated, "The FPPC was just about done with it and didn't find anything. I'm glad it's with the DA now; they're closer. It's been fun working with them." His final statement on the DA's investigation read, "These things, they're just used as a way of smearing a person, and they can't be cleaned up until afterward."

When the election rolled around in November 2010, Dan's extra-curricular activities resulted in his defenestration from the council. The electorate had had enough. In February of the following year, he pled guilty to breaking state conflict of interest laws and was fined $1,000 and sentenced to three years' probation as part of a plea deal. Gordon escaped any charges, as the DA couldn't prove beyond a doubt that a quid-pro-quo agreement had occurred.

CHAPTER 25

A Mystery of Holy Proportion

Where the sunset falls, where the sunset dies
She gave me love, she told me lies
That most mischievous ghost
She was in disguise, she was in disguise, she was in disguise
Elvis Costello – "Mischievous Ghost"

With all the hanky panky taking place on the council front, it was a masterful act of civil and artistic mischief that would capture the community's attention with an act of exquisite design and clinical execution.

On the morning of April 23, 2011, residents awoke to a town that had been mysteriously visited by the Virgen de Guadalupe. It was not a religious sighting, or a ghostly manifestation in the form of her image on a piece of toast. This appearance was more tangible. And it arrived in the form of a complete ten-foot-by-ten-foot mosaic featuring the deity herself standing on a white surfboard, hands clasped in prayer, with her green cloak afloat on the wind behind her. The piece had been erected the previous afternoon, by what had at first appeared to be two workers from the City's Engineering Department. As it turned out, these supposed City employees were the artist and his partner in crime. The two rascals had emerged the previous day clothed in bright-green safety vests and regulation hard hats to install the artwork in plain sight of anyone passing by. And they garnered about as much attention as any other legitimate City worker. The duo had cleverly installed the substantial piece on one of the supporting walls of a span of railroad overpass that crossed the main road into the city. The wall now provided the background for the Surfing Madonna, complete with wetsuit booties to protect her extremities from the cold. Down one side of the mosaic read the slogan "Save the Ocean."

Word soon spread, and the news ignited a procession of residents and tourists all eager to view the religious "miracle." Pilgrims were seen eagerly snapping the obligatory selfies so they could display their proximity to such a soulful creation on social media. Others brought flowers and candles. And it wasn't long before the space beneath the bridge began to look more like a shrine than a shady support for the city's main rail artery. Whether they liked the Surfing Madonna or not, no one could ignore the chutzpah of the perpetrators for pulling off such an audacious act of civil disobedience.

It wasn't long before news of this latest addition to the city's art scene reached the City. And the media gathered to find out how the council was going to deal with this new, and unplanned, attraction. Graffiti was the judgment from the authority. Mayor James Bond informed the public that there was an established process for getting permission to display art in public. And that the artists had not followed the correct procedures. His comments suggested that the Madonna was heading for a wipeout, and the community nervously awaited news from the discussions that would follow.

Maggie had an established history of supporting the arts along with local organizations, such as Arts Alive and the Artists' Colony. She was privately delighted at the act and quickly drove down to take a look. In public, she explored ways that the piece could be relocated since the bridge would not be a feasible option due to safety concerns.

As the discussions continued, experts were summoned to evaluate how to remove the mosaic without damaging it. During their analysis, they uncovered a signature on a remote segment of the background, and the name Mark Patterson was exposed.

With the jig clearly up, the artist and erstwhile engineer duly stepped out from the shadows to not only accept the consequences of his actions, but also ensure that the mosaic's removal didn't result in any damage to the finely interwoven pieces of stone and glass that made up the scene. In interviews, Mark expressed his desire to give the mural to the city, even though there had been several substantial financial offers to purchase it.

Maggie contacted Mark, and it wasn't long before she came home, clutching a selfie featuring a beaming council member shoulder to shoulder with the smiling artist. She and others talked with people in the arts community about how to find a home for the piece, and an idea soon emerged to post it at the entrance to one of the city's beaches. However, with the depiction of a religious theme, the separation of church and state was blurred. That location was nixed. In the meantime, Mark was fined $500 for the illegal activity along with $6,000 in costs to have the piece removed.

After much hand-wringing and multiple offers of real estate upon which to post the mosaic, it traveled to an interim location before finding its first real home on a wall adjoining a nearby coffee shop. Later on, it would make its way onto its current resting place on the side of a pizza restaurant, only a few feet away from its original illegal roost. For her involvement, Mark made Maggie a small mosaic as a memento of an adventure that would, in time, turn into a successful 501c3 nonprofit organization called the Surfing Madonna Oceans Project. Today this nonprofit hosts beach runs and other events to raise funds for multiple charities, including the disabled, special needs kids, veterans, marine mammal rescue, and coastline protection. What had started as a prank had become an enduring source of civic pride and charitable giving.

CHAPTER 26

Two for the Price of One

I stare into
Some great abyss
And calculate
The things I'd miss
If I could only
Make some sense of this
Sheryl Crow – "Make It Go Away"

T he appointment for my cancer blood test was in the same modern five-story glass and concrete building that Maggie visited for her chemo infusions. I checked in and took my seat in the waiting room, selecting a magazine from the stack of periodicals that lay on a nearby table. Sifting through the wad, I purposely avoided the golf journals and picked up one that focused on travel. With all the golf articles I'd read in medical establishments, Tiger Woods had begun to feel more like a family member than a sporting icon, and by now I could hold an informed conversation regarding his problems with his tee shot, his contract with Nike, and even the seamier side of his private life.

As I waited, the daily procession of patients showing up for their infusion of chemicals shuffled past. I assumed that the few who still had hair and sported healthy complexions must be newbies. The others appeared pale and gaunt, some behind cotton facemasks to guard against infection and many wearing a headscarf or beanie hat, the uniform of a long-term cancer patient. The cheerful staff welcomed many of them more like regulars at the local pub than beleaguered patients fighting for their lives. However, their chipper *Hi, Mr. or Ms. X* rarely received the same upbeat response.

Eventually, my name rang out over the intercom, and I went into a room where four chairs were flanked by phlebotomists busily working on extracting blood from their unsmiling visitors. "Name? Date of birth?" Everything checked out, and after the application of a rubber tourniquet and the insertion of a needle into an accommodating vein, the small vial on the end of the syringe slowly filled with deep-red fluid. It only took a couple of minutes, and I was soon in the parking lot and on my way back to work.

At home, Maggie was preparing her speech for Saturday's Surfrider Foundation awards ceremony, where she was going to receive the Clean Water Award for her work in protecting local water resources. Work that included a smoking ban on the city's beaches, a tax to support clean water initiatives, and protection for the nearby shoreline, bays, and watersheds. The smoking ban had been hard-fought, while the clean water tax had ultimately failed. But her advocacy and tireless efforts had caught the attention of Surfrider, who tracked the work and voting records of local politicians when it came to ocean-related activities.

The following week the doctor's office called to let me know my blood test results were in and that the doctor would like to schedule an appointment to go over them. It occurred to me that this was a bit elaborate since they could have told me the results over the phone. Still, I dutifully made an appointment for later that week. As with most people waiting to find out information from a doctor, I wondered why he wanted to go over the findings. Had the analysis confirmed that cancer was present? Had the test revealed some other issue besides cancer? Was this just a formality to tell me about some problems with cholesterol or a lack of iron?

I showed up at the office on the appointed date and walked into the same room where the notorious latex glove assault had occurred. A few minutes later, the doctor came in, clutching the standard manila folder under his arm.

After some brief small talk, he got into the analysis of the results. He gave me the background on the protein-specific antigen, or PSA, test, a procedure that provides an indicator as to whether or not cancer is present. "For a man of your age, your PSA should be in the range of 0 to 4," said the doctor. "Your results show you have a PSA of 44." It didn't take long to realize that this was not the confirmation of robust health that I was expecting.

After a moment of thought and using my best matter-of-fact voice, I asked the doctor the obvious question. "So, is this a death sentence?"

"No," he replied. "I've had patients in here with a PSA of a thousand, and I have a much different conversation with them. I'd like you to go for a biopsy to confirm what is going on, and if there is something, then we need to know what stage of development it's at." He gave me a number to call, and with that, the appointment was over.

This wasn't welcome information because at the time, Maggie was starting to have trouble breathing and had scheduled some scans to see what was causing the problem. Her news was equally as disappointing; the diagnosis was a pleural effusion, which is a build-up of fluid in the membrane that sits just outside the lungs. And it had begun to restrict her ability to breathe. The subsequent visit to the hospital entailed a doctor inserting a large needle into her back so that it would enter the pleural area in a procedure called a thoracentesis. The fluid was then drained off into a large plastic bladder, which ended up filled with over two pints of amber liquid. The norm for fluid in this area of the lungs is four teaspoonfuls. Her response was immediate: "It feels like I can breathe again," she said as we made our way out through the lobby. *Good news,* I thought, *but for how long?*

At this stage, I could see that the clouds were gathering. Maggie's diagnosis had escalated, and we were now dealing with malignant neoplasm of corpus uteri, excluding isthmus. The cancer was growing stronger, and it was invading other areas of her body. The names of the drugs she was taking began to read like a chapter from the *Selected Works* of Cicero: Lidocaine, Prilocaine, Aprepitant, Dexamethasone, Heparin, and on and on. Inserted into her upper chest was a port catheter containing a valve to which the drug delivery mechanism could be attached, thereby facilitating the introduction of chemicals into her body. The upside of a port was that it eliminated the need for the multiple injections that would otherwise be necessary. The downside was that the patient had a plastic valve stuck in the upper left quadrant of their chest.

The fluid removed from her lung was sent to the lab for analysis, and sure enough, the pathologist confirmed that it contained "abundant aggregates of pleomorphic, malignant glandular cells." In other words, there was a lot of cancer in the fluid. It was apparent at this stage that the multiple efforts made by the medical community to cure her disease had failed. What was worse, the procedures she'd endured had made matters worse and were now shortening her life.

What was becoming evident was that Maggie was going to die. The only question left was one that no doctor seemed able or willing to pin down: how long did she have? And how much time did I have to spend with a woman who, through a simple twist of fate, had become my wife, friend, confidant, and lover?

Typically, when at home, Maggie was always busy, reading documents, talking on the phone, tending to animals, or watching the occasional late-night TV show. One evening I spied her lying on the couch in the front room staring off into space, chewing on the side of her thumb. It must have been that time when a person comes to terms with their future and reflects on their mortality. When thoughts turn to the experience of dying and what life has meant. And to the world that will be left behind.

Without the fluid in her lungs, Maggie's strength, along with her spirits, rose. And she continued her breakneck involvement with City issues and the ongoing fight for the rights of those without a voice. For my part, I'd undergone the recommended biopsy, and the diagnosis was very aggressive prostate cancer. Surgery would be the next step, and a week later, I went under the knife. After returning home, I awaited the analysis on eleven lymph nodes that had been extracted, along with the prostate. It turned out that seven of them turned out to be cancerous, which meant the disease was spreading. In technical terms, the cancer had metastasized.

Later that week, I asked a visitor to take a picture of the two of us standing in the front yard. It was a glorious late-spring day with the sun filtering through the branches of a majestic Jacaranda tree that cast its shade over the front garden. The picture shows a smiling Maggie wearing her pale-green Disney pajamas along with a completely bald head, the result of her second round of chemo. For my part, I'm wearing a T-shirt and shorts while modeling a Foleys catheter, an appliance that was busily draining urine from my bladder into a large plastic bag that hung down below the hemline of my shorts. Not a shot for the typical family album.

If there was one bright light amidst the gathering gloom filled with doctor's visits, drugs, and test results, it was that on two occasions, Maggie got to meet her newborn grandson, Charlie Oliver. Chris and his wife. Laura, brought their new baby down for a visit and, on a separate trip, Maggie was strong enough to fly to Sun Valley, Idaho to spend some time with the family and take in the natural beauty of the area, with Charlie Oliver being spoiled and fawned over by his grandmother as only a grandmother can.

I looked at the two of them as she hoisted the child into her arms and reflected on the contrast between one approaching the finality of her time on earth and the other just embarking on his journey into a world where he would cut an as yet unknown path.

During the following weeks, I underwent regular blood tests to ensure that my PSA count stayed close to zero. It turned out that this was not the case. And the PSA number started to creep up. This meant the surgery had failed. The next step was a thirty-day course of radiation. The goal was to stem the march of the disease by killing off the last of the cancer cells that were floating around uncontested within my body.

When I was finished being zapped, and a waiting period had expired, I went in for more tests. Maggie and I returned a week later to discuss the results with the doctor. The news wasn't good. The oncologist informed me that the procedures had not stopped the cancer. I asked what the probable passage of events would be from here and was told that the disease would manifest itself in the bones or a major organ, at which time I would receive palliative care, which was the last mile before boarding the bus to paradise. "How long?" I asked. "Five years, maybe more," came the professionally vague reply. There we sat. Now both of us had had our tickets punched for Never Never Land.

Over the next few weeks, I became increasingly disillusioned with Western medicine, and I was not about to embark on a series of hormone treatments that the doctor recommended. Having experienced them once before, just before the initial surgery, I was familiar with all the hideous side effects they brought: weight gain, hot flushes, and a lack of stamina. After my earlier experience with these drugs, no one could accuse me of not being sympathetic to women when they undergo the female change of life.

With all the money spent in the medical sphere, here I was facing two strikeouts. Both my wife's mortality and my own were now laid bare. And after multiple attempts by Western-educated doctors, with all of their high-tech machinery and multi-billion-dollar pharmaceutical backup, they had come up with a very expensive zero. They had also shortened Maggie's life due to the toxic effects of the chemo on her immune system. Finally, realizing that a genuinely informed fight against cancer rests in the patient's hands, and not by handing the strategy over to a doctor trained in a single medical discipline, I began to research not only Western medicine, and what it contains at its core, but also what alternatives we both may have missed. However, I feared it might be too late.

What I found was both illuminating and disheartening. And it gave me second thoughts about all of the procedures the two of us had endured. Procedures that had absolutely nothing to show for all the pain and suffering they had inflicted. My research led to a discovery that the basis for Western medicine was determined after the American Medical Association created the Council on Medical Education, or CME. In 1904, the CME asked the Carnegie Foundation for the Advancement of Teaching to survey American and Canadian medical education, in support of its reformist agenda. Abraham Flexner carried out the survey, publishing his report in 1910. Flexner, with no medical training in his background, was asked to evaluate the mishmash of education that qualified students to dispense medical care. A further directive was for him to provide guidance on how to train the doctors of the future. Flexner's findings led to recommendations on establishing a single basis for medical tuition. It required pre-med education along with a grounding in biology and chemistry followed by an internship before achieving the qualification to be an MD. All crucial improvements.

A key recommendation in the report, however, was that all doctors should practice allopathy. Allopathy is a form of medicine where a doctor diagnoses a symptom and, when confirmed, administers a pharmaceutical or surgical solution to resolve or manage that symptom. This practice seemed reasonable until I came across conflicting research from other medical disciplines. They recommended evaluating the entire person, because when we become ill, the symptom is often an indicator of something else wrong in our lives. This influence on the illness could involve diet, lifestyle, the result of a traumatic event, stress, exposure to chemicals, or even another part of the body creating a symptom in a separate limb, organ, or system.

Digging deeper, I also discovered a more sinister side of Flexner's recommendations. Once his report was released, Carnegie, along with fellow industrialist John Rockefeller, used their foundations to donate large sums of money to universities and medical institutions that adopted this "approved" system of teaching—and also adhered to the requirements of allopathic medicine, thereby promoting the use of prescription drugs.[4] The industrialists then inserted chosen surrogates onto the boards of these organizations so they could continue to influence and monitor their progress. Now they had institutionalized medical training and the adoption of allopathic remedies. Both Carnegie and Rockefeller proceeded to invest heavily in the pharmaceutical arena, thereby creating a lucrative and closed-loop financial ecosystem.

Not content with locking down the supply chain for their economic advancement, the new medical community, triggered by Flexner's report and eager to cut out any competition, set about vilifying all alternative methods of treating the sick. These modalities included homeopathy, osteopathy, naturopathy, acupuncture, Chinese medicine, Ayurvedic medicine, and so on. Some of these forms of what in the west we now call "alternative" treatments have been in existence for thousands of years, with many peer-reviewed cases proving the efficacy of a number of their remedies.

The ongoing barrage of damaging misinformation forced on the public by the western medical community is why today, the general population is inclined to view these disciplines as quackery, which is, of course, the intent. Unfortunately, through this suppression, many potentially life-saving adjuncts, or even alternatives, to the Western dogma of drugs, surgery, and the use of radiation go unexplored by patients who receive only allopathic relief. It's also worth noting that allopathy is the predominant, and often the only, form of medical treatment that insurance companies will cover. This was quite a departure from the turn of the twentieth century, when 30 percent of the medical schools in the U.S. taught homeopathy, a discipline that contains far less opportunity for financial gain since many of the solutions it uses are natural substances that are inexpensive to obtain.

I was also alarmed to find that as recently as 1976, five Chiropractors sued the American Medical Association accusing them of participating, for years, in an illegal conspiracy to destroy the chiropractic profession. After a lengthy legal battle,[5] on August 24, 1987, US District Court Judge Susan Getzendanner ruled that the AMA and its officials were guilty as charged of attempting to eliminate the chiropractic profession. During the proceedings, evidence revealed that the AMA:

- Tried to undermine chiropractic schools
- Tried to undercut insurance programs for chiropractic patients
- Concealed proof of the effectiveness of chiropractic care
- Subverted government inquiries into the effectiveness of chiropractic
- Promoted other activities that would control the monopoly that the AMA had on health care

The 7th United States Circuit Court of Appeals upheld the judgment.

My next discovery was about the financial relationship between doctors and the pharmaceutical industry. Oncologists are the only doctors who get a commission on the chemo drugs they prescribe, and chemotherapy drugs are the only category of prescription drugs where this practice is allowed. The payouts are substantial. The hospital buys the drugs for around $5,000; they then sell them to the patient for $18,000. The insurance company pays $15,000. The hospital writes off the $3,000 as a loss, and the MD oncologist gets a percentage of the profit. At the very least, the doctor will pocket $3,000 for every prescription. In 2006, NBC nightly news ran a segment that questioned the propriety of these payments.[6] Having this kind of financial upside to prescribing a very toxic drug or cocktail of drugs is concerning. However, it's a concern that's tempered if the drugs are effective in curing the disease.

In 1956, Hardin B Jones, a former professor of medical physics and physiology at the University of California Berkeley, published a highly controversial report in the journal *Transactions of the New York Academy of Sciences.*[7] In the report he details how he studied the life expectancy of patients for more than twenty-five years and concluded that chemotherapy does more harm than good. "People who refused chemotherapy treatment live on average twelve and a half years longer than people who are undergoing chemotherapy." Said Dr. Jones of his study. Another article in *Clinical Oncology,* a journal of the Royal College of Radiologists in Great Britain,[8] discovered that the overall contribution of chemotherapy to five-year survival in adults was estimated to be 2.3 percent in Australia and 2.1 percent in the USA. It concluded that cytotoxic chemotherapy only makes a minor contribution to cancer survival.

With these and other discoveries in hand, I decided to walk away from Western medicine as a treatment for my cancer and passed up any further tests or visits to the oncologist. Who would take their car back to the same mechanic if they had failed to fix it on multiple earlier visits?

The conclusion I drew from my actual experience, coupled with my investigations, was that handing a cancer diagnosis over to a doctor who uses a single medical discipline was not a fight against the disease, but the surrender of a person's ability to seek out all forms of cure and to determine for themselves which ones to pursue. An astute patient, with access to the right tools and information, can be an independent broker for their strategy and select remedies that come from an understanding of all the medical modalities that are publicly available, Western or otherwise. Unfortunately, this approach also involves some financial investment, which is not an option for many in our society; as I mentioned earlier, insurance companies only, or predominantly, cover allopathic medicine.

Maggie and I began to adopt other natural methodologies to combat the disease. However, by this time, the chances of saving her life were remote. She was starting to lose weight, and I could see that the cancer was beginning to visibly ravage her body. She visited an MD who specialized in looking beyond the standard treatments for cancer and instead focused on options such as amino acid infusions. He recommended a regimen of various kinds of herbal supplementation, so, along with our plant-based regimen, we both embraced this new rigor with increased hopes of hitting on a cure. However, after only a few days of wheatgrass shots, we both declared that dying of cancer would be a far better option than one more day of having to feel this pungent liquid slip down our throats, leaving a piquancy in the mouth that bore a strong comparison to the bottom of a compost heap.

The word had spread that Maggie, in a departure from the other struggles in her life, was probably not going to make it through this one. People wanted to say goodbye and to thank her for all she'd done to enhance the city. And for her tireless work on behalf of animals and those less fortunate than most of society. Many cards that appeared in our mailbox, or accompanied the numerous flower arrangements, spoke of a person who had inspired them on many different fronts. People wrote about starting to separate recyclable materials from household trash or being encouraged to adopt a homeless animal from a shelter rather than from a retail pet store, and how that rescue animal had become an integral and much-loved member of their family. Cards spoke of the guilt that the author now felt if a plastic bag or piece of cardboard packaging was to ever stare up at them from within their collection of household trash. Or that they now felt compelled to stop and care for injured animals, some even crediting Maggie with their becoming vegetarian. One spoke to how Maggie's work had moved their child so much that they had started to volunteer at the local animal shelter. And the cards kept coming and coming.

Realizing that any realistic hope of recovering from the disease had come to an end, we now faced the question of our resident animal population. This group now included sixty-four turtles and tortoises, a dog, three cats, two guinea pigs, an unknown number of rats, two rabbits, a cockatiel, and a chinchilla. I didn't want to broach the subject, as I knew how near and dear the animals were to Maggie's heart. But she'd already realized that with a management job consuming at least ten hours a day, I wouldn't be able to see to the care and feeding of all the critters, which up to this point had been a team effort. Seemingly small things could be a big deal; a turtle ending up on its back for an extended period could collapse its lungs. And Rose, the pit bull mix, would need to be in a kennel for the time I was at work, which would be hard on any dog. The reality was that most of the animals would need to go to new homes.

Maggie had seen this day coming, and with a few phone calls, she tapped into the animal rescue network in the county, each group specializing in a specific species from rabbits to birds to turtles, cats, and dogs. Many of the people she contacted knew of her situation and were aware that all of the animals in question were rescues. And it wasn't long before trucks and cars started appearing in the driveway with crates and boxes that were soon loaded with irritated tortoises or inquisitive rats. The Turtle and Tortoise Society responded. The House Rabbit Society also stepped up, as did many individuals, as the word spread amongst people who recognized Maggie's considerable contributions to animal welfare, and her years of housing and caring for unwanted creatures.

Within a couple of weeks, the only animals left were Rose, the dog; and Grumpy, Dexter, and Bullet, the cats. Some weeks later, and with regret, I would transport Rose up to Idaho, where she would join Chris and his family in the mountains. The cats were to remain with me. Without shedding a tear or complaining, Maggie orchestrated each departure with a stoicism that surprised me. To Maggie, this was like giving away her children. And she did so without displaying the emotions that must have been simmering below the surface.

CHAPTER 27

All Is Said and Done

There's a train leavin' nightly called "When All is Said and Done"
Keep me in your heart for a while
Warren Zevon – "Keep Me in Your Heart"

Seeing that the end was drawing near, a small group of supporters started to plan a celebration of life event, where residents, friends, fellow UCSD workers, politicians, and well-wishers could gather and say goodbye. This industrious band of Maggie's closest friends and political confidants had big ideas, and they set about putting them into practice.

After scoping out suitable locations, they approached the CEO of the Quail Botanic Gardens. Quail is a thirty-seven-acre urban retreat that had been deeded to the County of San Diego in 1957 by its original owners, the Larabees. They had created an urban oasis of drought-tolerant plants, shrubs, and trees, which had been enhanced over the years. And now the gardens had grown to include four miles of trails that weaved their way through twenty-nine uniquely themed areas offering flowering shrubs, majestic palms, restful vistas, and the country's most extensive bamboo collection. All of which thrived in the mild climate. Julian, the CEO, agreed to have the party right in the center of the gardens, where a lush lawn lay fringed by towering trees, subtropical plants, dahlias, and succulents. All of this natural beauty was accompanied by the sounds of nearby streams and waterfalls. It was a fitting paradise, and one of the few places that could handle the crowd that would show up on the day of the event.

The organizing committee found a chef and catering company to supply food. Then they went in search of musicians to entertain the guests. It didn't take much to persuade singer-songwriter Jack Tempchin to bring his band to the event. Jack had written the song "Peaceful Easy Feeling" and co-written "Already Gone" for the Eagles, along with penning the 1977 hit "Swayin' to the Music" for Johnny Rivers, and songs for Glen Campbell, Emmylou Harris, and others. Jack generously waived any payment for his band's performance.

The day of the event rolled around accompanied by warm temperatures and a cloudless sky. Family members had made the trip south, and by mid-morning, our house was chaos. People were in various stages of preparation: taking showers, dressing, doing hair, and offering suggestions about accessorizing. Finally, it came time to leave for the gardens. I watched Maggie as I realized this was not only the community's opportunity to say thanks and farewell. It was also her chance to say goodbye to friends and the city she loved. However, in the hubbub of activity, there was little time for introspection, and we were soon on our way.

As we left the house, I was almost surprised by how spectacular Maggie looked considering the advanced nature of her disease.

Wearing a borrowed Hawaiian-themed jacket, with a pink-and-white lei around her shoulders and professionally styled hair, she looked vibrant. An unknowing bystander would be hard-pressed to realize that a terminal disease, in the final stages of its relentless journey, hovered just below the surface.

When we arrived, the center of the gardens was alive with people. Lines of white chairs faced a podium that was topped with a microphone to accommodate the speeches that were to come. Off to one side, nestled against the surrounding foliage, lay a gazebo from which Jack and his band were warming up the crowd. A bar, bustling with the activity of guests and manned by bartenders dressed in crisp white shirts and black slacks, stood beneath one of the nearby trees. Adjacent to the bar, four long tables had been set up and were now groaning under the weight of steaming entrees and a host of delicate desserts. More thank you cards started to accumulate behind the podium, along with mementos her friends and co-workers had purchased or created. Tributes signed by those present, and by others who couldn't attend the event but who were still eager to embrace the memory of a friendship, successful political endeavor, or animal lives saved, added to the pile.

As the festivities wore on, it was time for the speeches, including one from her son, Chris. He had flown down from Idaho with his family and quickly had the crowd chuckling with tales of a childhood surrounded by animals and plants and highlighted by the various potluck parties that punctuated his youth. He spoke of an understanding mother who, amongst other considerations, had allowed him to sport a prominent Mohawk hairdo during a rebellious period in his youth. It was a creation that required copious amounts of hairspray every time he left the house, under the curious stares of the neighbors.

Area politicians stepped up to the mic to compliment Maggie on her ability to change the city while remaining cordial in her dealings with those who didn't agree with her. Friends stepped up and emphasized character traits and replayed conversations or actions that had changed their thinking on a political initiative, animal issue, or environmental challenge, with many describing their amazement at the level of energy and involvement that could come from a single person.

Interspersed amongst all the raucous laughter that rang through the surrounding foliage, tears began to flow. Both from those at the podium and, less obviously, from guests within the crowd, who realized that this life, which had become a source of such inspiration, would shortly be coming to a close.

As the sun began to set, the party started to wind down. But not until the band had played some country and western numbers that had guests on their feet with many following Maggie's lead, some learning how to line dance for the first time. Her years spent as a dance teacher were on full view as she yelled out instructions and grabbed participants, twisting and turning them with the ease of a seasoned veteran.

The crowd continued to thin, and the laughter and noise died down as the final tearful embraces took place. Guests slowly filtered out after expressing their appreciation for times past along with their love and support for the future.

We left the event and returned home, along with what seemed like half of the attendees, all eager to push the party well into the night. And it wasn't until around 10 p.m. that just a few family members and Maggie and I remained to reminisce about the day.

The following morning, we awoke and looked through some of the mementos stacked up in piles in the front room. There were large cardboard posters signed by numerous friends and admirers, framed photographs, cards, and flowers. It had been quite a day. Now the last of our overnight visitors were leaving, and the house would be quiet again.

On Monday, Maggie returned to the City, and as the days slipped by, her strength began to ebb. It became impossible for her to physically attend the council meetings. Instead, she would insist on joining the proceedings through a conference line. She was determined to throw her last efforts into ensuring that there was a balanced dialogue on City issues, as long as she could muster the strength.

It was only a couple of weeks later that she became too weak to walk more than a few steps. And she would sit in a reclining chair that became her sanctuary while entertaining a steady stream of visitors and friends who would come to chat or read to her, some taking her for a drive so she could get out of the house for an hour or so.

I'd taken a leave of absence from work so I could be with her. And it was during these last weeks of consciousness that she decided to sell off her considerable collection of mostly American Indian jewelry, along with her wardrobe of Western clothing, so she could retire her outstanding debts. Since our unusual wedding circumstances, we had always maintained some personal as well as joint financial accounts. Now she wanted to put her house in order before it was too late. I implored her not to sell her collection, promising to take care of any outstanding bills. However, I quickly recognized signs of the determination that had shaped her life, and she would not be dissuaded.

As she took a slow inventory of the jewelry, I recalled a trip to San Juan Capistrano some years prior, where the main street was home to several stores selling American Indian wares. As we strolled past the historic Franciscan mission founded by the priest Junipero Serra, Maggie paused, looking at the adobe walls of the building. She recounted the terrible human toll the missions in California had taken on the Native tribes. And how they had subjugated the indigenous people by forcing them into slavery and concentrating them into tightly packed groups, thereby facilitating the transmission of pathogens, including those borne by Europeans and Mexicans, to which the American Indians had little immunity.

In these missions, one in three infants didn't live to see their first birthday, and four out of ten Indian children who survived their first year perished before their fifth. At the same time, between 10 and 20 percent of the adults died each year, with the sexes separated so they couldn't procreate.[9] She went on to complain that even today, we marginalize these tribes when we could still learn so much from their respect and maintenance of the land, instead of our generation's decades-long quest to destroy much of it for the support of a growing population and for capital gain.

The jewelry collection she had amassed over several years now contained antique and modern pieces from some well-regarded American Indian artists—intricate works of silver supporting jade, coral, and lapis inserts. Rings, ornate necklaces, bracelets, earrings all went up for sale to buyers who would come to the house by appointment. I watched as she sat in the front room and described the history of each piece to the various shoppers and was amazed by the focus she'd brought to creating the collection and the fortitude that she exhibited as she parted with the treasures she'd valued for so many years. It wasn't long before only a few of the less notable pieces remained.

As time went by, it became more difficult for her to digest food. And it was necessary to have a bag inserted through her side and into her stomach. This setup allowed food into her system, but the food was then diverted into the bag as, by now, her digestive tract had failed. I was often called to fix a blockage at the bag's valve that would cause the food to back up. And I would conduct a quick procedure to ensure that the contents exited unimpeded until the next stoppage occurred. Another medical complication that had appeared was evidence of clotting in her legs, probably attributable to the chemotherapy. To avoid a heart attack, she had to have blood thinners injected into her abdomen daily, something she hated receiving as much as I dreaded administering it. She would pull up her top and expose her midsection, only to grimace and look away as I inserted the needle, along with the contents of the syringe, into her midsection.

Slowly she continued to weaken and was confined to bed. Although her body was failing, her mind was still sharp. And she welcomed the constant flow of visitors that came to her bedside with some callers bringing their children who would hold her hand and tell her they loved her. Others, unable to keep their composure, would break down. Throughout the entire length of her struggle, Maggie never shed a tear and never voiced a complaint about her condition. And even now, in the final stage of her illness, she was still able to display one of her signature smiles for each visitor.

Notably absent from the list of people wishing to share a last moment with Maggie, and from the list of those who sent flowers or cards, were the people with whom she'd been at political odds on the City Council. There were no communications or messages of support from Stocks, Bond, Guerin, or Dalager. The dislike that had been evident throughout her tenure on the City Council continued. Even in the face of imminent death. One surprise did arrive, however, in the form of a bouquet from Paul Ecke III, the flower grower, developer, and head of the Ecke clan. The card wished Maggie well in her struggle. I remember her being touched by this unexpected gesture. At least one old adversary had sufficient strength of character to rise above old scores and recognize an opponent who had stood true to her belief in a government of the people, by the people, and for the people. And who had fought tirelessly, often in the face of ferocious opposition, for the well-being of all residents.

To soften her transition from life, someone had recommended a spiritualist, and Maggie asked her to come to the house during her final days. Bianca was her name, and she would take a seat next to Maggie's bedside and close the door so that they could be alone. I never knew much about what they talked about, but it seemed to give Maggie great comfort. One day, when her time was drawing near, she shared with me that Bianca had pointed toward the large bedroom window that looked out over the front yard and said, "Look, there are all the animals that you've rescued and cared for over the years. They're all here at the window waiting for you to join them."

A couple of days later, Maggie had a seizure and lapsed into a coma from which she would never recover. And it was only a few days later that, surrounded by her son, daughter-in-law, sister, and me, she drew her last shallow breaths. With her heart still fighting to stay with us, her body failed. She could fight no more, and it was death that finally broke her stride.

Epilogue

Art ranging from painting and jewelry to clothing and dance held a particular fascination for the three-term council member. And she frequently supported local art groups by serving as a celebrity MC at their events or helping them raise money at art sales. The most notable of these was the "Arts Alive" banner auction, held annually, where Maggie would auction off fine art that had been painted on vinyl and hung from lampposts along the town's main thoroughfare.

Six months after her passing, the 101 Artists' Colony, organizers of the banner celebration, decided that for 2012, they would recognize the late Mayor's ongoing support of their efforts and her work on behalf of the community. And they determined the best way to provide such an honor would be to place her likeness on the back of the banners and dedicate the event to her memory.

Before the permit could be issued and the banners raised, however, the City administration caught wind of what was about to happen and dusted off an obscure piece of municipal code, called a view ordinance, that threatened to derail the tribute. The code stated,

"Banners over public rights-of-way shall be permitted subject to the standards established by the City and approved by the City Manager or designee. Said banners are for civic and nonprofit City-wide recognized special events."

This language was reviewed by the City, where, following discussions, it was determined that Maggie's likeness on the banners was a political statement and therefore violated the ordinance. The local newspaper published a quote: "Mayor Jerome Stocks, who was often at odds with Houlihan when she was on the council, has said he considers the Houlihan image to be "political" and thus shouldn't be allowed to be displayed on City-owned property." The result was that the City would withhold the permit for the banners if her image was present.

Rather than see the work of the artists withheld from public view and cancel the event, the group offered to cover up her image with squares of peel and stick opaque Mylar, which would effectively block her out, along with any printed references.

With the banners altered, the permit was issued, and volunteers installed the artwork along Highway 101, which ran through the center of town, but not until one of the key organizers of the event was overheard to say, "They have just simply tried to erase her from the history books of Encinitas."

This situation didn't sit well with many members of the community, and one day I received an email from Jim Kydd, the publisher of the local paper, the *Coast News*. Jim questioned the wording of the City code and how it didn't seem to cover the tribute that was on the back of the banners. It was this email that triggered a course of action that would once again lead to conflict with the City Council, only this time it would be without the physical presence of the late council member.

I made a call to the American Civil Liberties Union (ACLU), described the situation, and provided a copy of the specific municipal code that was in question. After taking a few days to evaluate the legal implications, the ACLU came back with a judgment that the City was violating the First Amendment of the U.S. Constitution, the right to free speech and that the language saying "banners are for civic and nonprofit City-wide recognized special events" did not rule out using a deceased political figure's likeness to advertise a special event. The letter quoted numerous precedent-setting legal cases, and their determination provided the smoking gun needed to confront the City Council.

Not wishing to take any chances, I also retained a local law firm that came to the same conclusion as the ACLU. They agreed that the actions of the City not only violated First Amendment rights but, in addition, didn't comply with the language of their own municipal code. They also provided a number of legal precedents to prove that the City had made the wrong decision.

With this legal backing and with a letter from the ACLU that detailed their findings, I attended the next City Council meeting to demand that the council allow the display of Maggie Houlihan's image.

That evening, the council chambers were packed while others watched the proceedings from home on their TVs. When the banner item came up for discussion, I approached the podium and posted the letter from the ACLU on a monitor positioned so that the audience and council could see what it said. After pointing out the findings of the ACLU and their judgment that the City was in violation of the First Amendment, I posted a second letter from the law firm, which contained a similar legal assessment. The law firm's attorney had come to the meeting, and she followed up my presentation by educating the City Council on the particulars of the legal precedent set from earlier cases. She concluded by instructing the council to allow Ms. Houlihan's image to be displayed.

It didn't take long for the council to realize their tenuous legal position, and after feigning a lack of knowledge as to why the original permit had directed the arts group to conceal the picture of the late Mayor, they agreed to allow the removal of the Mylar patches.

The next day a new permit was issued. And shortly thereafter, the banners were displayed as originally intended, but this time with a heartfelt and now hard-earned tribute to the late Mayor proudly on display. I think that she would have been pleased to win one last battle.

Appendix

1. Russell Thornton. American Indian Holocaust and Survival: A Population History Since 1492. (Norman: University of Oklahoma Press, 1987) xx, 292.

A sociologist, Thornton has written a thorough and balanced demographic account of Native American societies in what became the United States from before the arrival of Europeans to the present. There is still no agreement on pre-European population size north of Mexico, but everyone now agrees that Mooney's estimate of about 1 million is too low. Thornton rejects the highest estimates but chooses 7 million as the most reasonable. Since there is agreement that Indians in the United States were reduced to about 250,000 by the end of the nineteenth century, the loss was of staggering proportions.

The classic estimate of aboriginal population size for this area is James Mooney's 1,152,000 million for North America north of the Rio Grande River at first (extensive) European contact (see Mooney 1928). Subsequent scholars generally accepted Mooney's estimate until 1966, when Henry Dobyns (1966) asserted an aboriginal population size for North America north of Mexico of between 9.8 and 12.25 million; in 1983, he increased his asserted size to 18 million (north of Mesoamerica) (see Dobyns 1983).

Kirkpatrick Sale. 1992 – "The Conquest of Paradise." Sale asserted that the best working number for pre-contact population should be closer to 15 million. According to Sale's estimates, the total population decline in North America from 1492 to 1900 was between 95 and 99 percent.

Lucy Dawidowicz. 1975 – "The War Against the Jews." Dawidowicz used prewar birth and death records to come up with a figure of 5,933,900. And one of the more authoritative German scholars of the subject, Wolfgang Benz, offered a range of 5.3 to 6.2 million.

2. Benjamin Madley. 2016 – "An American Genocide." The United States and the California Indian Catastrophe. Yale University Press.

3. Jack Weatherford. 1988 – "Indian Givers - How the Indians of the Americas Transformed the World." Three Rivers Press.

    David Hurst Thomas, Jay Miller, Richard White, Peter Nabokov, Philip J. Deloria. 1993 – "The Native Americans." Turner Publishing Inc.

4. E. Richard Brown. 1979 – "Rockefeller Medicine Men." University of California Press.

    Abraham Flexner. 1910 – "Medical Education in the United States and Canada." The Merrymount Press.

5. Phyllis Mensing. 1987 – "AMA Found Guilty of Anti-trust Conspiracy Against Chiropractors." Associated Press. https://apnews.com/e4f9f342f302528cfbebb81e1e2224f2 Wilkes vs. the AMA

6. NBC Nightly News with Brian Williams. 2006. – http://www.nbcnews.com/id/14944098.XmkUFZNKiu4

7. Hardin B. Jones. 1956 – Transactions, New York Academy of Science, series 2, v. 18, n.3, p.322.

8. Graeme Morgan, Robyn Ward, Michael Barton. 2004 – "Clinical Oncology." A journal of the Royal College of Radiologists.

9. Benjamin Madley. 2016 – "An American Genocide." The United States and the California Indian Catastrophe. Yale University Press.

About the Author

IAN THOMPSON was born and raised in England. He began his career doing menial jobs before starting a surfboard company. He has traveled all over the world, mostly on surfing adventures.

A freelance journalist, Ian has published articles in *Surfer Magazine,* in British sports journals, and in local U.S. newspapers. He is also a retired manager and technology executive from the cybersecurity field.

He wrote this memoir about his wife because, as he puts it, "Maggie Houlihan was an inspiration, and her life has many lessons to teach us." He currently resides in Encinitas, California.